Praise for

THE SISTER

"An extraordinarily well researched, invaluable resource for understanding one of the most intriguing and least known figures in today's North Korea."

Stephen E. Biegun, former United States
Special Representative for North Korea and
Deputy Secretary of State

"[R]eads like Shakespeare brushed with William F. Buckley and the 1980s TV hit 'Dynasty.' A must read for policy practitioners, Hollywood writers, and Martha's Vineyard A-listers alike: meet *The Sister*."

Alexis Dudden, Professor of History, University
of Connecticut, and author of *The Opening and
Closing and Japan, 1850–2020* (forthcoming)

"In explaining the rise to power of Kim Yo Jong, Lee displays his deep knowledge and understanding of North Korea's extreme, ruthless and self-obsessed dynastic autocracy.... Not a reassuring story."

Sir John Scarlett, former Chief of the
Secret Intelligence Service (MI6) and co-founder, SC Strategy

"This is a stunningly good book. I look forward to everything that Sung-Yoon Lee writes—everything. His understanding of the North Korean regime is almost uncanny. His writing is spellbinding.... an unforgettable tutorial in how North Korea actually works."

Dr. Nicholas Eberstadt, Henry Wendt Chair
in Political Economy, American Enterprise Institute, and
author of *The North Korean Economy: Between Crisis and Catastrophe*

"*The Sister* is revelatory. It is a most astute, acerbic, and, at times, even amusing exposé of the pathological ways of the North Korean dynasty."

Ri Jong Ho, former Chairman of the Korea
Kum-Kang Economic Development Group,
National Defense Commission, DPRK

"A stellar analyst and wordsmith, Lee combines his profound knowledge of North Korean culture, history, and regime dynamics to write a must-read page-turner for North Korea scholars, students, and policymakers alike."

Greg Scarlatoiu, Executive Director,
Committee for Human Rights in North Korea

"It reads like a thriller novel and informs like the best textbook."

Gordon Chang, author of
Nuclear Showdown: North Korea Takes On the World

"Lee's impeccably arranged sentences are not only a joy to read, but they apply his native proficiency, historical depth, and extraordinary perceptiveness to reveal the danger and the horror that Kim Yo Jong represents."

Joshua Stanton, Attorney, drafter of U.S.
sanctions laws on North Korea

"With the precision of a surgeon's scalpel, Dr. Lee cuts open the Kim regime's seven decades–old cloak to reveal its grotesque nature, forbidden secrets, and intentions for the future. *The Sister* is pregnant history that casts a long light on tomorrow—a stupendous achievement."

Jihyun Park, author of *The Hard Road Out:
One Woman's Escape from North Korea*

"Engrossing account of the enigmatic Kim Yo-Jong....Through a masterful narrative, Lee delves into her influence on the regime....captivating, well-researched portrait of one of the world's most secretive and powerful women."

Bradley Hope, author of *The Rebel and the Kingdom*
and co-founder of Project Brazen

"*The Sister* is a literary tour de force....the book bears testament to Dr. Lee as one of the few remaining bastions of truth about the realities of the Kim dictatorship."   Dr. Soo Kim, former CIA North Korea Analyst

THE
SISTER

NORTH KOREA'S KIM YO JONG, THE MOST DANGEROUS WOMAN IN THE WORLD

SUNG-YOON LEE

PUBLICAFFAIRS

New York

PublicAffairs
Hachette Book Group
1290 Avenue of the Americas, New York, NY 10104
www.publicaffairsbooks.com
@Public_Affairs

Printed in the United States of America

Originally published in the United Kingdom in 2023 by Macmillan, an imprint of Pan Macmillan

First US Edition: September 2023

Published by PublicAffairs, an imprint of Hachette Book Group, Inc. The PublicAffairs name and logo is a trademark of the Hachette Book Group.

The Hachette Speakers Bureau provides a wide range of authors for speaking events. To find out more, go to hachettespeakersbureau.com or email HachetteSpeakers@hbgusa.com.

PublicAffairs books may be purchased in bulk for business, educational, or promotional use. For more information, please contact your local bookseller or the Hachette Book Group Special Markets Department at special.markets@hbgusa.com.

The publisher is not responsible for websites (or their content) that are not owned by the publisher.

Image 1 © Bloomberg/Getty; Image 2 © Matthias Hangst/Getty; Image 3 © Universal History Archive/Getty; Image 4 © REUTERS/Alamy; Image 5 © Pool/ Getty; Image 6 © Korean Central News Agency; Image 7 © Sopa Images/Getty.

Typeset by Palimpsest Book Production Ltd, Falkirk, Stirlingshire

Library of Congress Control Number: 2023937288

ISBNs: 9781541704121 (hardcover), 9781541704138 (ebook)

LSC-C

Printing 1, 2023

Contents

Principal Characters vii
Family Tree x

CHAPTER 1
The Princess Cometh 1

CHAPTER 2
The Mount Paektu Bloodline 13

CHAPTER 3
Peninsular Predominance: Pyongyang's Ultimate Mission 28

CHAPTER 4
All in the Family 40

CHAPTER 5
The Narcissistic Psychopath Father 51

CHAPTER 6
State Secrets 73

CHAPTER 7
The Apprentice Years: 2007–2009 88

CHAPTER 8
Funeral and Rebirth 107

CHAPTER 9
The Vile Ventriloquist 113

CHAPTER 10
The Pyongyang Games 120

CHAPTER 11
The Blue House Visit 131

CHAPTER 12
A Korean Comedy of Errors 144

CHAPTER 13
Who Trumped Whom? 160

CHAPTER 14
The Ascent: Mounted Paektu Princess 185

CHAPTER 15
Weaponizing Food: A Family Practice 201

CHAPTER 16
Twisted Sister 213

CHAPTER 17
They Call Her 'Devil Woman' 225

Acknowledgements 249
Notes 251
Index 281

PRINCIPAL CHARACTERS

North Korea

The Mount Paektu Bloodline

Kim Il Sung: founder of North Korea and the 'Mount Paektu Bloodline'. Grandfather of Kim Yo Jong. Died 1994.

Kim Jong Il: Son of Kim Il Sung and Supreme Leader from 1994 until his death in 2011. Father of Kim Jong Un and Kim Yo Jong.

Kim Jong Un: Son of Kim Jong Il and Supreme Leader since 2011. Older brother of Kim Yo Jong.

Kim Yo Jong: Daughter of Kim Jong Il and younger sister of Kim Jong Un.

Kim Jong Chol: Son of Kim Jong Il and older brother of Jong Un and Yo Jong.

Kim Ju Un *or* Ju Ae: Daughter of Kim Jong Un. Born *c.* 2010.

Other Kim family members

Hong Il Chon: First wife of Kim Jong Il. Married 1966, but estranged shortly after birth of Kim Hye Kyong.

Jang Song Thaek: Husband of Kim Kyong Hui and long-time number two of Kim Jong Il. Executed in 2013 or 2014.

Kim Chun Song: Younger daughter of Kim Jong Il and Kim Yong Suk. Half-sister of Jong Un and Yo Jong.

Kim Hye Kyong: First-born child of Kim Jong Il. Mother is Hong Il Chon.

Kim Jong Nam: Kim Jong Il's eldest son, born to Song Hye Him. Once presumed to be his father's nominated heir. Assassinated in 2017 on the orders of his younger half-brother, Jong Un.

Kim Kyong Hui: Younger sister of Kim Jong Il.

Kim Sol Song: Older daughter of Kim Jong Il and Kim Yong Suk. Half-sister of Jong Un and Yo Jong.

Kim Yong Suk: Second wife of Kim Jong Il. Mother of Sol Song and Chun Song.

Ko Yong Hui: Kim Jong Il's common-law wife. Mother of Jong Chul, Jong Un and Yo Jong.

Ri Sol Ju: Wife of Kim Jong Un.

Song Hye Rim: Mistress of Kim Jong Il and mother of Kim Jong Nam.

Senior North Korean officials

Choe Hwi
Choe Son Hui
Choe Thae Bok
Hyon Song Wol
Jo Yong Won
Kim Chang Son
Kim Hyok Chol

Kim Jong Gak
Kim Ki Nam
Kim Song Hye
Kim Yang Gon
Kim Yong Chun
Kim Yong Nam
Pak Jong Chon
Ri Myong Je
Ri Son Gwon
Ri Yong Ho
U Dong Chuk

South Korea

Presidents

Kim Dae Jung (1998–2003)
Roh Moo Hyun (2003–2008)
Lee Myung Bak (2008–2013)
Park Geun Hye (2013–2017)
Moon Jae-In (2017–2022)
Yoon Suk Yeol (2022–present)

Other South Korean officials

Cho Myoung-gyon: Unification Minister from 2017 to 2019.
Chung Sye-Kyun: prime minister during Moon Jae-In's presidency.

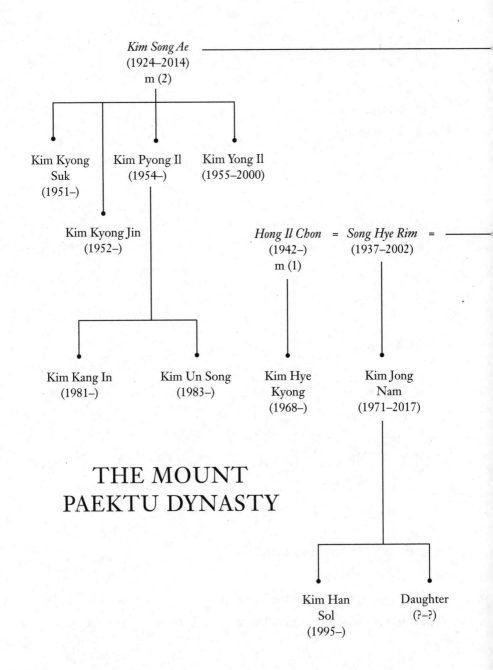

Kim Song Ae
(1924–2014)
m (2)

Kim Kyong
Suk
(1951–)

Kim Pyong Il
(1954–)

Kim Yong Il
(1955–2000)

Kim Kyong Jin
(1952–)

Hong Il Chon = Song Hye Rim =
(1942–)   (1937–2002)
m (1)

Kim Kang In
(1981–)

Kim Un Song
(1983–)

Kim Hye
Kyong
(1968–)

Kim Jong
Nam
(1971–2017)

THE MOUNT
PAEKTU DYNASTY

Kim Han
Sol
(1995–)

Daughter
(?–?)

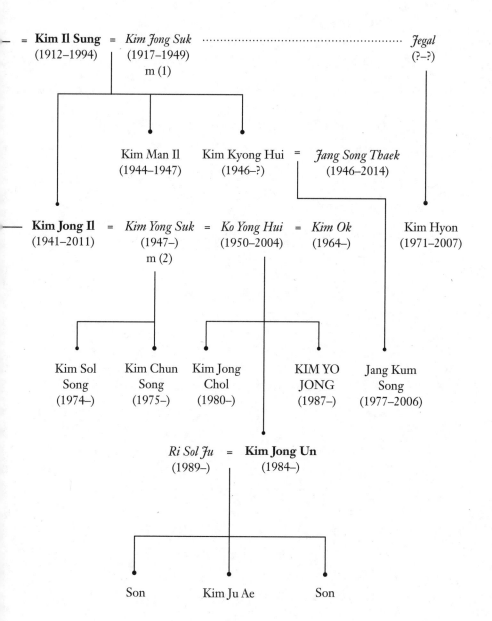

To my mentor, Professor John Curtis Perry

CHAPTER 1

The Princess Cometh

Under a foggy February sky, a plane made its descent towards Incheon International Airport in South Korea. Inside sat twenty-three passengers – five officials, three reporters, and the rest bodyguards. But one mattered above all.

At 1.46 p.m. Korea Standard Time, on 9 February 2018, the Soviet-era Ilyushin-62 that was the North Korean leader's personal plane, *Chammae-2* (Goshawk-2, after the national bird of North Korea), touched down. It was the first time an individual of the 'Mount Paektu Bloodline', as the direct descendants of North Korea's dynastic founder Kim Il Sung style themselves, had set foot on South Korean soil since North Korea's founder himself in July 1950, one month after invading the South. But it was not the current North Korean leader, Kim Jong Un, and this was an entirely different kind of North Korean 'invasion' – one the majority of South Koreans embraced.

From touchdown, it was nine minutes of taxiing to reach the gate. Television viewers eager to catch the first on-screen glimpse of the very important personage were then treated to a further thirty-five minutes of the contours of the parked plane and nothing else: the tail featuring a big red star, the national emblem; 'Democratic People's Republic of Korea' in Korean stretched along the fuselage.

When an air bridge began extending itself towards the plane, a news anchor on one of the major South Korean networks covering the proceedings live gasped in disappointment. Viewers would not, after all, witness the important person grandly exiting the plane.

The very first image of the visitor, depending on the TV channel, came more than forty minutes into the coverage. The nominal head of the North Korean mission, Kim Yong Nam, emerged from the airport building and got into the first of two black sedans. Then, shadowed by a tall, male North Korean bodyguard and a female South Korean bodyguard, a slightly built young woman walked the dozen steps to the second car. Her gaze was still and her posture erect, as though at ease with being the centre of a historic moment like this.

It had happened so quickly, lamented the TV commentators – and that fleeting glimpse was partially blocked by a structure. But even in those few seconds, something was clear. The visitor was known for her eschewal of heavy make-up, an expert noted – yet here she seemed to be wearing her thickest make-up yet. What could this mean? Were they sure it was she? Still, it was exciting, the expert mused, because the thickness of her eye shadow must mean something positive – that she, in her commitment to inter-Korean rapprochement, took her mission most seriously.

A few minutes later, as the motorcade began to move, another North Korean bodyguard came into view on the other side of the young woman's car and, along with the first one, jogged alongside the vehicle before jumping into a trailing black SUV. The destination was the KTX (Korea Train eXpress) station within the airport complex, from where the delegation would travel east by South Korea's state-of-the-art high-speed train to Gangneung. The train, no doubt, would be a first-hand experience of the numerous painful points of stark contrast between the two Korean states.

Television networks played and replayed those precious brief seconds of the walk to the car. Some commentators identified a couple of the North Korean officials who had walked out of the airport afterwards. 'But wait!' one newscaster burst out. 'We have a video clip of her earlier, in the VIP room!'

The new clip, again played over and over, did not disappoint. At last viewers got a good look at the debutante as she made her highly anticipated 'stage entrance' into the VIP Reception Room in the airport terminal. Kim Yong Nam entered first, escorted by his South Korean host, Unification Minister Cho Myoung-gyon. After a few steps, Kim stopped mid-stride and looked back, as if slightly concerned that he was walking ahead of his more important colleague. The glance caused all heads to turn, and then the woman of the hour walked in with a faint smile on her face. Cameras whirred. She maintained her flawlessly erect carriage, her eyes steadily focused on just two or three spots in the room, to avoid giving the least impression that she was either excited or anxious.

3

This was Kim Yo Jong, the younger sister of North Korea's Supreme Leader Kim Jong Un. Her brother rules like an absolute monarch, but she was not a mere royal sibling without real power, like Jong Un's older brother, Jong Chol. Since at least 2014, she had run her nation's powerful Propaganda and Agitation Department. She was ambitious. As the youngest child of Kim Jong Il, North Korea's second-generational leader, she had been doted on lavishly since her earliest days. Both her father and mother addressed her as 'My Sweet Princess Yo Jong' or 'Princess Yo Jong'. Her father had long recognized her talents and political acumen. The world, too, would soon see them at last.

While the main North Korean delegates were being led off the plane, commentators on the TV networks had noted the historical significance of the moment, and filled viewers in on Kim Yo Jong's expected itinerary over the next fifty-six hours, although much still remained to be finalized. One thing, however, was certain. The most important event was Ms Kim's visit the next day with South Korean President Moon Jae-In in the Blue House, the presidential office and mansion, followed by a luncheon. Perhaps she would bring a personal letter from her brother? Perhaps Kim Jong Un might even suggest the two leaders meet in person sometime? Another inter-Korean summit, the first in over a decade – how exciting would that be for the prospects for peace in the Korean peninsula? (The next day, she did indeed deliver such a letter.)

It had also been confirmed that later that evening the North Korean delegation would attend the opening ceremony of the

Winter Olympics in Pyeongchang on the east coast, some two and a half hours by high-speed train from Incheon. The historical irony of Kim Yo Jong landing at Incheon, the city on the western coast of the peninsula where a pivotal military operation in 1950 had turned the tide in the Korean War to Pyongyang's detriment, could not have been lost on the delegation. That evening, the North Koreans would meet President Moon for the first time, if only for a photo-op. Kim Yong Nam, the ninety-year-old nominal head of the delegation, would attend the pre-opening ceremony reception and dinner and mingle a bit with other world leaders; Kim Yo Jong would show up later, at the opening ceremony itself. She would be in the royal box in the stands, presumably seated quite close to President Moon.

The South Korean host had many dignitaries to attend to: US Vice President Mike Pence; German President Frank-Walter Steinmeier, whom few outside Europe were familiar with; the Japanese Prime Minister Shinzo Abe, whom many South Koreans reviled; the International Olympic Committee president, Thomas Bach, who delighted in the North Koreans' attendance; and others with perhaps less at stake. During the ceremony, athletes from both Koreas would make their entrance together under a single blue peninsular flag – this symbolism also called for a historic inter-Korean handshake between Kim Yo Jong and President Moon. Perhaps Ms Kim would be seated with Kim Yong Nam a few seats down from President Moon? Might she be seated somewhere in the vicinity of the US vice president? Perhaps she would have to walk past Mr Pence, or he past her, as seats were being taken – would *they* end up shaking hands? A very special moment that would be.

In the airport VIP room, the South Korean hosts indicated to Kim Yong Nam to take the centre seat across the table from Minister Cho, the head of the receiving corps. But the seasoned nonagenarian knew better, and motioned to the thirty-year-old princess to take the head seat instead. With a wide, generous smile, she gestured to the older man, pointing with her left hand at the centre seat to concede the honour. He protested mildly; she opened her hand and her eyes returned a reassuring smile. 'How gracious she is!' remarked the South Korean pundits ad nauseum, too thrilled to notice that Kim Yo Jong's outstretched fingers were less a gesture of respect than the boss telling her underling to sit down. Had her gesture signified true deference to age, Kim Yo Jong would have motioned with both hands cupped slightly.

Imperiousness, authority, and self-confidence bred from an early age do not lend themselves to modesty, unless the occasion calls for it. In this moment, she was calmly exuding arrogance rather than respect. Three months later, on the other hand, visiting China with her brother, Ms Kim would willingly give President Xi Jinping of China a deep, ninety-degree bow, as she would again in June 2019 during Xi's visit to Pyongyang: the Chinese head of state needed to be shown deference. But South Koreans were her inferiors. The Mount Paektu royalty was the true Korean leadership, while the South was a mere puppet of the United States. After all, the dynasty was named for the fabled mountain home of the military camps from which

Kim Il Sung had finally vanquished the Japanese colonialists in 1945, before founding the North Korean state, according to the official North Korean narrative. And Kim Yong Nam, valued official as he was, could only ever be a junior to the granddaughter of Kim Il Sung.

But at this moment, many South Koreans, who had learned all this at school, had suddenly forgotten. 'She is not only pretty but also polite!' declaimed the commentators, over-looking, in this rare, exciting moment, that Ms Kim's 'simple, unassuming image' was the product of an extremely entitled lifestyle and a studied royal decorum. Like her brother, she knew how to comport herself with the appropriate level of imperiousness in public.

Ms Kim took her seat with Kim Yong Nam on her left. On his left was Ri Son Gwon, a foul-mouthed army colonel turned chief of the Committee for the Peaceful Reunification of the Fatherland, the key North Korean agency that deals in talks with the South, who in January 2020 would be appointed Minister of Foreign Affairs. To Ms Kim's right sat her former subordinate in the Propaganda and Agitation Department, Choe Hwi, at the time Chairman of the State Physical Culture and Sports Guidance Commission. Like Ms Kim herself, Choe had been sanctioned by the US Department of the Treasury since January 2017 in response to the North Korean regime's 'serious human rights abuses and censorship activities'.[1] Such matters were not raised before, during, or after the special visit.

The sit-down made for awkward optics, as the North Koreans kept their winter coats on over their suits. The South Korean officials would have offered to take their coats, but the Northern guests – who could also have left their coats with their own staff – would have politely declined, not because they felt cold inside the airport, but to signal that they would rather be on their way and were agreeing to this photo-op as a gesture of goodwill. Kim Chang Son, Kim Jong Un's chief secretary of the Secretariat of the State Affairs Commission, who occasionally led North Korean delegations in talks with the South, and whose priority on the trip was to tend to the princess, remained standing by the door. The royal family's trusted – and therefore powerful – butler, he had served them for decades.

Minister Cho made a little small talk, remarking how the weather had suddenly turned warmer. 'The very important Northern guests brought to South Korea warm weather,' he said with a smile. In fact, by Korean winter standards, it was now a balmy 45°F (7°C). Kim Yo Jong sat silently, her back straight and her face impressively expressionless. Across the table, her South Korean hosts maintained their wide grins.

Ms Kim wore a black coat with a wide fur collar and fur trim around the wrists, accentuated by a single big round button on her bare neckline. No necklace or earrings; ears unpierced; a black handbag over her left shoulder. A faint trace of peach eye shadow was now visible, as was a touch of eyeliner. Light peach leggings and black fur boots were sighted. Later, it became clear she wore a silver watch and no bracelets. How revealing was her chaste taste in fashion, cooed reporters. According to *The Washington Post*, viewers 'marveled at [Kim Yo Jong's] barely-there makeup and her lack of bling. They commented on her plain black outfits and simple purse. They noted the flower-shaped clip that kept her hair back in a no-nonsense style.'[2]

Another close-up shot of Kim Yo Jong that played over and over on South Korean networks was her escalator ride at Incheon Airport. Kim Yong Nam was the first among the North Korean delegation to come down, wearing his immovable faint smile, with two bodyguards staying close. Kim Yo Jong was surrounded by three North Korean bodyguards and a South Korean bodyguard as she descended, holding her chin up and projecting that catwalk-model style and purposeful fixed gaze. Behind her was Kim Song Hye, a rare female senior official from the Committee for the Peaceful Reunification of the Fatherland who had participated in several rounds of talks with South Korea and who would also be on the North Korean delegation visiting President Donald Trump in the White House on 1 June 2018, just eleven days before Trump's first summit meeting with Kim Jong Un in Singapore. Kim Chang Son followed, and then the more nominally senior officials, Choe Hwi and Ri Son Gwon.

The sequence was a snapshot not only of Kim Yo Jong's position in the North Korean delegation, but also of a peculiarity in North Korean political culture, in which official ranks and titles often belie the true hierarchy and power dynamics, and the lives of cabinet members and four-star generals often hang on the whims of a real powerholder of a much lower rank. Kim Yo Jong's position, of course, was unique: even if she were ranked at the bottom of the 250-strong Central

Committee of the Workers' Party of Korea, she could, on a whim, order the execution of any one of them but one, her brother. Similarly, Kim Chang Son and the princess's personal secretary, Kim Song Hye, held greater sway than higher-ranked officials on the delegation, such as Choe and Ri.

For the next two days, the mysterious young princess from Pyongyang had South Korea enthralled by not doing anything much besides walking, sitting, dining, occasionally talking, infrequently smiling, shaking hands, ghosting Mike Pence while sitting above him in the Olympic stands, and quite frequently looking down her nose at the South Koreans she met – including President Moon Jae-In. She didn't give a single public statement or interview.

Yet she was the talk of the nation, and far beyond the peninsula. Press coverage of Kim Yo Jong remained intensely over-the-top from the first moment of her visit until she took off aboard her brother's plane late on the night of 11 February. As the press kept reminding the public, hers was the first-ever visit-by-invitation to South Korea by a member of the North Korean royalty. The world, including President Moon and his officials, gawked. Fascination bordering on fetishism followed her wherever she went, swelled by her femininity and the South's hopes of communing with her brother. That she simply showed up in the South made her an international star. Princess-watchers from Tokyo to Washington opined on her simple taste in fashion, royal comportment, modesty, imperiousness, self-confidence, demureness, and her Mona Lisa smirk-smile.

She herself gave no overt message to the South Korean people or to the world. But she brought that personal letter from her brother inviting President Moon to Pyongyang, which made her presence all the more tantalizing. Whether the Kim siblings were scheming to use the softest target in their geopolitical neighbourhood – i.e. whoever occupies the Blue House as South Korea's elected leader – with a view to moving up to a slightly harder target in President Donald Trump, was a consideration complicated to the point of being unnecessary. The Princess of Mount Paektu was here, in South Korea! Her flesh and blood presence, keenly tailed and surrounded by her brother's royal bodyguards, could only mean the two Koreas stood on the verge of an epoch-making event. It presaged, at the very least, reconciliation and peace – perhaps even eventual reunification.

The sensational optics trumped the cold reality. The majority of South Koreans did not favour making even a small financial sacrifice to underwrite the long-term economic cost of reunification. And the eventual reunification dreamed of by Kim Yo Jong and her brother would be only on *their* terms: dominated by the Kim dynasty, antithetical in turn to South Koreans grown used to basic freedoms and relative affluence. But to raise such sober points in the euphoria of the moment seemed downright curmudgeonly.

That Kim Yong Nam, a veteran of six decades in high government positions, had been for the past twenty years President of the Presidium of the Supreme People's Assembly, North Korea's rubber-stamp parliament, was of interest only to a few specialists. Most South Korean viewers knew that it was the

First Sister of North Korea who wielded the real power. Kim Jong Un actually sending *his own sister*, went the logic, could only mean she was bringing peace.

The public also intuitively knew that in North Korea, the Supreme Leader's word carried far greater authority than any written statutes or government rank. Kim Jong Un was the state and his words the inviolable law. But what the public largely missed was that his sister was far more than just a pretty face at her brother's party meetings and on-the-spot guidance tours. Her brother was the face of the nation, but she was the chief censor, the enforcer. Her visit to the Olympics was not as a tourist or messenger. The sister had a purpose.

This book will document Kim Yo Jong's rise in power since her visit to South Korea. Her role in government has dramatically increased since 2018, but was foretold as early as 2009. We'll see how she has played an integral part in statecraft, expanding her dynasty's power by utilizing lessons learned from her father, Kim Jong Il. At the time of writing, she is second in power only to her brother Kim Jong Un, and the fate of the 'Mount Paektu Bloodline' may yet lie in her hands.

CHAPTER 2

The Mount Paektu Bloodline

Since its founding in 1948, the Democratic People's Republic of Korea (DPRK) has neither been a democracy nor a republic. Rather, it has existed as a totalitarian hereditary kingdom cloaked under the trappings of democracy, with a constitution that purportedly protects all basic rights and a government that, since the mid-1950s, has determinedly met even the tiniest dissent with banishment or death. Handing down power from father to son is heresy in Communism, but the so-called Communist DPRK has done it twice: first, in the wake of Kim Il Sung's death in 1994, and again after Kim Jong Il's death in 2011. This hereditary rule is legitimized by the purported greatness of the Mount Paektu Bloodline.

The first of the Mount Paektu Bloodline was, of course, the founder of the DPRK, Kim Il Sung. A small-time anti-Japanese guerrilla since the early 1930s, supposedly operating out of camps in the foothills of Mount Paektu, Kim Il Sung's heroic feats against Korea's Japanese colonial masters were hyper-inflated by his propagandists who declared him the greatest patriot and war hero bar none. This fictitious narrative has long formed the ideological foundation for his and his progeny's right to rule. Like the divine right of medieval monarchs, this is derived from the grace of God. In North Korea, where no religious freedom or deity is allowed, God is Kim Il Sung. While he was alive, Kim Il Sung was infallible. In death, his legacy is so sacred that it cannot be challenged or recognized in an individual outside his direct descendants.

Mount Paektu is a real place, a stratovolcano with a stunningly beautiful crater lake, called Heaven Lake ('Cheonji' in Korean and 'Tianchi' in Chinese), which sits on the border between North Korea's Ryanggang Province and China's Jilin Province. Mount Paektu is the North Korean spelling for what in South Korea is transcribed as Baekdusan (White Head Mountain) and in China Changbaishan (Ever White Mountain – its peaks are visibly snow-capped for much of the year). Historically, the present border between Korea and China, over 1,300 km (808 miles) long, was undelimited. In September 1909, when Korea was Japan's protectorate and bereft of sovereignty, Japan and China signed the Gando ('Jiandao' in Chinese) Treaty, under which Heaven Lake and its adjacent peaks became Chinese territory.

In the early 1960s, when China was embroiled in the famine induced by the Great Leap Forward, and in serious stand-offs with the Soviet Union and India, North Korea took the chance to negotiate a new border treaty. On 12 October 1962, the two communist neighbours settled on a redrawn border more favourable to North Korea. The two sides split the mountain into approximately equal parts, but North Korea gained more of the Heaven Lake summit caldera (55.5 per cent to 45.5 per cent). China also conceded approximately 500 km² of land.[1] It was a major victory for North Korean diplomacy, and further inflated the Mount Paektu myth.

In Korean creation mythology, Dangun, the purported progenitor of the Korean people, was born atop the mountain in 2333 BCE. In North Korean mythology, it is where, in February 1942 in a wooden hut on a foothill near the Heaven Lake crater, Kim Jong Il, the second-generation ruler, was born, during the period of heroic struggle against Japan led by his father.[*2] In 1988, Kim Jong Il had one of the peaks, Jangsu Peak, renamed Jong Il Peak, and the words carved into it in red. In wintertime, the snow-capped mountain and its ice-covered summit caldera appear mysterious and majestic, but bitingly cold 'knife winds', as North Koreans say, swirl around it for much of the year, eternally underlining the indomitable spirit of the freedom fighters under Kim Il Sung's command. February is one of the colder months, when the temperature near the peak of Mount Paektu often falls well below -29°C, and sometimes as low as -50°C. It is unlikely that Kim Jong Il's mother would have chosen such an inhospitable place to give birth to her first child.

---

* Throughout the book, the official North Korean English translation is used, except where it is indicated that the translation is incorrect, inadequate or unidiomatic.

And, of course, she didn't. He wasn't born there, but on a Soviet army base in the Russian Far East, and not in 1942 but on 16 February 1941, and not even as Kim Jong Il, but as Yuri Irsenovich Kim.[3] By then, Kim Il Sung had joined the Soviet 25th Army.

Mount Paektu is referred to in the national anthems of both Korean states. It is the most celebrated and symbolically important mountain in Korean history. Koreans on both sides of the border regard it as the birthplace of the Korean nation – the unique Korean ethnic identity, with its autonomous history and culture, set apart from its gargantuan and occasionally threatening neighbour, China.

For this reason, North Korean leaders have determinedly milked the mountain's imaginary mythical qualities. In the North Korean national emblem, its image appears just under the five-pointed red star. Mount Paektu is often referred to as the 'Sacred Mountain of the Revolution'. Kim's 'historical resistance' from his base in this Sacred Mountain of the Revolution, overstated as it is, affords the despotic dynasty its single most important source of legitimacy. Again, Kim Il Sung was the greatest patriot and war hero, bar none. It is only a matter of time before each scion of the dynasty undergoes a symbolic 'christening' as a child of Mount Paektu.

The earliest image of the current ruler Kim Jong Un riding a white horse with a silver star in its headstall appeared in 2014. It shows the boy Jong Un, seemingly no older than ten, riding next to his father. The photograph may be from around 1994, not long after Kim Jong Il had assumed power as Supreme Leader in the wake of his father's death.

It was November 2012, not quite a year into Kim Jong Un's reign, when Kim Yo Jong, then twenty-five, was shown riding a white horse with her paternal aunt, Kim Kyong Hui. Her aunt's white horse featured a five-pointed silver star on its headstall, as did the niece's: the emblem of the Kim dynasty, and also the nation it rules. Both women were of the Mount Paektu Bloodline: one the daughter of Kim Il Sung, the 'Sun of the Korean Nation', the other his granddaughter. While Kim Kyong Hui had long been a known entity, having run the party's Light Industry Department for more than two decades, Kim Yo Jong was not. But state media showing the younger sister of the incumbent Supreme Leader horse-riding genially with her aunt was a clear suggestion that Kim Yo Jong's official role in the dynasty was set to expand. It also implied a link between the two women: each was a princess and the sister of a Supreme Leader. At the same time, the difference between the two women was as stark as sunset and sunrise. Each offshoot of the 'Sun' will one day have reached its zenith, and the aunt was of a bygone era. The young niece's zenith is yet to be reached, and its height unknown.

A further indication of her importance came in October 2019, when Kim Jong Un and Kim Yo Jong were photographed riding up Mount Paektu together, each on horseback. At the time, the significance of the event went virtually unnoticed but, as I will argue in Chapter 14, it was a clear sign that plans to vastly strengthen and normalize Kim Yo Jong's official role in government were already in place. The pandemic only accelerated them.

Kim Yo Jong attends a wreath-laying ceremony at the Ho Chi Minh Mausoleum in Hanoi, Vietnam, on Saturday 2 March 2019.

Unlike famine or foreign attack, a pandemic kills prince and pauper alike. It can kill even the unassailable bearer of the Mount Paektu mantle. Since the end of the Korean War in 1953, North Korea's ruling family has never faced any serious existential challenge: not a popular uprising or even organized public protest worthy of the name. Despite countless stand-offs and rhetorical bellicosity, it has not been attacked by the United States or South Korea, beyond self-defence against armed attacks by the North. Between 1965 and 1971 there were over two thousand significant incidents south of the Military Demarcation Line, including in the Demilitarized Zone (DMZ) and inside the Republic of Korea (the formal name for South Korea), resulting in the deaths of 395 United Nations Command personnel.[4] And between 1954 and 1992, the North infiltrated approximately 3,700 armed agents into the South, 20 per cent of them sneaking in during 1967 and 1968 while the US was bogged down in the unwinnable war in Vietnam.[5]

But a silent, invisible, deadly enemy like Covid was one the North Korean leader had never seen before, and he is not in optimal health. Like his father and grandfather, Kim Jong Un suffers from heart disease, diabetes and obesity, and those are just his known ailments. Unless he suffers from delusion, too, he must believe that a succession plan to install his most trusted aide, his sister, should he become incapacitated, is essential to the security of his nation, and the safety of his wife and young children.

Even in the rigidly patriarchal, male-dominated society that is the Democratic People's Republic of Korea, Yo Jong's gender is not an impediment to rule – her blood is what matters above all else. Her mother was Ko Yong Hui, Kim Jong Il's most favoured consort, who gave birth to three children. The oldest, Jong Chol, might seem a more likely candidate to take over just by being male, but he has long been passed over as heir and has not appeared in public with Kim Jong Un since the death of their father in December 2011. Her half-brother, Jong Nam, the eldest son among the seven children Kim Jong Il fathered by four different women, fell victim in February 2017 to a sinister plot – assassinated by a chemical weapon attack in Kuala Lumpur International Airport in broad daylight. None of her three older half-sisters have held any significant government roles, or been given public acknowledgement.

Kim Jong Un himself is reported to have three young children, a son and two daughters. In November 2022, he publicly revealed one of his children for the first time, a daughter approximately ten years of age, at an event no less family friendly than the launch of a powerful intercontinental ballistic missile that could hit every part of the continental United States. The girl, reportedly named Ju Ae, bore a remarkable resemblance in facial features to both her mum, Ri Sol Ju, and her dad.* North Korean state media released several photos of

---

* In 2013, Dennis Rodman, the former US basketball star, revealed that Kim Jong Un had a baby girl named Ju Ae and that Kim had allowed him to hold her in his arms. However, the Chinese character 'Ae' (Beauty) is seldom used in naming girls among North Korea's millennial generation. According to Hyunseung Lee, a former North Korean party member of elite background, the girl's first name may actually be 'Ju Un', a combination of the second character from the first names of each parent (Ri Sol Ju and Kim Jong Un), and that Ju Ae may be a term of endearment.

the Kim family – dad, mum, daughter, and Aunt Yo Jong – joyously applauding the missile flight. Eight days later, North Korea released more photos of the girl at a photo-op with dad, this time dressed and made-up in the style of her mother, at the recent test-fire of what state media called 'the world's strongest strategic weapon.'[6]

Kim Jong Un's public rollout of his young daughter led some North Korea watchers to predict that she had already been chosen as his successor. In fact, Kim may have brought his child along to the spectacle just to gloat over the democratically elected leaders in Washington and Seoul, bound as they are by term limits. She is a symbol that his power, unlike theirs, is held for life and, in due course, will be passed on to one of his children. Moreover, Kim must have thought that the juxtaposition of a powerful missile that can hit the US with nuclear warheads and a wholesome parent–daughter ensemble might sow in his adversaries' subconscious a resigned acceptance of his nukes: 'He obviously cares about his daughter. He couldn't possibly start a nuclear war. Perhaps, in time, he'll become a responsible custodian of his nuclear weapons.'

In February 2023, Kim Jong Un had his girl sit centre-stage at a banquet, between her mother and himself, with generals in full dress uniform adorned with multiple shiny medals as the backdrop for a family photo shoot. Moments before, Kim had made his entrance on the red carpet holding his daughter's hand while his wife walked half a pace behind. The guests in attendance cheered and clapped wildly, as the ritual called for. All but one, who stood with her hands by her side looking on with a smile – Kim Yo Jong. She was the sole individual in the banquet hall who didn't need to applaud rapturously. Just days later, Kim Jong Un had his little girl sit next to him in the reviewing stand at a night-time military parade. At one point, she placed her little black-gloved hands on her daddy's grinning face, further reinforcing the loving father–daughter image.

Even if Kim Jong Un has decided his daughter is his most suitable successor, it will be some time before she grows into adulthood and is able, like Aunt Yo Jong, to issue formal statements in her own name or lead a delegation to Seoul or a foreign country. Among Kim Il Sung's seven grandchildren by direct hereditary lineage, it is therefore the youngest, Yo Jong, who stands as the sole heir to the throne. At least until well into the 2030s. In the event of such a sudden power transition, whether North Korea's first female Supreme Leader chooses to settle for the role of regent until her nephew or niece comes of age, or decides to rule for life – the rest of her life and *for* her own life – is a question to which there is no clear answer. But the wrathful nipping winter of 2013 could give her sobering pause for thought: Kim Jong Un's uncle, Jang Song Thaek, had served as the new, young Supreme Leader's regent for the previous two years, but that winter his utility and life together expired. Suddenly accused of being a traitorous counter-revolutionary, and also guilty of 'clapping half-heartedly' at his nephew's formal events, Jang was stripped of all his titles and executed – at the same time as which, or soon after, the process of digitally removing him from articles and photos was completed.

Memories of avunculicide and fratricide may deter any indiscretion on Ms Kim's part.

At least Kim Yo Jong is far better prepared to be the torchbearer than Kim Jong Un was on 17 December 2011, when, three weeks shy of his twenty-eighth birthday, he was thrust onto the throne in the wake of their father's sudden death from cardiac arrest. Until 2020, Yo Jong's day job was as her nation's 'Censor-in-Chief',[7] leading the Department of Propaganda and Agitation, also known as the Information and Publicity Department of the Central Committee of the Workers' Party of Korea. 'Department' belies its power and reach: it is more of a ministry, its mission to ensure that the North Korean people are properly indoctrinated with the state ideology and remain, to the greatest extent possible, ignorant of the outside world. Her father had also led the department from 1967 to 1972, when he was being groomed for power.

In 2020, Kim Yo Jong assumed more powerful roles, and effectively become 'Deputy Dear Leader'. Further following in her father's footsteps, she became the de facto head of the Department of Organization and Guidance, her nation's central locus of political power, overseeing all daily decisions on key personnel matters, including in the military.[8] In this most powerful department, political surveillance, punishment and commendation were her prerogatives. In theory she could decide who was monitored, demoted, promoted, punished, rewarded, banished or even tied up to be executed in the town square or in a sports stadium behind closed doors. The final word on which official or royal family member was to be purged, reinstated, suicided, demonstrably executed, or assassinated next still lies with her brother, but for many years she has clearly had his ear, and he has delegated foreign policy to her. As she declared in June 2020, she had been authorized by 'the Supreme Leader, [the] party and the state' to run policy towards the 'enemy', which means South Korea, Japan, much of Europe and, pointedly, the United States.[9] In other words, Kim Yo Jong now looms large as her nation's 'supreme deputy' – second only to her brother, and a powerful internal administrator and foreign policymaker.

Her spheres of influence have grown correspondingly in power, reach and, above all, visibility. In early 2021, she returned to her old job in the Propaganda and Agitation Department and, on 30 March, excoriated South Korean President Moon Jae-In in a written statement signed as 'Vice Director' of the department. Moon's crime? He had dared, four days earlier, to raise a mild objection to her nation's recent flight test of a 'new-type tactical guided' ballistic missile. Moon, she said, was 'a parrot raised by America' who 'doesn't have even the elementary logic and face.'[10]

The move back to her old haunt is neither a promotion nor demotion, but rather suggests that the Kim siblings, pleased with her work at the Department of Organization and Guidance in tightening control over key officials and punishing the undesirables, wanted to return to the task of putting their dynastic house in order vis-à-vis external enemies. They did this through pronouncements, vituperation and threats – including, as of early 2022, nuclear threats. (As of March 2023, Kim Yo Jong has issued nearly thirty statements, each of which is accentuated by her signature snark).

Later in 2021, Kim Jong Un pushed her higher still. In September, he appointed his sister to the State Affairs Commission, the top governing body and successor to the National Defence Commission, an entity Kim Jong Il had created.[11] Becoming one of thirteen members of the Commission, alongside Kim Jong Un, gave Kim Yo Jong a new official title when engaging with foreign heads of state, but as described above, titles and ranks often have little bearing on the actual power dynamics in North Korea. She was already the second-in-command, and will remain so even after she leaves the Commission, as she will whether she becomes a full member of the Political Bureau of the Central Committee of the Workers' Party of Korea, or merely an alternate member – as her brother appointed her in 2017 – or indeed is 'stripped' of the position altogether, as Kim Jong Un is rumoured to have done in January 2021.[12]

In short, as a divine princess of Mount Paektu Bloodline, Kim Yo Jong is immune to the vicissitudes of political appointments and dismissals of which the rest of DPRK officialdom must live in fear.

What Kim Yo Jong has shown so far suggests, moreover, that were she ever to become the Supreme Leader, she may prove fiercer and more ruthless than even her brother, their father or their grandfather. In her written statements she has repeatedly berated the South Korean president, calling him 'impudent', 'shameless', 'deranged', a 'frightened dog', an 'imbecile' and 'foolish' man who 'put his neck' into the 'noose of pro-U.S. flunkeyism'. In June 2020, she threatened to move troops into border regions that had previously been demilitarized. Although this threat was 'suspended' by Kim Jong Un later the same month, as though he was a restraining factor against his sister's wild impulses, it still loomed, as intended, as a psychological threat, further conditioning South Korea to docility.

In his 2018 New Year's Address, her brother had spoken of the 'nuclear button' on his desk. Of the heads of the world's nine nuclear states it is only one, the North Korean dictator, who remains unencumbered by any institutional checks and balances. Kim Yo Jong has already prefigured her own finger resting on that button. In April 2022, the First Sister threatened to nuke South Korea were the South to shoot first. If the South's military 'violated even an inch of our territory', she warned, 'our nuclear combat force will have to inevitably carry out its duty'. 'If the situation reaches such a phase,' she went on, in language as clear and bombastic as can be, 'a dreadful attack will be launched, and the South Korean army will have to face a miserable fate little short of total destruction and ruin. This is not just a threat.'[13]

Despite South Korean and Western media cooing over her charming smile and deportment during her Olympic visit, her gender denotes neither a softer streak nor a propensity towards denuclearization. In fact, to presume this first female co-dictator with her finger on the nuclear button in history – the world's first 'nuclear despotess' – may be more prone to parting ways with nukes by virtue of her gender is at best patronizing. Her youth – the other characteristic that disarms her interlocuters – in reality portends a prolonged reign of repression, as did her brother's when he took the reins at twenty-seven.[14]

At twenty-seven years of age, Kim Yo Jong, as the de facto leader of her nation's powerful Propaganda and Agitation Department, was spewing racist and sexist attacks, respectively, on US President Barack Obama and South Korea's first female president, Park Geun Hye. At thirty-five, in January 2023, she assumed the larger role of chief spokesperson on Russia's war on Ukraine and the renewed Cold War dynamics. Warning the US that any tanks supplied to Ukraine for defence against Russia will be 'burnt into pieces in the face of the indomitable fighting spirit and might of the heroic Russian army and people,' she added that her nation will 'always stand in the same trench with the service personnel and people of Russia.'[15]

Her dynasty's kinship with Russia, born when Josef Stalin designated Kim Il Sung the leader of what would become the North Korean state, was further consolidated by the greatest gamble to reunify Korea to date: the devastating war started by her ambitious grandfather.

CHAPTER 3

Peninsular Predominance: Pyongyang's Ultimate Mission

The continued division of Korea into the North and South is a living reminder today to Kim Jong Un and whoever may follow him that his family has unfinished business. North Korea's 'supreme national task', as stipulated in its constitution,[1] and referred to in the Charter of the Workers' Party of Korea, the Communist Party, is 'completing the cause of reunification through the united efforts of the whole nation.' In plain language, that means the obliteration of the democratic south, bringing the whole peninsula under the rule of the Kim dynasty.

If not for the United States thwarting the Soviet Union's plan to take over the whole peninsula, Kim Il Sung would most likely have become the Supreme Leader of a united Korean state, albeit a satellite state of the USSR, before handing over that power to his progeny. The partitioning of the Korean peninsula in August 1945 by the United States and the Soviet Union, the two principal powers emerging from the Second World War, was never meant to be permanent, but a temporary measure to facilitate the surrender of the Japanese troops dispersed throughout the region.

For the US, the broader strategic goal was to prevent the Soviet forces taking over all of Korea. The Soviet Union had declared war on Japan on 8 August 1945, and the very next day Soviet forces began attacking the Japanese Kwantung Army in Manchuria on three fronts. The Soviet–Japanese War lasted only a week, but the battles were intense, with heavy casualties on both sides. As the Red Army rapidly made its way south towards the Korean peninsula, the US belatedly sought to gain a foothold on the Asian mainland. Korea suddenly became a potential barrier to further unilateral Soviet land acquisition.

On 10 August, Soviet Foreign Minister Vyacheslav Molotov made it clear to the US Ambassador in Moscow, William Averell Harriman, that the Soviets were determined to take over the entire Korean peninsula.[2] Senior US officials scrambled to come up with a plan for partitioning Korea that would be acceptable to Stalin. At the time, the closest US troops to the Korean peninsula lay 600 miles (966 km) away in Okinawa.[3] Time was not on their side.

The few days between the US atomic attacks on Japan, on 6 and 9 August, and Japanese Emperor Hirohito's announcement of surrender on 15 August were hectic for senior US officials in Washington, their agenda consumed with the terms of surrender and the consequent US occupation of Japan. Korea, Japan's colony since 1910 and, thereafter, largely forgotten by Americans, suddenly took on an unprecedented importance.

At approximately 2 a.m. on 11 August, at a State-War-Navy Coordinating Committee meeting at the Pentagon, Brigadier General George Lincoln, together with Colonels Dean Rusk and Charles Bonesteel, was charged with coming up with a plan to block further southward advance by the Red Army. Poring over a small *National Geographic* map of East Asia, the three men less-than-methodically determined that the thirty-eighth parallel running east–west across the peninsula was likely to be the northernmost line acceptable to Stalin. In his memoir, *As I Saw It*, Dean Rusk, who went on to become Secretary of State in the 1960s, would recall that '[W]e looked just north of Seoul for a convenient dividing line but could not find a natural geographic line. We saw instead the thirty-eighth parallel and decided to recommend that.'[4] Persuading the Soviet leader to concede nearly half the peninsula to US administration even as Soviet forces stood on the verge of entering northern Korea seemed overly ambitious.[5] It was a frantic, last-minute, Hail Mary effort.

To the Americans' surprise, Stalin, his eyes set on winning American concessions on the post-war division of Europe, accepted the US proposal in less than forty-eight hours. In truth, neither the US nor the Soviet Union were inclined to go to war with each other in the very last days of history's greatest conflict over such a secondary prize as Korea. Thus a country that had remained undivided for over 1,000 years was split in two, and Brigadier General George Lincoln came to be referred to by his fellow West Point Military Academy alumni as 'the man who drew the thirty-eighth parallel.'[6]

The flippant manner in which the division of Korea was conceived and executed still grates on many Koreans' nerves.[7] At the same time, it prevented the full Communization of the peninsula, and made it possible for at least South Korea to develop into a prosperous democracy. The totalitarian Mount Paektu clan has prevented that in the North, yet through three generations remains just as determined to extend its rule over the South.

So, even before Kim Il Sung was chosen by the Soviets in 1945 to be their proxy in northern Korea, the United States had blocked the most direct route to his becoming the Supreme Leader of a *united* Democratic People's Republic of Korea. But the partition was still a line drawn on a map – not an insurmountable obstacle to the DPRK's unification agenda. Yet, to Kim Il Sung's surprise and much dismay, the US, which by 1949 had almost abandoned South Korea, would be mobilizing the United Nations to defend the South against his forces in the Korean War he started on 25 June 1950.

North Korea is a state built on bold and blatant falsehoods. The bald-faced lies that Kim Il Sung liberated Korea from Japanese colonial rule in 1945 and defeated the United States in the Korean War are the foundation of the state, and are both vigorously promoted to English readers abroad. In 1973, North Korea published an English translation of a biography of Kim Il Sung by Baik Bong, a government-employed writer, which was first published in Korean in 1968.

'On August 8, 1945, the Soviet Union finally declared war on Japan,' writes Baik. Of the events leading up to Korea's liberation, he states that:

General Kim Il Sung, who had already completed his operational plan for the final decisive offensives against Japanese imperialism, ordered the mobilization of all units under the Korean People's Revolutionary Army. Under the command of the General, the units began conducting courageous military operations in many areas in North, East and South Manchuria and the homeland, together with the Soviet Army.[8]

The acknowledgement of Soviet support in the book is noteworthy, not only because it is perhaps the only fact that is actually true, but also because for much of the first half of the 1960s, North Korea's relations with the Soviet Union had soured. Kim Il Sung had supported China in Beijing's stand-off against Moscow and also in the 1962 Sino–Indian War. And during the Cuban Missile Crisis in late 1962, which was contemporaneous with the Sino–Indian clash, North Korea denounced the Soviet Union for 'revisionism' – that is, giving in to the US imperialists instead of being yet more militant.

However, in the latter half of the 1960s, North Korea moved away from Beijing and cozied up to Moscow. By 1965, Nikita Khrushchev, with whom Kim Il Sung had had a frosty relationship, was out of power and Soviet arms aid to North Korea resumed. Moscow generously supplied Pyongyang with tanks, submarines, missiles, and jet fighters. Exploiting the acrimonious Sino–Soviet relationship in the 1960s, North Korea heavily leaned on the Soviet Union and openly criticized China, especially once China descended into the chaos of the Cultural Revolution in 1966. During the most radical early phase of the violent socio-political movement, which for three years engulfed so much of China from the north all the way to Yunnan and Guangdong,[9] Pyongyang and Beijing hurled insults at each other.

Although Kim Il Sung himself was a seasoned purveyor of vicious political purges, killing thousands of pro-Soviet and pro-China officials (i.e. his potential rivals) between 1956 and 1962, perhaps even he was awed by the sheer scale of attacks and killings in China's Cultural Revolution, masterminded by Mao Zedong and his fourth wife, Jiang Qing.[10] People were killed and disappeared on a scale never seen before.[11] Senior North Korean officials told the Soviet ambassador in Pyongyang that Mao is 'an old fool who has gone out of his mind', and that the Cultural Revolution was a 'great madness, having nothing in common with either culture or revolution.'[12] In return, Chinese Red Guards, the vanguards of the revolution, called Kim Il Sung a 'fat revisionist' and 'Khrushchev's disciple',[13] and in posters depicted him as a 'millionaire, an aristocrat, and a leading bourgeois element.'[14]

Hence Kim Il Sung's biography, much of it written during the absolute nadir in North Korea–China relations, completely omits the critical role of China in saving the DPRK from state collapse in the early phase of the Korean War, when the US-led

UN coalition captured Pyongyang and much of North Korea. China's entry into the war completely turned the tide, from the DPRK flailing on the precipice of extinction to once again repelling its adversaries south of the border. China inflicted a heavy toll on its adversaries, and also paid for it dearly in Chinese lives. Without question, Mao Zedong saved Kim Il Sung and his kingdom, as the United States had saved South Korea months before, in the wake of the North Korean invasion. Mao was Kim's deus ex machina. Yet in his 1968 authorized biography, the North Korean leader refused to acknowledge any Chinese role in what he would call 'the Fatherland Liberation War':

> During the Fatherland Liberation War, Premier Kim Il Sung, as Chairman of the Military Committee of the Democratic People's Republic of Korea and Supreme Commander of the Korean People's Army, commanded the infant People's Army and the entire people with super-ior commanding art and operational tactics acquired in the anti-Japanese armed struggle, and mercilessly crushed the reactionary armed forces composed of 16 countries led by the U.S. imperialists.
>
> . . . While the entire land had been turned into a sea of flame, the rocks burnt, and when even the rivers boiled, the Korean people, in response to the call of the Leader, converted the whole land into an impregnable fortress of enemy-smashing heights, badly mauled the large forces of the enemy attacking from the air and ground, and buried all of them in the mountains and rivers of the fatherland.

U.S. imperialism was defeated . . . As a result, the name of Premier Kim Il Sung, ever-victorious, iron-willed brilliant commander, coupled with the name of Heroic Korea, became a symbol of justice, courage, and might to the whole world.[15]

Neither is there any mention in the biography that Kim Il Sung had assiduously implored both Stalin and Mao to give him the green light to invade the South. In April 1950, two months before launching the invasion of the South, Kim Il Sung had told Stalin in Moscow that, in the very unlikely event the American imperialists became involved, Chairman Mao was ready to send Chinese troops. Even then, Stalin only reluctantly came on board. Later, in May, Kim Il Sung visited Mao in Beijing and sold the Chinese leader the same tall tale, this time that Comrade Stalin had agreed to send Soviet forces into Korea should the Americans intervene (which, he was sure, they wouldn't). Only then did Mao – who had more pressing duties on his mind, such as the post-Chinese Civil War reconstruction of his own vast country, the People's Republic of China being not quite eight months old – tell Kim to go for it.

As Kim had foretold, the South Korean military was utterly helpless. By the summer of 1949, the US, after three years of governing the South, had, as previously mentioned, effectively abandoned the country, withdrawing its troops aside from a few hundred military advisors. Seoul fell within three days of the invasion, just as Kim had predicted. In 1950, Seoul prefigured the taking of Saigon in 1975 and Kabul in 2021, both

American-supported regimes falling helplessly to their foes in spite of years of US military and financial assistance. In late June and July, as North Korean troops overran the vast majority of South Korean territory, Kim Il Sung, not quite forty years of age, stood on the cusp of unifying the fatherland by absorbing the American 'puppet state' in the South in a heroic war for the 'Liberation of the Fatherland'.

However, in a strange twist of fate, the Americans spoiled Kim's ultimate mission of communizing the entire Korean peninsula by coming back to defend South Korea. The Harry Truman administration completely misread the cause of Kim Il Sung's invasion of South Korea. The US saw the invasion across the thirty-eighth parallel as a test of the United States by the Soviet Union: a prelude to a general military expansion in Europe and other strategic outposts throughout the world. Should the US sit idly by, the Americans thought, it would only embolden Moscow. In their misguided and patronizing reading of the North Korean leader and his ambitious agenda, they saw Kim Il Sung as a puppet of Stalin and Mao, doing what he was told by his Communist patrons.

For example, Edward Barrett, Assistant Secretary of State for Public Affairs, told reporters after a National Security Council meeting soon after news of the outbreak of the war in Korea that the relationship between Stalin and Kim Il Sung was the same as that between Walt Disney and Donald Duck. Such misunderstanding of the funny-looking North Korean leader, a profound condescension bordering on racism, has plagued successive American administrations for more than thirty years in their inadequate efforts to cope with the North Korean nuclear problem.

US forces came to defend South Korea, therefore, not necessarily to save South Korea itself, but to deter Moscow and Beijing from further military aggression by proxy, thereby upholding the United Nations Charter and the concept of collective security, and to protect US national interests by shoring up Japan, still under US occupation but by then considered a key ally in the making. Whatever the motive, the US led a sixteen-nation coalition under the banner of the nascent United Nations to defend South Korea from the North. After three years of feral fighting against the combined Sino–North Korean forces (and undeclared participation by Soviet pilots) and a tremendous death and casualty toll, the war came to an end with a truce: a ceasefire agreement that left the two Korean states divided along virtually the same line that was in place before Kim Il Sung's invasion. South Korea was saved, and North Korea's war of liberation was thwarted.

On 27 July 1953, the armistice agreement between North Korea, the United States, the United Nations Command and China was signed. The North Korean General Nam Il and US Army Lieutenant General William K. Harrison, Jr. signed the document at the border village Panmunjom, at 10 a.m. Later, Kim Il Sung, Chinese Commander Peng Dehuai, and US Army General Mark W. Clark, Commander of the United Nations Command, separately affixed their own names.[16] South Korean President Syngman Rhee, out of concern that the ceasefire agreement would, if not perpetuate the division of the Korean peninsula, then give the North time to rebuild its military for another invasion, as well as out of his personal desire to unify Korea, refused to sign.

The armistice agreement is not a peace treaty. Neither is it an Instrument of Surrender, as signed by Nazi Germany and Imperial Japan, respectively, in May and September 1945. At the same time, North Korea claims victory over the US and celebrates 27 July each year as Victory in the Great Fatherland Liberation War. Oddly, despite its 'victory', North Korea since the early 1970s has persistently called on the US for a peace treaty. Just why a 'victor' would call on its 'vanquished foe' to sign a peace treaty remains unexplained by Pyongyang. But the reason lies in plain sight. A formal peace treaty would render the United Nations Command, a United Nations Security Council-mandated multinational command in South Korea that has enforced the de facto peace in the Korean peninsula since 1953, unnecessary, if not illegitimate. More importantly, it would deprive the US troops stationed in South Korea of their very raison d'être. Under the euphoric rubric of 'peace', pressure would then build within South Korea as well as in some circles in the United States, goes the thinking, to withdraw American troops and downgrade US military support for South Korea.

To North Korea, therefore, the United States is, by its continued commitment to the defence of South Korea against North Korean adventurism, 'the fundamental obstacle to the development of our revolution and our principal enemy,' as Kim Jong Un stated in his January 2021 Eight Party Congress speech. The United States, North Koreans remind each other daily, is a jackal constantly eyeing their righteous victim state. It must be resisted at all costs.

What is not apparent to the ordinary North Korean, or even many South Koreans, is that the Kim dynasty are motivated by more than their duty somehow to fulfil the 'supreme national task' of unification. Trying, alone, is not enough, for it implies remaining perpetually the inferior Korean state. The mere existence of a Korean state immensely more legitimate, freer, and richer presents the Mount Paektu clan with a long-term existential threat. By conservative estimates, South Korea is fifty times richer than the North. It is also a beacon to the North Korean people, having attracted since the 1953 armistice over 34,000 North Koreans to risk the dangerous escape from their brutal native land to resettle there. For the Kim dynasty to endure, rather than see the North absorbed by its prosperous neighbour, it must eliminate this alternate Korean state either by force or peaceful merger, and South Koreans will not willingly choose to live under the Kims and the Workers' Party of Korea.

On the other hand, reunification by a mixture of force and blackmail seems feasible, armed with nuclear weapons as the North is – except that the US stands in the way. In this existential game, Kim Yo Jong has assumed the grave responsibilities of threatening, censoring and manipulating the richer Korean state and its sole treaty ally, her dynasty's 'principal enemy'.

CHAPTER 4

All in the Family

When, in July 1994, with the secretive kingdom plunged into histrionic mourning in the wake of his father's death, Kim Jong Il rose to become the Supreme Leader, the outside world – even foreign intelligence agencies – knew very little about the new man. They knew virtually nothing about his children, either, except for Jong Nam, the eldest son, who was in his early twenties. Of Kim Jong Il's two youngest children, Jong Un and Yo Jong, they knew nothing at all.

Kim Jong Il's first biological child is Hye Kyong. She is the daughter of Kim and his first wife, Hong Il Chon. Kim Jong Il married Ms Hong in 1966 upon the urging of his father. The next year, Ms Hong gave birth to Hye Kyong. Soon thereafter, Ms Hong became estranged from her husband, possibly due to his philandering.*

---

* Hye Kyong has reportedly been a central figure in Kim Jong Un's Secretariat of the Workers' Party of Korea for several years, the central office of the nation's leader (see Song Hong-geun, 'The Big Shot in North Korea's Secretariat is the Daughter of Kim Jong Il and Hong Il Chon' [Korean], *Shin Donga*, 29 April 2020). She – or one of her two younger

One of the results of Kim Jong Il's womanizing was the birth of his oldest son, Kim Jong Nam, at Ponghwa Clinic and Hospital in Pyongyang, an exclusive facility for the elites, on 10 May 1971. Kim Jong Il was overjoyed to have a son, but could not tell his father as that would mean confessing to his illicit affair with the famous actress, Song Hye Rim, Jong Nam's mother. When Kim Jong Il propositioned Ms Song in the late 1960s, she was married to another man. Kim Il Sung, although he had a wandering eye himself, may have frowned on his son's behaviour. Kim Jong Il would have feared his father's disapproval all the more as he had yet to be designated heir.

In the early 1970s, at one of his lavish evening parties, Kim Jong Il met Ko Yong Hui, a trained dancer with the Mansudae Art Troupe. Thereafter, he often called on Ko to sit next to him at dinners and late-night parties. In 1974, Kim Jong Il was internally designated heir apparent. That year, while living with Song and carrying on an affair with Ko, Kim Jong Il married his typist, Kim Yong Suk. At the end of the year, Yong Suk gave birth to a daughter, Sol Song. For many years, Sol Song was mistaken by South Koreans and others as Kim Jong Il's eldest daughter. Her younger sister, Chun Song, was born in 1975.

Ultimately, Ko Yong Hui won over Kim Jong Il, beating her competitors, and in 1979 moved in with him at Residence No. 15 in Pyongyang, an extravagant mansion with a zoo

---

half-sisters (excluding Yo Jong) – may also be the female figure spotted tending to Kim Jong Un as an aide during official events in 2022. But, as with all her siblings besides Jong Un and Yo Jong, she has not been presented to the public explicitly as a member of the royal family.

inside its precincts where Kim had previously lived with Song Hye Rim.[1] Kim Jong Il never married Song, but he treated her as his common-law wife, as he did Ko Yong Hui, whom Song, in private conversations, referred to unflatteringly as 'hammer nose'.

As we have seen, Ko Yong Hui had three children with Kim Jong Un. All three are presumed to have been born in North Korea. But the places of their birth remain unconfirmed. The date and month of Kim Jong Un's birth, 8 January, is an accepted fact. But North Korea has yet to confirm his year of birth. This is not unusual. The only royal birthdays – day, month, and year – explicitly stated are those of Kim Il Sung, his first – officially, that is – wife Kim Jong Suk, and Kim Jong Il. Kim Il Sung's birthday, the 'Day of the Sun', is the most important national holiday. Kim Jong Il's birthday is the second most important. Both are celebrated each year as the 'grand festival of the Korean nation', although Kim Jong Il's real birth year, 1941, has never been acknowledged. In 1974, when Kim Jong Il was internally designated heir, North Korea announced his birth year for the first time – as 1942. By making the son's birth year exactly thirty years after his father (who was born in 1912) they would tidily reach key milestones together. So, when Kim Jong Il turned forty, Dad turned seventy. When the son turned fifty, Dad turned eighty. There were big celebrations for both events, accentuating the hereditary greatness passed down from father to son. The birthday of Kim Jong Il's mother, Kim Jong Suk, 24 December 1917, has not been designated a holiday, although it is mentioned reverently in the state media on Christmas Eve.

In time, the state will make Jong Un's birthday into a national holiday on a par with the birthdays of his two predecessors. But the third-generational ruler's relative youth, having inherited his kingdom in his late twenties, has to date tempered such solipsistic impulses.

As for Kim Jong Un's purported year of birth, South Korea's Ministry of Unification has listed it as 1984, with the acknowledgement that it is disputed and that the correct year of birth 'may be 1982 or 1983'. The National Intelligence Service, South Korea's top spy agency, states Kim Jong Un's birth year is still unconfirmable. But Ko Yong Suk, Kim Jong Un's aunt and caretaker who defected to the US with her family in 1998, has said on record that she knows for a fact that Kim Jong Un was born in 1984, the same year as the birth of her first son. There could be no doubt because, as Ko Yong Suk told a *Washington Post* reporter in April 2016: '[Kim Jong Un] and my son were playmates from birth. I changed both of their diapers.'[2]

Another family defector, Jong Nam's cousin, Lee Han-Young, revealed some telling details about the imperiousness and notions of entitlement that sprouted early within the Mount Paektu clan. Lee Han-Young escaped to South Korea in 1982 and published an exposé on the North Korean royal family in 1996. Whereas, in Korean culture, for a child to address an adult by his or her first name would be tantamount to blasphemy, Kim Jong Il's offspring, of course, were no ordinary kids. Lee Han-Young revealed that Kim Jong Nam, the eldest son, called adults by their first name. Adults addressed the boy respectfully by his military rank, which rose with each birthday.

On his third birthday, Jong Nam was given the title of one-star brigadier general. The next year, he was promoted to major general. When he turned five, he became lieutenant general. At six, a full four-star general. At seven, marshal. And on his eighth birthday, generalissimo. From age eight, adults around Jong Nam thus addressed him as 'Comrade Generalissimo', while the little, spoiled prince always used the informal way of speech with grown-ups.[3]

Lee Han-Young, whose given name was Yi Il Nam, was born to Jong Nam's maternal aunt, Song Hye Rang. Lee wrote in his memoir that he, too, as a member of the royal family, addressed adults by their first name even though he was just a juvenile. Lee was feared by virtually all adults he met as a result of who his uncle was. As a teenager, he could kick a general in the shin or slap the North Korean ambassador to Moscow in the face with impunity.

Some other credible details on the childhood of Kim Jong Un and Kim Yo Jong are available, courtesy of Kim Jong Il's Japanese sushi chef of thirteen years. Kenji Fujimoto (a pseudonym) worked for Kim Jong Il from 1988 to 2001, and was paid handsomely and granted many perks by the Dear Leader. For years, he frequently enjoyed direct personal access to Kim Jong Il and his three youngest children, Jong Chol, Jong Un, and Yo Jong. He never saw any of the Supreme Leader's other children – not at home, official party meetings, or any family outings, since Kim Jong Il during Fujimoto's years of employment forbade his children from different mothers from meeting each other. Fujimoto was invited to attend Kim Jong Il's banquets and late-night drinking parties. He played games with the royal family. He was allowed to ride on Kim Jong Il's luxury yacht off Wonsan harbour. Even though the chef was in his forties, in the late 1980s and early 1990s he served as the boys' 'play date', teaching them games and how to fly kites and, when Kim Jong Un grew into his mid-teens, was the boy's secret smoking buddy.*

According to Fujimoto, Yo Jong's parents addressed their daughter as 'Princess' or 'Princess Yo Jong' from early childhood. What's more, they addressed and referred to Yo Jong's two older brothers as 'Big Brother' (Jong Chol) and 'Little Brother' (Jong Un) – that is, from Yo Jong's vantage point.[4] The princess, soon after birth, became the axis of the royal family. At meals, she always sat next to her father, on Kim Jong Il's left, while mother sat to the Dear Leader's right. To mother's right sat Jong Un, and on Yo Jong's left sat Jong Chol. This was always the seating configuration at the dinner table.

Fujimoto paints Yo Jong as a strong-willed girl. Not quite yet 'iron-willed', a favourite epithet of the Mount Paektu family which has been passed down the generations, but determined and stubborn. For example, Kim Jong Nyo, a singer with the Pochonbo Electronic Ensemble, a once favourite band of Kim Jong Il, was stationed at Kim Jong Il's Wonsan estate to tend to Kim Yo Jong and serve as the little princess's playmate. The singer even accompanied Yo Jong on her foreign trips with her

* Kim Jong Il allowed his teenaged son to drink alcohol but prohibited him from smoking – as with many other less renowned families around the world, the father's exhortation proved futile, as Kim Jong Un remains a chain smoker, as his father had been for most of his adult life.

mother and brothers. Ko Yong Hui would occasionally take her three children on pleasure trips to Japan aboard the ferry *Man Gyong Bong* (named after a neighbourhood in Pyongyang where Kim Il Sung was reportedly born). Japan banned the ferry service in the wake of North Korea's first nuclear test in October 2006, but in its heyday the ship was a regular conduit for passengers as well as illicit drugs, counterfeit US currency, and electronic gadgets. As soon as the ship's crew were alerted that important personages were approaching the dock by car, they would order all passengers aboard to draw the curtains and desist from peering outside at the motorcade. Ms Ko and her children would arrive at the Wonsan port in a Mercedes sedan with heavily tinted windows, surrounded by other cars, and come on board right before the ship would set sail. Those intrepid enough to take a peep would see a well-dressed and apparently powerful woman with small children and a female aide or two. Once the ship dropped anchor in Japan, Ho Jong Man, Chairman of the General Association of Korean Residents in Japan (also known as Chongryon or Chosen Soren), the de facto North Korean representative organization in that country, would be waiting on the dock to greet the royal visitors.[5]

One day, Fujimoto found Kim Jong Nyo, the princess's aide, gone. Princess Yo Jong, then around eight or nine, had fired her.[6] Another time, Yo Jong scolded her brother, Jong Chol. Fujimoto observed that Jong Chol, like teenaged boys around the world, showed a keen interest in girls, whereas Jong Un, even at sixteen, was far more engrossed in sports and video games. When Jong Chol was about sixteen, he developed a crush on one of Yo Jong's female aides, who was very pretty and only a year older than him. One day, Jong Chol made the mistake of sneaking into a women-only theatre inside one of his father's estates, where Yo Jong liked to watch movies with her female aides, to steal glimpses of his sister's aide. About ten minutes later, Yo Jong dragged the secret intruder, her brother who was seven years her senior, out of the theatre, thus restoring order.[7]

When Ko Yong Hui was absent from home, away in Europe for months at a time seeking medical care for breast cancer and other ailments, Kim Ok (born 1964), Kim Jong Il's last and youngest live-in consort, took Ko's seat at the table, with the three children in their usual seats. Kim Jong Il had an open intimate relationship simultaneously with Ko Yong Hui and Kim Ok, who worked as his personal assistant. The two ladies had a good mutual relationship, according to Fujimoto. Ko even saw Kim Ok as a potential caretaker of her three children. In fact, when Ko was home, all three adults and the three children had dinner together, with Kim Ok seated next to Jong Un. The children called their father's mistress-cum-secretary by her first name, albeit affectionately, as they did all adults other than their parents.

Ko Yong Hui had sought medical care in France for several years before succumbing to cancer in May 2004. She died in Paris. Kim Jong Il sent a special coffin on his personal plane to transport Ko's body from Paris back to Pyongyang. As France did not have diplomatic relations with North Korea, the South Korean embassy in Paris facilitated communication between

Paris and Pyongyang and helped with logistics for the North Korean delegation, the head of which was none other than the lady-in-waiting, Kim Ok.[8]

While Kim Jong Il spent more time with Ko Yong Hui than any of the other mothers of his children, he kept tabs on all his offspring. During their twenty-four-day journey by train through Russia in July and August of 2001, Kim Jong Il mentioned to Konstantin Pulikovsky, President Vladimir Putin's Russian Far East envoy, that Sol Song was 'very capable'. Pulikovsky wrote a book about the experience, *Orient Express: Through Russia with Kim Jong Il.*[9] He did not mention it in the book, but later said that Kim Jong Il told him on the train that he had two very capable daughters, whereas his sons were basically 'useless'. It's unclear which daughters Kim Jong Il had in mind. He certainly could have been referring to Sol Song and her sister, Chun Song. Kim Yo Jong, in August 2001, would have been a month shy of turning thirteen, likely too young for her father to be assessing her leadership potential with confidence but, as we've seen, neither of Yo Jong's older half-sisters has been confirmed to have held a high office or led a prominent public life in either the Kim Jong Il or Kim Jong Un era.

To Kim Jong Un and his sister, their three half-sisters are 'side branches', which is a phrase Kim Il Sung used for the first time in 1973. Kim Il Sung was referring to his own wife, Kim Song Ae – his second or third wife – and her younger brother, Kim Song Gap. Kim Il Sung had grown indignant that his wife and brother-in-law were amassing power by appointing and promoting their own people in key positions within the party and the military without his approval. By then, Kim Song Ae had, first, as the vice chair of the Central Committee of the Korean Democratic Women's League in the mid-1960s and then as its chair in 1971, started to build her own cult of personality. Photographs of her giving on-the-spot guidance tours and articles and books about her were published without her husband's permission, the Supreme Leader's fastidious son dutifully informed him.

Kim Jong Il, who lost his mother in 1949 when he was only eight and fondly remembered her throughout his adult life,[10] counselled his father that his stepmother's self-idolization projects were an offence to his biological mother's memory as a hero of the revolution, as well as a direct challenge to his father's monolithic ideological system of leadership. The ideological system was an elaborate set of principles calling for the absolute worship of the Supreme Leader, which Kim Jong Il's uncle, Kim Yong Ju, had first developed in 1967. By the early 1970s, Kim Jong Il had appropriated the dogma himself and propagated it widely, calling for absolute loyalty to his father.

Side branches grow out of the core of the Mount Paektu Bloodline. When necessary, they need to be trimmed. Kim Il Sung prevented his wife from appearing at formal events for the next two years. Her influence waned as party officials caught on. Her brother was not heard from again. In North Korea, catching drift of who's in and who's out is a vital survival skill. When he was still heir, Kim Jong Il saw his two half-brothers and two half-sisters as side branches to be watched closely. As leader, he made sure that these 'side branch' half-siblings, Kim Song Ae's four children, would not occupy powerful positions in government but be sent abroad as diplomats in semi-exile.

His youngest brother was not so lucky. In 1971, when Kim Jong Il became for the first time the proud father of baby boy (Jong Nam), so too did his dad, Kim Il Sung, become the father of a newborn son (albeit not for the first time). Kim Il Sung, nearing sixty, acquired that year both a grandson in Jong Nam and an eighth child in Hyon, born to his considerably younger nurse-cum-masseuse.[11]

In 2007, Kim Jong Il, presumably out of fatherly love and an abundance of caution, had his half-brother Hyon, at the time thirty-six years of age and living in comfort in a mansion in Pyongyang, killed.[12]

To Kim Jong Un, beyond his own children only his sister, Yo Jong, and brother, Jong Chol, belong to the core trunk of the Mount Paektu tree. His three older half-sisters inhabit a space within the royal family outside the direct line of descendants while, as we have seen, his half-brother Kim Jong Nam met an altogether darker fate. His older brother Kim Jong Chol appears quite content to live out of the spotlight. But Yo Jong, capable and trusted, is of an entirely different mould.

CHAPTER 5

The Narcissistic Psychopath Father

Kim Jong Il's children had the kind of rich and pampered royal lifestyle that would tend to engender a sense of supreme entitlement. Did they also inherit some of their father's worst traits?

When Kim Jong Il became his father's heir, what most observers saw, or chose to see, was merely a playboy devoted to hard drinking, womanizing and watching Hollywood movies. His nephew Lee Han-Young revealed much about the ultra-lavish and deified lifestyle of North Korea's royal family, including the frequent parties Kim Jong Il threw for up to forty of his closest aides. These featured young female singers and dancers with whom the men drank, sang, and danced into the night. The 'admission fee' to these exclusive parties, an affirmation of one's privileged status as a member of Kim Jong Il's inner circle, was to gulp down at the door to the banquet hall a full glass of hard liquor. On some nights, the revelry led to drinking games, in which the loser had to shave off a part of his hair – pubic hair for women. In the Kim Jong Un era, too, senior officials have occasionally been seen at formal events with a streak of their hair missing.[1]

But with his accession to power in 1994, darker rumours resurfaced – of Kim Jong Il ordering the kidnappings of foreign women from East Asia, Europe and the Middle East to serve as compliant attendants at his parties. Now it all seemed plain to see: the new Great Leader was, well, nuts. How could such a depraved, downright crazy kook possibly succeed in holding his strange nation together, mused knowledgeable people with touching earnestness.

Belief in Kim's fondness for the sybaritic lifestyle was not without foundation, but the allegations of insanity were mostly the product of unsophisticated inferences. Those familiar with Western frat-house culture might have concluded ruefully that Kim Jong Il's penchant for partying hard and chasing after women was not necessarily incompatible with success, and fell woefully short as evidence of insanity or even incompetence. But the centuries-old stereotype of the cruel, wily, inscrutable Oriental dictator clouded judgements. The North Korean leader was an incomprehensible oddity to be mocked and endlessly patronized.

The long and disorienting journey Kim Yo Jong and Kim Jong Un's father had been on is, to a considerable extent, instructive in explaining the formation of the person he was on his ascension to leader. At the age of just four, when Kim Jong Il's parents were still calling him affectionately by his Russian name, Yura, his father became the most powerful indigenous leader in the land. North Korea may have been just one half of a land divided into two, and still occupied by the Soviet Union, but Kim Il Sung was the one the Soviets most favoured. Most of the time, when Father was not meeting with the Russians, he was surrounded by fawning subordinates. For the young prince, life in destitute Korea was bounteous and privileged far beyond that of any other child.

As a young boy, however, Yura suffered two personal tragedies. First, in 1947, his three-year-old brother Shura drowned in an accident. Two years later, in September 1949, his mother died, possibly from complications while giving birth. The following year, still only nine, Kim Jong Il found himself living through the terrifying travails of war – albeit one started by his own father.

When the North invaded the South on 25 June 1950, Seoul fell without much resistance, in just three days. Under Kim Il Sung's personal command, the Korean People's Army drove south, taking town after town, and by early August the territory controlled by South Korea had shrunk, despite incipient military support from United Nations forces, to a small part of the south-eastern tip of the peninsula behind the 'Pusan Perimeter', a 140-mile-long defensive line, and Jeju Island further south.

However, in mid-September, the tide turned. The western flank of the peninsula saw the Incheon Landing, an amphibious assault on North Korean forces by the United Nations Command under General Douglas MacArthur, its commander-in-chief. In October, having cut off North Korea's supply lines, the US-led UN forces marched north into North Korean territory.

Yura, or Kim Jong Il, and his younger sister, Kyong Hui, were forced to retreat from Pyongyang to the city of Kanggye in Chagang Province, near the border with China. Their father's trusted friend, Ri Ul Sol, a partisan comrade of Kim Il Sung in the Soviet 25th Army, was charged with seeing the young prince and princess to safety. For both Kim Il Sung and Ri Ul Sol, joining the Soviet Army had proved a once-in-a-lifetime career move. Following the end of the Korean War, both men lived a long life of immense power and privilege. In 1995, Kim Jong Il appointed Ri as Marshal of the Korean People's Army – at the time only one of three officers to be granted the honour in the nation's history, excluding Kim Jong Il himself. In fact, Ri even outlived Jong Il, once his ward, by some four years.

As an extra precaution, Kim Jong Il and Kim Kyong Hui were taken out of the warzone to Jilin, China, where as a teenager their father had been schooled in the late 1920s.[2] Kim Il Sung had spent much of his youth and young adulthood, 1919 to 1940, in China. While he would later talk and even write about his awakening to communism in China, his son, Jong Il, would be more reticent about his inglorious sojourn there as a young boy during the war.

In August 2010, however, sensing his own mortality creeping up on him after suffering a major stroke in August 2008, and just three months after his previous visit, Kim Jong Il took his youngest son, Jong Un, to China for a proper introduction to the Chinese leadership (both the outgoing president Hu Jintao and the incoming leader, Vice President Xi Jinping) upon whom he depended for political support and his country's material sustenance.[3] The next month, Kim Jong Un's name appeared in North Korean media for the first time, as none less than a four-star general.

During their China visit, Kim Jong Il took his son to his old hometown, and the most important stop was Jilin Yuwen High School, where his father Kim Il Sung had studied from 1927 to 1929. That day, according to North Korea's official news agency, the Korean Central News Agency (KCNA), Kim Jong Il 'laid a floral basket before the statue of the President [Kim Il Sung] . . . and was overcome with deep emotion.' The school choir sang for the special guest a 'Song of General Kim Il Sung' and the 'school song in humble reverence for the President, a peerlessly great man.'[4] The North Korean leader also left an inspiring signed statement for the school and its students, both present and future: 'I wish Yuwen Middle School, which is symbolic of DPRK–China friendship and has a long history and tradition, will train many more excellent personnel. August 26, 2010. Kim Jong Il.'[5]

Not far from the school was father and son's next port of call: the Catholic Church of Jilin. As children, Kim Jong Il and his sister Kyong Hui lived on its compound under pseudonyms for much of the duration of the Korean War. Kim Jong Il reportedly told a priest, 'I once lived here.'[6]

Kim Jong Il's stopover in Jilin was not entirely out of respect for his father's awakening to Communist thought at Yuwen Middle School, as it was called in the 1920s. Neither was it primarily triggered by nostalgia as he approached the end of his life. It was principally intended to re-confirm to the Chinese leadership the old historical bond between the Mount Paektu family and the leadership of the Communist Party of China. Winning the Chinese leaders' good graces towards his son, who would one day inherit his kingdom, was an act of fatherly love. The next day, President Hu Jintao told the North Korean leader that his visit to Jilin Province was 'where the historical roots of Sino–DPRK friendship were provided amid the common struggle against foreign aggressors', and 'is of particular importance in boosting the traditional bilateral relations of friendship and cooperation onto a new higher stage.'[7]

Further insight into Kim Jong Il's priorities came from the fact that father and son embarked on their China trip by train on 25 August, just hours after the former US President Jimmy Carter had landed in Pyongyang on a mission to retrieve a US citizen, Aijalon Gomes, a Boston-based missionary who had been detained since January for illegally entering North Korea. Kim Jong Il's snub was not due to conflicting schedules – even last-minute rescue missions entail several days of planning and mutual communication between the two parties, the hostage-taker and hostage-rescuer. He'd also decided not to leave so much as a courtesy note for Carter or give even the slightest indication that he would be wholly unavailable for the former US president during his visit. Kim Jong Il had, in fact, already issued a signed amnesty for Gomes before taking off for China close to midnight.[8] But Carter waited an extra day in the hope of meeting Kim Jong Il, before departing for Boston with Gomes only after it had become clear that Kim would not be back any time soon.

After the war ended in 1953, Kim Jong Il had lived the pampered life of a prince and, later, from his early thirties on, the unchallenged imperious life of the heir apparent. Outwardly, he was far less gregarious than his father. He seldom travelled abroad and, on the few foreign trips he made once he'd become the Supreme Leader, he travelled only to China and Russia, always on his customized personal train. Domestically, Kim Jong Il never once addressed his nation on television – never even gave speeches to be aired on TV or radio, bar one at a military parade in Kim Il Sung Square in April 1992, on the occasion of the sixtieth anniversary of the founding of the Korean People's Revolutionary Army, the band of anti-Japanese fighters supposedly founded by Kim Il Sung. Appointed by his father Supreme Commander of the Korean People's Army (the regular North Korean Army) the previous December, he faced the columns of soldiers below from the reviewing platform, leaned towards the seven raised microphones before him, hands awkwardly taking his weight on the rim of the podium, and blurted out, 'Glory to the heroic soldiers of the Korean People's Army!'

That was it. The whole speech. Lasting precisely five seconds.[9] Perhaps the new supreme commander believed brevity a virtue.

In private settings, however, Kim Jong Il was talkative, decidedly not shy, and often quite charming. He could be both kind and cruel, amiable and offensive, narcissistic and generous. To his forty or so favourite male officials and also their female entertainers – singers, musicians, and attendants – often 'invited' to his exclusive late-night revelries, Kim Jong Il gave, by North Korean standards, lavish gifts. Almost monthly, Kim Jong Il dished out to the men imported suits, socks, shoes, and pens. From the Dear Leader, the women – some of them movie stars, some there to provide sexual favours to select men – received Japanese underwear, make-up, soap, and winter scarves. Once a year, Kim gave away Swiss-made Omega and Rolex luxury watches. There was just one gift that topped the watches: fancy imported sedans given only rarely to the most favoured in his circle.[10]

With generosity came discipline. Kim Jong Il rigorously enforced his own rules of non-disclosure about these drunken parties, during which he often sang the same South Korean pop songs he had banned throughout his nation. In 1979 or 1980, Kim Jong Il had the wife of a senior official, Ri Myong Je, a frequent attendee of these parties, executed at a State Security Department (secret police) shooting range. The victim, a professor at Kim Il Sung University, had written an anony-mous letter of complaint to Kim Il Sung, describing in detail the frequent, debauched parties his son was hosting, and imploring the Supreme Leader to put an end to such vileness. In an attempt to hide her own identity, she wrote the letter with her left hand, although she was right-handed.

The letter never reached Kim Il Sung's desk. The secret police sent it straight to Kim Jong Il. By then, all documents submitted to Kim Il Sung were screened first by Kim Jong Il, Kim Il Sung having by 1980 been relegated by his son to merely the public face of the state, reduced to carrying out 'guidance tours' of factories, farms and schools to exhort his subjects to 'work harder and raise productivity', receiving foreign dignitaries, and putting his name to diplomatic documents. Kim Jong Il had gained full control of the powerful Organization and Guidance Department (OGD) by appointing his cronies and classmates from Kim Il Sung University. By the time Kim Il Sung formally declared Jong Il his successor at the Sixth Party Congress in October 1980, the son had almost monopolized power, especially the power to appoint key personnel to government and the military, by removing that final authority from all other branches of government and concentrating it in the OGD. Even the chief officers of Section 1 of the Supreme Guard Command, the division of the Korean People's Army tasked with protecting Kim Il Sung, answered directly to the OGD. Following the 1980 party congress, Kim Jong Il forbade the party from calling another congress, a move that would only consolidate power in the formal rank of the party's general secretary, Kim Il Sung, and other top party members of the presidium of the politburo.[11] It would be thirty-six years before the next party congress would be convened, by which time Kim Jong Il had been embalmed for several years.

It took two months of investigation to identify the letter writer as Ri Myong Je's wife. She was then shot dead at the shooting range by her own husband, who volunteered to take on the job of executing the 'enemy' traitor himself. Kim Jong Il, there in attendance, personally approved the request. After Ri had shot his wife, he turned to Kim and asked the de facto Supreme Leader to shoot him next, for being the husband of the 'enemy'. In all likelihood, it had been Ri who had blabbed to his wife about Kim Jong Il's parties after coming home from one of them in a state of inebriation.

'I'll forgive you just this one time,' replied Kim, graciously sparing Ri's life.[12] Indeed, Ri was allowed to keep attending the late-night parties. A while later, the Dear Leader even hooked Ri up with a new wife – a young female nurse who worked in the party central committee, showing himself once again a benevolent leader. What his son, Ri Yong Ho, then in his mid-twenties, thought of his dad killing his mum and marrying a woman much closer to his age than Father's, may never be told. He, too, certainly prospered under the Kim regime – both under Kim Jong Il and Kim Jong Un – for a time. Ri Yong Ho is the foreign minister who, in September 2017, while standing outside a hotel in New York City, informed the world that Kim Jong Un had in mind an 'unprecedented powerful hydrogen bomb test above the Pacific'. He also accompanied Kim Jong Un to summit meetings with Donald Trump in 2018 and 2019. But then, in January 2023, reports surfaced that Ri had been executed the previous year. Days later, South Korea's top intelligence agency confirmed Ri had been purged, though it could not confirm whether he had been killed. Kim Jong Il had condemned Ri Yong Ho's mum while sparing his dad, his close aide. Jong Il's son, Jong Un, for whom Ri junior had worked very hard, proved less charitable.

To Kim Jong Il, public executions and forced disappearance of persons were essential tools of inner-circle control, as well as serving a broader rule of state control by terror. By his thirties, Kim Jong Il was showing ample signs of a solipsistic, manipulative personality – even, or especially, in acts of superficial generosity like dispensing gifts to his cronies. He was a perfect example of a self-absorbed, conniving psychopath, embodying the 'dark triad personality – Narcissism, Machiavellianism, and psychopathy' in spades, which would in turn become apparent in his own children, Kim Jong Un and Kim Yo Jong.[13] They have shown the same enthusiasm for trampling on the rights of the North Korean people, enslaving millions and determinedly persecuting Christians. Such extreme moral turpitude marks the core personality of the Mount Paektu leadership, from grandfather, to father, down to the son and daughter.

Christians are persecuted in North Korea arguably more than in any other state on Earth. Open Doors, a non-denominational Christian mission that has monitored the persecution of Christianity worldwide since 1992 and ranked persecutor states around the world since 2002, crowned North Korea as number one – worst in the world – for twenty years straight.[14]

The North Korean leadership's persecution of Christianity is virtually coeval with its entire political existence. It predates the founding of the Democratic People's Republic of Korea in 1948, which took place just three weeks after the founding of the Republic of Korea, or South Korea, on August 15. As soon as his Soviet supporters had designated him as the leader of northern Korea, Kim Il Sung targeted religious organizations. Alongside landowning capitalists under Japanese rule, the would-be Great Leader, through various 'reform' measures, confiscated religious groups' assets and land.[15] Since Christians preached that there was an authority higher than the king, that ancestor worship and Christianity are incompatible, and that the Kingdom of God was the ultimate salvation, to Kim Il Sung, Christianity was the ultimate ideological threat.

Kim Il Sung went on a politico-religious killing spree. Mass killings of Christians also took place during the Korean War and in the post-war years. He started a family tradition that his heir later upheld. Public executions of Christian converts became routine. A North Korean escapee gave a first-hand account of watching a gruesome public execution from the front row. In 1996, five Protestant Christians, their hands and feet bound, were thrown before a large steam roller. Twenty fellow parishioners, arrested together with the condemned five, were forced to watch the execution. Some fainted at the 'popping sound' of skulls being crushed beneath the steam roller.[16]

It was Taliban-run Afghanistan that finally toppled North Korea from its position of world number-one persecutor of Christians in 2022, but North Korea's fanatical hatred for Christianity evokes the extremist fundamentalism of the Taliban. Indeed, the North Korean cult of personality and the Taliban's theocracy are both animated by a spirit of extreme intolerance and share several similarities, from egregious human rights abuses like summary executions to the lethal suppression of basic freedoms such as those of religion, speech, the press, assembly, and consumption of foreign culture and information. North Korea, with its highly regimented state, is just slicker and more discreet in its mass murder and torture. And in the North Korean officialdom, there is no one who can disguise this brutish ethos as effectively as the young, beautiful, and occasionally smiling princess of Pyongyang.

But while historically the Taliban has been formally recognized by just three nations – Pakistan, Saudi Arabia, and the United Arab Emirates – North Korea is recognized diplomatically by over 160. Arguably, each enjoys a 'comparative advantage' in its particular abuses. The Taliban, for example, exceeds North Korea in cultural genocide and the prohibition of education for girls and women. But though North Korea provides public education for girls and speaks of Communist gender equality, in practice the chauvinistic state is far from a paragon of equality between the sexes. The sexual abuse of girls and women has long been a regular tool of the North Korean arsenal of terror.[17] For decades, routine rape and torture of female prisoners in North Korea's inhumane prisons have taken place out of sight of the outside world, and with the knowledge and connivance of the state. North Korea's 'religious police', the state security agents who hunt down Christians, may refrain from the Taliban's public flogging of victims, but they still make targets, including women and children, disappear – both from home and this secular world.

In the 1970s, even before his appointment as heir apparent, Kim Jong Il had overseen Pyongyang's proliferation of international terrorism. Once appointed successor, he became more blatant in his use of state violence as well as fake peace overtures. Throughout the 1980s, North Korea abducted Japanese nationals, attempted to assassinate the South Korean president, and blew up a South Korean civilian aircraft in mid-air – all while Kim Jong Il was his nation's de facto first-in-command under the de jure Supreme Leader, his father.

The faux peace overtures through China to the Reagan administration in 1983 were also the work of Kim Jong Il. They lasted until October that year, when North Korean agents detonated a bomb at the Martyrs' Mausoleum in Rangoon, Burma, targeting the visiting South Korean President Chun Doo Hwan, who was spared by his late arrival. Seventeen of his fellow countrymen and four Burmese nationals were not so lucky.

Rumours of Kim Jong Il's hobby of collecting foreign women were given credibility when the story of two former abductees came to light. Choi Eun-Hee, a famous South Korean movie star, and her ex-husband, Shin Sang-Ok, a renowned South Korean film director, were abducted by North Korean agents in 1978 on the express orders of Kim Jong Il. A film buff, Jong Il was in search of artistic inspiration and guidance for his upgrade of North Korea's film industry.

The sensational news of Kim Jong Il having ordered the abduction of the glamorous South Korean couple broke in March 1986. After eight years of detainment in North Korea, Choi and Shin were finally free to tell their story.

In January 1978, Choi Eun-Hee disappeared while on a visit to Hong Kong. She had been captured and sedated and, when she woke up, found herself in a luxurious villa in Pyongyang surrounded by guards. Shin Sang-Ok, her former husband, disappeared six months later. The disappearance of the South Korean celebrities remained an unsolved mystery until 12 April

1984, when they appeared together at a news conference in Belgrade, capital of the former Yugoslavia. The couple, by then having remarried in Pyongyang, claimed that they had voluntarily left South Korea for the North to escape from harassment by the South Korean authorities. The South Korean military government rebutted with the inference that Kim Jong Il had had them abducted.[18] The next month, Choi and Shin appeared at a news conference in Pyongyang, as if to confirm that they were still entirely pleased with their decision to seek a new life in North Korea.

Two years later, the truth would be unveiled to the US authorities. For the first five years of their captivity, Kim Jong Il did not inform either of the other's detainment. The two were kept apart from each other. Choi was well taken care of and often invited by Kim Jong Il to movies and concerts. At first, Shin was also treated lavishly. But after he was twice caught trying to escape, he was imprisoned and tortured. In 1982, after writing a forced apology and paeans to the Great Leader Kim Il Sung, he found the North Korean authorities' treatment of him improved markedly. The next year, it was time for Kim Jong Il to put the two captives, by then thoroughly tamed, to work.

In March 1983, Kim Jong Il brought Choi and Shin together and threw a party for them, at which he apologized for the enforced invitation to his country and his prolonged radio silence on each other's whereabouts. He also told the former husband and wife to remarry one another, even though Shin already had a new wife and children in South Korea.[19] By 1984, having made movies together for Kim Jong Il's delectation,

Choi and Shin had won his trust. Nonetheless, whenever they went abroad, the couple were always watched at close range by North Korean agents.

On 13 March 1986, during a visit to Vienna on the way to Hungary to start on a new film about Genghis Khan, the couple ran away from their hotel, jumped into a taxi and, having called ahead, sprinted into the US embassy, where their request for political asylum was granted.

In due course, Choi and Shin began to speak of Kim Jong Il's fondness for wild parties. Sinister and salacious tales followed of Kim Jong Il ordering the kidnapping of many others, including young women and girls to work as hostesses and dancers. Choi said she had met a Jordanian woman in Pyongyang who most likely was an abductee. Ms Choi had also heard from her North Korean hairdresser of a young French woman who had been tricked into coming to Pyongyang by a male agent posing as a 'rich Asian heir'.[20] Her accounts lent credence to suspicions that North Korea was engaged in the systematic and widespread abduction of foreign citizens.

On 17 September 2002, at his summit meeting with the Japanese Prime Minister Junichiro Koizumi in Pyongyang, Kim Jong Il, in the hope of securing a significant infusion of cash from Tokyo, came clean about North Korean agents having previously abducted thirteen Japanese nationals. Naturally, he described these agents as rogue elements, acting without his knowledge. But the real number of abductees was much higher, and included a thirteen-year-old girl, Megumi Yokota, whom North Korea had hitherto claimed had killed herself while mentally ill. Her alleged suicide at the age of twenty-nine has never been independently confirmed. DNA tests on her cremated remains, which had been sent by Pyongyang to Tokyo in 2004, were inconclusive. What is known is that she had been groomed to act as a Japanese language and culture teacher for North Korean spies. She was also paired up with a South Korean abductee, and the two had children together.

Although the exact number of Japanese abductees, or the total number of victims of North Korean kidnapping globally, remains unknown, what can be said with confidence is that from the late 1970s, Kim Jong Il had men and women abducted from a variety of regions – South Korea, Japan, China, Macau, Hong Kong, Thailand, Singapore, Malaysia, Jordan, Lebanon, Romania, France, Italy, Austria, and the Netherlands.[21] These acts of international terrorism – committed with impunity – were a grim reminder of what North Korea, through denials, threats, partial 'confessions' and, notably, the occasional swerve towards dialogue, is capable of getting away with.

Back in 1972, Kim Jong Il was but an apprentice to his father, observing at first-hand how his convivial father charmed foreign visitors to his office, even Americans. The dramatic thaw in Sino–US relations that began in July 1971 with the stunning visit to Beijing by Henry Kissinger, President Richard Nixon's National Security Advisor, followed by Nixon himself visiting China the next February, necessitated a similar shift on the part of both North and South Korea as, respectively, client states of China and the United States.

The original Great Leader could read the weather in the geopolitical sphere well, and knew when to put on a charming facade. His son would prove a good pupil, hosting South Korean President Kim Dae Jung in 2000 for an inter-Korean summit and, just four months later, US Secretary of State Madeleine Albright, with an eye on the prize of hosting US President Bill Clinton himself soon afterwards. Both visits were unprecedented, both in fact and in creating tantalizing expectations of peace in the Korean peninsula, even if their essential futility predominantly favoured North Korea.

In early 2018, Kim Jong Un would confirm himself in turn as *his* father's pupil, when in February he unleashed his sister on South Korea, and the next month reached out to US President Donald Trump for a summit meeting: the same playbook, coming after two years of saturated threats and provocations, marked by three nuclear tests and nearly fifty missile launches, including three intercontinental ballistic missiles (ICBMs) in 2017 alone.[22]

When Kim Jong Il ascended to the throne in 1994, he was entirely comfortable in the role, as for the previous dozen years he had been de facto ruler. For the next six years, he did not meet with a single foreign leader. He did not even once set foot outside North Korea. He lived the good life. He was a prince, aesthete, author of thousands of treatises on just about every subject under the sun,[*23] gourmand, bon-vivant billionaire,

---

* He started writing in 1952, at the age of eleven (officially, ten). So polyhistoric and prolific was he, the Workers' Party of Korea Publishing House was still struggling to keep pace with his literary legacy in December 2021. Only the previous month, it had managed to release

womanizer, collector of foreign human subjects, nuclear bombs-wielding dictator, and deceiver par excellence.

In spite of his genius, Kim Jong Il shrouded his family in secrecy while visiting upon foes both domestic and foreign varying doses of cruelty and duplicity. Secrecy, inhumanity, and duplicity were all essential tools of statecraft, even some of life's most cherished principles, for a tyrant.

The common view that Kim Jong Il was insane and there-fore incapable of governing his decrepit country once he assumed power in 1994, and, furthermore, that the political construct known as the Democratic People's Republic of Korea must soon follow the fate of East Germany in 1990, became the orthodox view of the US Department of State. That in 1991 the Soviet Union, North Korea's patron state, had itself collapsed seemed only to 'prove' the theory. This rosy view was shattered by Kim Jong Il's unprecedented August 1998 missile launch over Japan. Unsettled by this threat to a key ally, the US set about enthusiastically placating him, increasing food aid to North Korea to almost $300 million the following year.

But the real cash cow lay much closer to home: south of the border. Like the United States, South Korea also needed to be taught a lesson. As with the US, the proper way to raise funds from his neighbour would not be as a polite supplicant but by discourteous military extortion. Then, after a period of threats

---

Volume 41 of the *Complete Collection* of his works. It may take until the 2030s before they release the last volume, taking the reader to 17 December 2011, when the indefatigable leader, while working hard in his moving train, breathed his last breath.

and low-level skirmishes, the Great Leader's mood would swing to sunny. Why follow conventional models of national development – research, innovation, development, investment, and free-market competition – when the Kims are so well practised in mafiosi-style coercion elevated to an international level? This was one of the most important lessons on foreign policy that Kim Jong Il imparted to his heir.

In June 1999, North Korean patrol boats, which escorted at times up to twenty North Korean fishing vessels, conducted a series of incursions into South Korean territorial waters west of the peninsula. Over the course of eight days, warnings, threats, and incidents of boats bumping one another escalated. On 15 June, a North Korean patrol boat opened fire on South Korean vessels. The South's sailors fired back, inflicting heavy damage and possibly killing dozens of North Korean sailors, while taking no casualties themselves. South Korea clearly won the skirmish, but it was the North Korean government, unencumbered by any regard for the lives of its own people, that had won the psychological victory. Even in defeat, North Korea had instilled in its enemy both the fear of escalation and an impulse towards appeasement. South Korea, an affluent democracy, had far more to lose, which meant that no peace overture from Pyongyang, however transparently false and manipulative, could be ignored – or, indeed, be anything other than embraced.

Next came an incident a week later off the far north-eastern city of Sokcho. South Korean fishermen sighted a surfaced North Korean submarine that had become entangled in a fishing net. Initially, the fishermen reported, the North Korean sailors were trying to free the submarine, to no avail. Days later, a South Korean corvette towed the disabled submarine back to its naval base in Donghae with the North Korean crew, now unresponsive, inside. While being towed into port, the submarine sank. Three days later it was salvaged, and inside were nine dead North Koreans, four with gunshot wounds to the head. Weapons and other military gear were found. Also found inside the submarine were South Korean-brand drinks, a sign of a completed mission on land.[24] This apparent evidence of murder-suicide unnerved the South Korean public. In December, another exchange of fire took place when a North Korean submersible was sighted off the southern coastal city of Yeosu.

At the year's end, after two years of Pyongyang toying with the US, Japan, and South Korea, it was time to make a bold switchover. The message had been sent to the South: confrontation could quickly escalate into lethal exchanges of gunfire, which might blow up into full-scale war. If you want to avoid war, come and talk to us, bearing gifts.

The following year, Dear Leader Kim Jong Il changed his tune from *molto agitato* to *placido*. He embarked on the very 'unarduous' journey of turning himself into a new man: affable, sociable, sensible, peace-prone, reform-minded, US forces in South Korea-tolerant, and quite willing to part with his nuclear and missile programmes. At least, that's what South Korean President Kim Dae Jung, who visited Kim Jong Il in Pyongyang in June 2000, maintained, prefiguring President Moon Jae-In, who, upon meeting several times with Kim Jong Un and Kim Yo Jong in 2018, would also appear to go out of his way to defend the North Korean royals.[25]

But perhaps Kim Jong Il's greatest legacy was that, unlike his own father before him, he fathered and trained not just one but two imperious leaders and, perhaps most importantly, one of them was a woman.

CHAPTER 6

State Secrets

Most North Koreans, even senior officials, do not know how many wives or children Kim Jong Il had. He had his children home-schooled initially, and then, to shroud them in mystery out of sight of their peers – who, as schoolchildren, would see them as thoroughly ordinary and undivine – he sent them to study abroad in Geneva, Bern, and Moscow. But it was also to protect his own interests: to minimize the spread of rumours among potential schoolmates about his lavish lifestyle and other excesses, like his penchant for the best food and wine money can buy or falling prey to 'reactionary thought', in North Korean terminology, by watching James Bond movies and South Korean soap operas even as he punished others caught engaging in such criminal acts.

Basic information on Kim Jong Il's children was a closely guarded secret until 2009, when Kim Jong Un was declared, at first only internally, as heir. In December 2011, for example, few people recognized the weeping young woman in traditional black dress at Kim Jong Il's wake as Kim Yo Jong. The first time the state media released a photo of Kim Jong Un, Kim Yo Jong and Kim Jong Chol was on 27 April 2009. None of them were named, but it was apparently Kim Jong Il's three children (then in their twenties) who had accompanied their father on his impromptu tour of Wonsan Agricultural University the previous day, photographed with Kim Ki Nam, the godfather of North Korean propaganda under all three Supreme Leaders, posed in front of a big pine tree against a sunlit backdrop.

Kim Jong Un is seen in his dark Mao suit striking his trademark tough-guy pose, arms stretched out with fists softly clenched, in a cross between a sumo wrestler and Superman. To his left is the venerable master propagandist, also in a Mao suit, and to *his* left stands his protégé, Kim Yo Jong, fists likewise bunched in a feminized version of the Kim Jong Un stance. Kim Jong Chol, the future leader's older brother, stands in a Western-style suit to the right of his younger brother. The children were apparently learning the intricacies of on-the-spot guidance from the master himself, Dad, before retreating to their favourite resort-home, Kim Jong Il's palatial estate in Wonsan. This is the first North Korean media-shown photo of either Kim Jong Un or Kim Yo Jong. At the time, few outside North Korea knew who they were or what they were called.

Until the North Korean state revealed Kim Jong Un's name for the first time in September 2010, just days before he stood next to his father in the reviewing stand at Kim Il Sung Square at the 10 October Party Foundation Day celebrations as his evident successor, few governments knew his correct name. The South Korean National Intelligence Service, the country's chief spy agency, believed his name was Kim Jong Woon. As for Kim Yo Jong, even the Chinese, who have more access to North Korea's royal family and top officials than anyone, kept getting her name wrong. In Chinese her name is pronounced Jin Yu Zheng, but for several years she was referred to in the Chinese media as Jin Ru Zhen or Jin Ru Jing, probably because even the Chinese authorities did not know her real name until KCNA announced it for the first time on 9 March 2014, when she accompanied her brother to cast his vote at Kim Il Sung University for the Supreme People's Assembly election.

On 5 April Korean Central TV, North Korea's main state TV station, connected Kim Yo Jong the name to the person for the first time, as the woman by Kim Jong Un's side, referring to her as a 'cadre of the Central Committee of the Workers' Party of Korea'. It was soon revealed that her brother had won 100 per cent of the votes at 'Mount Paektu Constituency No. 111'. His sister was shown in a close-up shot as she cast her vote, apparently for her brother, the previous month.

Such guarded secrecy was the norm. The *Rodong Sinmun*, the official newspaper of the Workers' Party of Korea, published the first official photograph of Kim Jong Un only on 30 September 2010, referring to him as Vice Chairman of the Central Defence Commission of the Workers' Party of Korea. Three days earlier, Kim Jong Il had appointed his youngest son as well as his own sister, Kim Kyong Hui, as four-star generals. It made the front page: the young heir apparent, just twenty-six, seated in front row centre, two seats to the right of his father, with General Ri Yong Ho (whom Kim Jong Un would purge in July 2012) between them, against the backdrop of Mount Kumsu Palace of the Sun, the world's most lavish mausoleum, which Kim Jong Il had built for his father on his death in 1994. It may have crossed Kim Jong Il's mind that one day he too would join his father there. Behind Kim Jong Un stood Choe Ryong Hae, long-time number three or four to Kim Jong Il, depending on the Dear Leader's mood. Kim Kyong Hui's husband, Uncle Jang Song Thaek, for decades the real number two, stood behind Kim Jong Il in a two-piece suit.

Outside North Korea, there was one person who would have immediately recognized Kim Jong Un in the Wonsan photograph, as he would the faces of Kim Jong Un's brother, Jong Chol, and sister, Yo Jong. That person is Kenji Fujimoto, who'd left Pyongyang on a supposed shopping trip to Tokyo in April 2001 and did not return. At the time, few knew of his special association with the North Korean royalty. But, in 2003, Fujimoto wrote a book on his experience. Many were sceptical of Fujimoto's claim in it that Kim Jong Il's youngest son, Jong Un, would be his successor. Kim Jong Il would affectionately call Jong Chol 'girlish', according to Fujimoto, who also claimed that the boy lacked both interest in and aptitude for political life. In the Kim Jong Un era, he seems content to play his guitar with fellow musicians in Pyongyang, occasionally attend Eric Clapton concerts abroad, as he has in Germany, Singapore, and England, and stay out of the spotlight. However, Kim Jong Il had always viewed his youngest son, Jong Un, and youngest daughter, Yo Jong, as leadership material, Fujimoto asserted in various media interviews.

By 2009 Fujimoto had gained a modestly prophetic status. As of September 2008, foreign governments were aware that Kim Jong Il had suffered a serious stroke the previous month. Considering its apparent severity, said medical experts, the Dear Leader probably had at most five years left. What hardly anyone outside North Korea knew even then was whom Kim Jong Il would choose as his heir. Most money was on Jong Chol, simply on the principle of primogeniture. (By now, the oldest son, Jong Nam, was out of the running thanks in part to being tainted by the defection of his aunt Song Hye Rang.) But in January 2009, South Korea was reporting that Kim Jong Il had notified the Organization and Guidance Department that he had anointed Kim Jong Un, most likely on 8 January – Jong Un's birthday – as his heir. Fujimoto became quite famous, as possibly the only person outside North Korea to have correctly predicted, on the record, who would succeed Kim Jong Il.

While at least some insider information on Kim Jong Il's wives, consorts and children has leaked into the international media, North Korea tries to mislead the outside world with false biographical information about them. When Kim Jong Il's children studied abroad, for example, they went under false names. In 1996, Jong Un and Yo Jong went to Switzerland, their brother, Kim Jong Chol, having started his schooling there two years earlier as 'Pak Chol'. As an elementary school student at a German-speaking state school, Liebefeld-Steinhölzli Schule in Bern, the Swiss capital, Kim Yo Jong was 'Pak Mi Hyang'. Kim Jong Un attended the same school under the name 'Pak Un'.[1]

Kim Yo Jong had at least one other false name, 'Pak Jong Sun', while Jong Un, it was discovered in February 2018, possessed a genuine Brazilian passport bearing the name 'Josef Pwag'. Kim Jong Il also had a Brazilian passport with the name, 'IJong Tchoi'. Both were issued at the Brazilian embassy in the Czech Republic's capital, Prague, on 26 February 1996.[2] Likewise, North Korean officials posted abroad have multiple passports under false names. Ri Su Yong, North Korea's foreign minister from 2014 to 2016, served as minister at the DPRK Mission to the United Nations in Geneva from 1980, the year that Kim Jong Nam, Kim Jong Il's eldest son, enrolled at the International School of Geneva. Ri stayed on in Switzerland at the DPRK embassy in Bern as ambassador until 2010. During those decades, his priority was serving as the senior guardian of Kim Jong Il's children in Switzerland, under the pseudonym 'Ri Chol'. Ri would have attended the opening ceremony on the first day of the school year at the International School of Geneva in 1980. It was late summer, and all the new students stood in the school's amphitheatre holding the flag of their nation. But one Asian boy stood there without a flag in hand. It was Kim Jong Nam, Kim Jong Il's eldest son, then aged nine. South Korea's ambassador, Llo Shin Yong, also was in attendance. Mistaking the prince from Pyongyang as an ordinary boy from South Korea, Mr Llo asked him where he was from. Kim Jong Nam, without hesitation, replied in a robust tone, 'I'm from the Democratic People's Republic of Korea', which promptly ended the conversation, much to the relief of the boy's bodyguards.[3] (This author was also there as a new student with a South Korean flag in hand.)

In May 2001, Kim Jong Nam, accompanied by two women and his young son, was detained at Tokyo Narita International Airport for carrying a fake Dominican passport with a Chinese name, Pang Xiong, which in Chinese means 'Fat Bear'. Asked what the purpose of the attempted visit was, Kim Jong Nam replied that he wished to take his son to Tokyo Disneyland. He and his fellow travellers were deported to China. Sometime thereafter, rumours swirled among elite circles in Pyongyang that Ko Yong Hui, Kim Jong Un's mum, had alerted the Japanese authorities through her Chosen Soren contacts in Japan that a North Korean with a fake passport would be trying to pass through.[4] Discrediting a potential rival to her own teenaged son could only be construed as an act of motherly love.

The Kims assume false identities primarily to fend off unwanted scrutiny by foreign authorities. But there is also essential biographical information that must be hidden from the North Korean people. Kim Jong Un and Kim Yo Jong's mother, Ko Yong Hui, presents some complex problems. She was never legally wed to Kim Jong Il, though that is of no great relevance to her legitimacy as Kim Jong Il's common-law wife or the mother of his children: she was Kim Jong Il's favourite partner, in both passion and longevity, and unquestionably his de facto wife. But few outside Kim Jong Il's inner circle ever knew of her existence, and North Korea has never released a photograph of Ko and Kim Jong Il together, nor one of her alone after she became Kim Jong Il's unofficial First Lady in the late 1970s. Such controlled anonymity applies to Kim Jong Il's other women too. Even in a quasi-theocracy, Kim Jong Il's complicated, concurrent romantic relationships with several women called for discretion, not necessarily out of the Supreme Leader's fears of possible embarrassment, but in order to protect the legitimacy of his heir.

Above all, it is Ko Yong Hui's place of birth that needs to remain a state secret: Japan. The North Korean people might even accept philandering as the divine right of princes, but Ko's birth in Japan could have implications for the succession. The sanctity of the Mount Paektu family, founded in large measure on Kim Il Sung's anti-Japanese resistance, might be compromised.

Ko Yong Hui was born in Osaka on 26 June, either in 1950 or 1952. Like many Koreans between 1910 and 1945, her father, Ko Kyong Thaek, a native of South Korea's Jeju Island, had moved with his family to Japan during Japan's colonial rule of Korea. Ko took up work in a Ministry of War-run textile factory. The family moved to North Korea in 1962 as part of a massive repatriation programme, and in 1971 Ko Yong Hui became a dancer in the elite Mansudae Art Troupe. If not for the good fortune of meeting Kim Jong Il while performing at one of his big parties, her life might have turned out very differently. For one thing, she would not have given birth to a future Supreme Leader of North Korea. In fact, once her dancing days were over, she and her entire family, including future children, might well have found themselves leading a challenging life in an isolated village. Why?

In North Korea's insidious political classification system,

known as *songbun* ('birth status'), there are broadly three classes: the favoured Core Class, the middle Wavering Class, and the lowest Hostile Class (as well as over fifty subclasses),[5] the names reflecting the viewpoint from the summit of Mount Paektu in descending degrees of distaste. This institutionalized political and social discrimination started in 1957, after the proclamation 'On the Transformation of the Struggle with Counterrevolutionary Elements into an All-People, All-Party Movement'.[6] Political class has lifelong implications for all the major decisions the state makes for each citizen's life: where you live, your education, your job, and your food rations are all determined by *songbun*.

From the royal family's viewpoint, the most trustworthy are the anti-Japanese revolutionaries and Korean War veterans and their families. These are in the top Core Class. Peasants before liberation, white-collar workers in the party, government and military are also viewed favourably, although intellectuals need to be surveilled. These groups also fall in the top class.

Post-liberation labourers, independent farmers, small-time business owners, and itinerant workers fall under the Wavering Class. Many are placed under general surveillance.

Koreans repatriated from Japan are relegated to the lowest Hostile Class, together with rich landlords, Christians, Buddhists, Shamans and other religious people identified in 1945–46, the time of Kim Il Sung's ascendance and the start of his public persecution of religion. The families of these groups were jailed or executed. Their progeny, too, are consigned at birth to the lowest class. Those who muster up the courage and resources to escape the country are branded traitors to the nation, and routinely vilified as 'human scum', 'human trash', and 'mongrel dogs', as in Kim Yo Jong's written diatribes of 4 June 2020 and 2 May 2021. Their families – those not jailed or executed – are placed under strict surveillance.

Had Kim Jong Un and Kim Yo Jong not been the children of the late Supreme Leader of North Korea, they, along with their brother, would likely have been thrust into the Hostile Class, depending on whom their mother married. Of course, had their mother not met Kim Jong Il there would not be a Kim Jong Un or Kim Yo Jong, but that the son of a Japanese-born repatriate was chosen to rule the state founded by a godlike anti-Japanese independence warrior is, to say the very least, a historical irony that must remain undisclosed to the North Korean public. It seems to have remained undisclosed to Kim Il Sung, too. Although he did find out about the birth of his eldest grandson, Jong Nam, and adored him, the news of his profligate son forming yet another alternate family with a Japanese-born woman would have been a matter of some sensitivity. A conversation the future Great Leader would avoid with the incumbent Great Leader.

In the Kim Jong Un era, the North Korean state has not released a single photograph of Kim Jong Un or his sister with their grandfather. Forgery, counterfeiting, falsification of records, and deleting 'unpersons' are some of the Propaganda and Agitation Department's specialities – North Korea has been caught in the past blatantly photoshopping pictures, like many other nations of a similar ilk. Manufacturing a photograph, say, circa 1992, with an eight-year-old Kim Jong Un and a five-year-old Kim Yo Jong sitting on grandpa's lap would not have been a technically burden-some task. Yet the state has eschewed such a gamble, presumably because the stakes are simply too high. Releasing such a doctored photograph is certain to invite international scrutiny. North Korean people know not to ask such questions, but those who escape and resettle in free countries like South Korea would most keenly air such news and try their best to transmit it to the North Korean people. Kim Jong Un may have concluded that it is in his best interests not to draw attention to his apparently tenuous personal connection with his grandfather.

There is an even bigger family problem that impedes, if not precludes, large-scale public idolization of Kim Jong Un's late mother. In 1998 her younger sister, Ko Yong Suk, who had looked after Jong Chol, Jong Un and Yo Jong when they lived in Switzerland,[7] defected with her husband and three children to the United States, North Korea's sworn enemy.

North Korea vigorously implements the medieval practice of 'guilt by association'; that is, if one is condemned as a 'counter-revolutionary', the alleged traitor's entire family across three generations are condemned to death or a concentration camp – including infants and small children. By North Korea's 'customary law', therefore, Kim Jong Un, his brother and sister, together with their mother and father, Kim Jong Il, and Ko Yong Hui's father, who in 1998 was still alive, should all have been whisked away to a gulag in the wake of his aunt's defection.

As if that was not enough, there's a third dark state secret. Kim Il Sung's parents were Christian churchgoers. His mother, Kang Ban Sok, was a deaconess. His father, Kim Hyong Jik, attended Soongsil Academy in Pyongyang, a Christian school founded by William Baird, an American Presbyterian missionary. The boy who would become the original Great Leader of North Korea played the church piano. Had Kim Il Sung obeyed his own rules, his son, Jong Il, might have opened his newborn eyes to the reality of a life of extreme privation as a member of the Hostile Class. Perhaps he would have disappeared in the middle of the night and found himself in a concentration camp once his family history had been discovered by the secret police. Politically vulnerable and economically marginalized as he would have been as a young man in the 1960s and 1970s, he might never have been able to develop a fondness for South Korean films and TV drama. But, if he had, and was caught at it, he could have been executed before a crowd of townspeople, including children, routinely dragooned to witness such wretched spectacles.

The family taboos of the Paektu clan are bitter ironies that, if they got out, not even the most talented propagandist in the land could spin. By Kim Il Sung's own sinister class system, Kim Jong Un is an illegitimate ruler, as are his own sister and his children. A gulag rather than palaces might have been their home. A life of extreme hardship and starvation rations should have been their fate, instead of power and opulence. This information, therefore, must never be divulged, and even if people did find out, they would know not to talk or even whisper. No one openly asks about the royal family: citizens are conditioned from early childhood to know that exhibiting curiosity about the Mount Paektu family tree beyond what one is told by the state is a blasphemy. More than that, divulging even unarguable facts about the royal family can be career-ending.

Defectors, though, are a problem. Those who escape North Korea and tell the truth, these 'human scum', as Kim Yo Jong and her equally discourteous officials brand them, must be silenced entirely. To reveal salacious facts about the royal family upon permanently leaving North Korea may be fulfilling. It is certainly in the public interest. But it can also be life-ending.

In February 1997, Kim Jong Il had his de facto nephew, Lee Han-Young (again, given name Ri Il Nam), who defected to South Korea in 1982, assassinated for publishing an exposé on the North Korean royal family. The victim, who in South Korea had changed his name to Lee Han-Young and undergone cosmetic surgery for personal safety, was shot in the head by two North Korean assassins waiting outside his temporary abode, a college friend's home near Seoul, on 15 February, the eve of Kim Jong Il's birthday. The timing is not a coincidence. Investigations showed that over the previous four months several North Korean spies had tried to ascertain their target's whereabouts. On the day of the killing, a woman called the victim's friend's home posing as reporter for a women's magazine and enquired what time Lee was expected back.

Twenty years later, on 13 February 2017, three days shy of Kim Jong Il's birthday, Kim Jong Un's half-brother, Kim Jong Nam, was assassinated in Kuala Lumpur International Airport. Suspicion fell on Kim Jong Un, with speculation that Kim Jong Nam's 'mortal sin' had been to openly criticize his father's designation of Kim Jong Un as heir in 2009. By 2017, he had become a marked man with no recourse to a statute of limitations. He had also been approached by the spy agencies of the US and South Korea. In both murder cases, the victims had crossed the line – North Korea's sinister omerta against revealing secrets about the royal family. The sacred inviolability of the Supreme Leader or Supreme Leader-in-waiting must be enforced, even if it takes years.

The victims were also connected by a common past. Lee Han-Young's mother, Song Hye Rang, had virtually raised her nephew Kim Jong Nam since he was three. Jong Nam's own mother, Song Hye Rim, had suffered prolonged mental illness, and from 1974 until her death in 2002 lived in Moscow for much of the year for medical treatment. Song Hye Rim often blamed her illness on the two other women with whom Kim Jong Il lived contemporaneously in different mansions soon after she had given birth to Jong Nam. In the 1980s and 1990s, the Song sisters correctly identified Ko Hong Hui's sons, Jong Chol and Jong Un, as a threat to Jong Nam.[8] Abandoned by Kim Jong Il, Song Hye Rim died virtually alone, and was buried in Troyekurovskoye Cemetery on the outskirts of Moscow.[9]

The murder of Lee Han-Young would have been a brutal reminder to Jong Nam of the risks of upsetting the Fatherly Great Leader. It was not the first time he'd lost a family member who was seen as a threat to Kim Jong Il. As we've seen, Jong Il had an uncomfortable relationship with his half-brothers and had arranged for the youngest, Hyon, to be killed. Jong Nam and Uncle Hyon, who were the same age, had briefly lived together in Moscow in 1979 under the care of Hyon's mum.

The fate of Hyon, Lee Han-Young and Jong Nam is a reminder of what is at stake for members of the Mount Paektu Bloodline, Yo Jong included. Loyalty and discretion are more likely to ensure a long life. Family secrets – including that the North Korean Supreme Leader is the son of a Japanese-born mother and the nephew of a defector – must be kept at all costs.

CHAPTER 7

The Apprentice Years: 2007–2009

In their high-profile meetings with foreign leaders, Kim Jong Un and Kim Yo Jong have been the significantly younger party. But they hardly ever look nervous during formal meetings with more experienced foreign counterparts. Like all princes and princesses, they have received special training since early childhood to act like the royalty they are and exude confidence in any setting. When it comes to interacting with South Koreans, the siblings come across as supremely confident to the point of imperious. They know just the right tone to strike, which ethno-nationalistic buttons to push, how many humblebrags to make. In short, they know how to show, through their body language, who's in charge. After all, they learned from the master himself: their own father.

When Kim Jong Il greeted the South Korean President, Kim Dae Jung, in 2000, Kim Jong Un would have been sixteen and his sister three months shy of thirteen, and neither astute enough yet to fully appreciate how completely their dear father dominated his older guest. Seven years later, though, there was the visit of another South Korean president, Roh Moo Hyun, the first South Korean leader to walk across the Military Demarcation Line into North Korea. The visit was a diplomatic rout from beginning to end and the young adults would have been thoroughly impressed by their father's work, and taught an invaluable lesson.

It was few minutes past 9 a.m. on 2 October 2007 when President Roh Moo Hyun, President Kim Dae Jung's hand-picked successor, gave a speech at the Blue House. 'If the first inter-Korean summit held in 2000 opened a new road in South–North Korean relations,' he announced, in a tone appropriate to the serious nature of his mission, 'then I hope this summit will be an occasion for removing the obstacles that still remain on the road and pushing forward the delayed footsteps.' He went on to vow that he would forge lasting peace in the Korean peninsula.

His motorcade departed the presidential compound, applauded and cheered by thousands of well-wishers lining the long driveway and, beyond the presidential compound, the streets of Seoul. At the land border, President Roh and the First Lady exited their vehicle and walked towards the dividing line, beyond which North Korean officials, led by Kim Jong Il's close aide, Choe Ryong Hae, stood waiting to greet them. Facing south, his wife next to him and the cloudy sky his backdrop, Roh said, 'Today, I cross this forbidden line as the president. After I return, many more people will be able to visit.' In deliberate slow motion, they stepped into the North.

The streets of Pyongyang were lined with people waving pom-pom-like pink plastic flowers as Roh Moo Hyun, Supreme

People's Assembly Chairman Kim Yong Nam standing next to him, rode in the open-car parade. The motorcade stopped at the 25 April House of Culture – a massive 176-metre-long building with a 6,000-capacity theatre – where Kim Jong Il greeted Roh for the usual handshake, although this time, unlike his greeting of Kim Dae Jung in June 2000 with both hands, with just his right hand extended. North Korean honour guards put on the customary show of goose-stepping.

Roh was in the last five months of his single five-year term, and keen to make his mark on history. He was trying hard to please his host. In his motorcade was an unusual retinue. In addition to his officials and bodyguards, Roh brought with him the sole proprietress of traditional Korean royal cuisine, Ms Han Bok-Ryeo, who in turn had brought nine more chefs, together with the finest delicacies harvested from each of the South's eight provinces and Jeju Island, for an elaborate play-acting of the sumptuous court banquets featured in the wildly popular TV series *Dae Jang Geum* ('Jewel in the Palace'). Kim Jong Il was reportedly a big fan of the show, and especially its star, the South Korean actress Lee Young-Ae.

Roh offered to 'host' his first night in Pyongyang, with his chefs preparing the kind of banquet seen in many episodes of the TV show. He even brought with him several copies of the DVD box set, along with other South Korean TV shows and movies, as well as Samsung and LG televisions and DVD players to watch them on, most likely in violation of UN Security Council Resolution 1718, passed in October 2006 in the wake of North Korea's first nuclear test. Roh also brought various dish sets and tea samples from all the different provinces of South Korea. But the most visible among the many gifts he brought Kim Jong Il was an eight-leafed painting featuring twelve inanimate objects and animals symbolizing, pointedly, eternal life, which for a cruel dictator may not have been the most tactful choice.[1]

The First Lady of South Korea wore a hanbok to the banquet, the traditional Korean costume accented by long, graceful lines. But the look she wore, like most of the South Koreans there, was one of muted pleasure. The star of the show, Kim Jong Il, was a no-show. No explanation or excuse was given. 'Let us rid ourselves of any mistrust that remains between South and North Korea,' said President Roh in his speech, without offering any basis for his aspiration, while back home an outdoor concert in Seoul saw the blue 'Unification Flag' waved and traditional Korean drums beaten, the audience blithely unaware that the South Korean faces at the reality-show banquet had grown uniformly long. The tone of the talks had been set.

Back in 2000, Kim Jong Il had allegedly charged South Korean President Kim Dae Jung $500 million – $450 million of it in cash and the rest in material aid – for the privilege of a Pyongyang visit.* At the last minute he had then pushed back the summit date by a day, as the full $450 million had still not been received due to a clerical error. He also made sure to show the world his 'human side' – basically he had smiled a lot –

---

* Officially this money was aid, but a secretive payment just before the first-ever inter-Korean summit raised questions. When news of the payment broke, charges of bribery were made and several South Korean officials ended up in jail, although President Kim was not among them.

enough for a degree of collective amnesia to descend over his regime's deliberate starvation of the population, public executions and concentration camps full of skeletal political prisoners. In 2007, the lesson Kim Jong Un and Kim Yo Jong would have learned on the first day of President Roh's visit to North Korea was: show them who's boss.

The next morning, Kim Jong Il paid Roh a visit at his guest house, and sat down with him for a two-hour session. During the portion of the meeting open to reporters, when Roh thanked Kim for greeting him in person the previous day, the Dear Leader smiled and replied, 'I had no reason to sit around and wait at home like a [sick] patient.' It is not known whether Kim gave Roh a plausible reason for not attending the banquet, although the South Korean government and press would surely have announced it to the world, if only to mitigate some of Roh's embarrassment.

By all accounts, the morning talks did not proceed as Roh had envisioned. Kim was 'unreceptive' to his proposals, and left at lunchtime, leaving his guest to dine with his entourage and the South Korean press corps.

At the afternoon meeting, to the sound of cameras clicking like crickets, the Dear Leader, sitting across the wooden conference table, made a typically Dear Leader-like proposition. 'Why don't we postpone today's agenda to tomorrow so that we can have a long, leisurely lunch tomorrow?' Kim Jong Il threw in an unscheduled dinner as well. Taken aback, President Roh declined, correctly surmising that staying an extra unscheduled night in North Korea would make him look like a puppet on a string.

But postponing the afternoon discussions to the next morning had seen Kim Jong Il win another round. The next morning's session would be all or nothing. Roh Moo Hyun needed at the very least a joint statement co-signed with Kim Jong Il. Otherwise, his critics at home would ask, 'What was the point of the trip?'

In the evening, President Roh was treated to a grand outdoor spectacle featuring tens of thousands of singers, musicians, dancers, gymnasts, and martial artists. His host was Kim Yong Nam, the titular head of state. Apparently, Kim Jong Il had other affairs to attend to. Roh Moo Hyun was not nearly as important a guest as US Secretary of State Madeleine Albright had been in October 2000, when Kim Jong Il sat next to her in the stands wearing a big smile.

On Roh's last day in North Korea, the psychological impact of Kim Jong Il's snub showed. Roh made all the concessions and his host none. Six years later, South Korea's governing party (the opposition party during Roh's tenure) revealed that Roh, in his four-hour-long talks with Kim Jong Il on 4 October, had gone overboard in trying to please his host by promising concessions not just of the economic sort, but also on national security. A leaked transcript appeared to show Roh agreeing that the de facto maritime border between the North and the South should be pushed further southward, as the North had insisted for decades. It was not a trite matter that could be explained away as the excitement of the summitry: deadly naval skirmishes had taken place in those waters in 1999 and 2002, and another would take place in 2009. In March 2010, a North

Korean submarine fired a torpedo at a South Korean corvette, killing forty-six crew. President Roh's supporters argued that the transcript must have been altered.

In the transcript, President Roh also told Kim Jong Il that in his many meetings with foreign heads of state he had acted as Kim Jong Il's 'spokesperson' on North Korea's nuclear weapons programmes, proudly recounting how he had 'defended the North's position in the Six-Party Talks' over the past five years, and had 'fought' with the Americans.* He had told Kim that the US blacklisting in 2005 of Banco Delta Asia, a small Macanese bank in which approximately $25 million of laundered North Korean funds had been deposited, was 'unjust' and a 'mistake', and even said he had quashed OPLAN 5029, a joint South Korea–United States contingency plan for responding to possible instability or near-collapse scenarios in North Korea.

For all the apparent desperation to strike an agreement, however, the result of Roh's visit was just another one-sided joint statement reaffirming that unification will be resolved 'by the Korean people themselves' – code for 'based on North Korean initiatives, independent of the United States'. The phrase 'by the Korean people themselves' – 'Uri minjok ggiri' – was even the name of a major North Korean propaganda body (spelled 'Uriminzokkiri').

South Korean supporters of the 2007 summit claimed soon after Roh's return home that the agreement to create a special

---

* These intermittent multilateral talks from 2003 to 2008 involved China, Japan, North Korea, Russia, South Korea, and the United States, and were aimed (at least from the US perspective) at ending North Korea's nuclear programmes.

'peace zone' in the sea between the two nations would allow North Korean and South Korean fishing boats to roam about freely, and the 'passage of civilian vessels via direct routes in Haeju' (paragraph five of the declaration). The problem was that the naval bases in these coastal areas were heavily fortified. Short of a drastic mutual disarmament – impossible – North Korea was exceedingly unlikely to grant the South's fishing boats and other civilian vessels access to Haeju, a major city just 60 km north of the border. For his part, Kim Jong Il, unprompted, promised Roh Moo Hyun that he would accept direct flights from Seoul to Samjiyon, the closest city to Mount Paektu, for tourism, which many moons later remain just a chimera.

The North Korean state's concerns about unregulated contact between North Korean citizens and South Koreans leading to unlicensed inflow of goods and information and an increase in defectors would always preclude such a future. The clause in the joint declaration is evidence of the fanciful optimism of the South, and the deceitful bait-dangling of the North.

Back home, President Roh declared he had won peace and pledged aid to secure the peace already won, to the tune of $13 billion in grants, low-interest loans, and investment (in addition to approximately $4.4 billion aid, more than half of it in cash, since taking office).[2] Kim Jong Il's children would have observed that it pays to sell fake peace, and studied their father's tactics: first, establish credibility by threatening war and building up weapons of mass destruction; second, play hard to get; third, set the tone from the outset and milk them for as many concessions as possible, while smiling and frowning appropriately. Above all, seize the momentum and remain in control.

They would follow this playbook perfectly in 2018 at the Pyeongchang Olympics.

Two years after watching their father dominate the 2007 inter-Korean summit, they would even get to see him engage in 'hostage diplomacy' towards the United States of America.

As previously mentioned, on 8 January 2009, Kim Jong Il reportedly informed the Organization and Guidance Department that he was anointing his youngest son, Jong Un, heir apparent. It was Jong Un's twenty-fifth birthday. All hailed the wisest of all decisions by their current Supreme Leader. State media now began to build up the young man who, obviously, had much to prove. Radio stations played ad nauseum a song called 'Footsteps', written for Kim Jong Un for his eighth birthday and played at his party by North Korea's first pop band, the Pochonbo Electronic Ensemble, no fewer than four times straight off, celebrating the advent of a new 'General Kim' who would 'spread the spirit of February', a reference to Kim Jong Il's birthday, 16 February:

Tramp tramp tramp,
The footsteps of our General Kim
Spreading the spirit of February.
Tramp tramp tramping onwards,
Footsteps, Footsteps,
Spreading out further the sound of a brilliant future ahead.

The regime had waited no less than seventeen years before actually releasing it.

A week later, in a short, sensational dispatch from South Korea's quasi-government news agency, *Yonhap News*, the big news was made public. At the time, few outside Kim Jong Il's inner circle even knew the future Supreme Leader's correct first name. With so much false and unconfirmed news on North Korea, it was not until June that the South Korean government confirmed the intelligence. The April 2009 photograph of Kim Jong Un, Kim Yo Jong, and Kim Jong Chol accompanying their father at Wonsan Agricultural University offered a glimpse of the Supreme Leader's children as apprentices or casual observers. In Kim Jong Un's case, it was far more likely the former. In Kim Yo Jong's case, it is likely she too was already playing a key role in government. In early August, an American eyewitness would see Kim Yo Jong, a month shy of turning twenty-two, in action, supporting her father at close range in his rather important meeting with none other than a former US president.

In August 2009, Bill Clinton made his first and, to date, only trip to Pyongyang, at the invitation of Kim Jong Il, nine years after his plan to make what would have been the first-ever visit to North Korea by an incumbent US president had been scuppered by a recount following the George W. Bush vs Al Gore election, to Clinton's regret.[3]

But now Clinton had a legitimate and pressing reason to make the trip: to win the release of two American women,

Laura Ling and Euna Lee, journalists working for Current TV, a media company co-owned by Al Gore, Clinton's former vice president. In March that year, they had been captured by North Korean border guards along the Tumen River, which separates north-eastern North Korea and China.

Along with a cameraman, the women were visiting the Yanbian Korean Autonomous Prefecture in China's north-eastern Jilin Province, where ethnic Korean women, many escapees from North Korea, ended up as victims of human trafficking and were forced to work in the sex industry. With the help of South Korean church organizations, Ling and Lee were making a documentary on the plight of these women. When they, with their cameraman and a male guide, had apparently crossed over to the North Korean side of the river border one night, they were chased by armed North Korean border guards. The men managed to outrun the guards, but the women were seized, despite having made it across the border into China, and beaten, in the case of Ling to the point of unconsciousness.[4] Ling and Lee were sentenced to twelve years' hard labour for illegal entry and so-called 'hostile acts' against the North Korean state.

Word had come to Clinton from Laura Ling's sister, Lisa, a well-known TV journalist, that the Dear Leader might release Ling and Lee if he came to Pyongyang. But it had to be Clinton – not former US President Jimmy Carter or any other retired dignitary. The situation was challenging. The US–North Korea relationship, never good, was at a particularly low ebb. Kim Jong Il had pushed the new Obama administration hard.

Just hours before Obama, on his first visit to Europe as president, was to deliver his first major foreign policy speech on a world without nuclear weapons, North Korea fired a long-range missile, its first launch in three years. The next month, on 25 May 2009, North Korea conducted the nation's second nuclear test. The date was Memorial Day in the United States that year, a day of remembrance for all Americans who paid the ultimate price in the defence of American freedom, including fighting against North Korean forces in the Korean War. It was hardly a coincidence.

For decades, North Korea had shown a keen sense of timing when it came to pressuring the US. In 2006, North Korea had given the George W. Bush administration a 'seven-rocket salute' on Independence Day, firing a long-range ballistic missile and six short-range missiles for good measure. Back in 1998, a previous three-stage rocket launch over Japan had triggered major concessions, almost $300 million USD worth of food aid, to the North by Clinton's own administration.

North Korean provocations also come in one-two punch packages. Three months after the Independence Day rockets in 2006, North Korea conducted its first nuclear test – for any would-be nuclear state, a seminal date never to be forgotten. Kim Jong Il chose 9 October, the eve of the Workers' Party of Korea Foundation Day anniversary, the third most important red-letter day in the North Korean calendar. It also coincided with – or was timed to occur during – the Columbus Day holiday in the US.

That Kim Jong Il would try his best to paint President Obama into a corner early in his term – barely four months into his administration – was virtually preordained as well. It's the North Korean way: put maximum pressure on at the start of the contest.

As a presidential candidate, Obama had spoken of his amenability to meeting with dictators without preconditions, including those in Pyongyang and Tehran. But being nice up front is not North Korea's game. The time for smiles comes after creating havoc, making threats, raising the temperature. North Korea only raises its net worth as an adversary when it creates political and military problems for its interlocuters. A new US administration led by a young, untested president, grappling with a global financial crisis and two unpopular wars in Iraq and Afghanistan, was the perfect time to put the pressure on. And now two American hostages lay stuck in Pyongyang.

Despite the optics of seeking a favour from a dictator, a former president on a humanitarian mission was politically acceptable. Clinton's mission was to be all business: get the hostages out safely[5] – no sightseeing, no concerts, no propaganda trophy for Kim Jong Il. 'Let's not embarrass ourselves,' the American delegation agreed, according to Clinton's closest White House aide, Doug Band. Just as Clinton, while president, had not welcomed former President Carter's visit with Kim Il Sung in 1994, so President Obama was less than effusive: a former president's photo-op with a decades-old adversary – whether Carter de-escalating a nuclear stand-off relatively early in Clintons' tenure, or Clinton winning the release of American hostages not even seven months into Obama's first term – tends to make the incumbent look less than stellar. President Obama insisted that the Clinton delegation spend no more than twenty hours in North Korea and not stay overnight. Kim Jong Il, on the other hand, called for an overnight preceded by an elaborate dinner.

In the end, Clinton spent a total of twenty hours in North Korea, including talks over dinner and an overnight stay. He flew into Pyongyang on a private jet provided by the Hollywood mogul Steve Bing. A hundred thousand dollars in cash that Doug Band brought proved essential: North Korea's charge of $97,000 was almost certainly the single most expensive landing fee in history.

When the plane touched down, it was Kim Yo Jong, unnerved by the heat and humidity, who was waiting on the tarmac. Ignoring the former American president, and neglecting to introduce herself to any of the American visitors, she went straight to Doug Band. No cordiality; she was all business. In English, she asked for the letter of thanks from President Obama that had been promised her father in return for releasing the two women. It was apparent she knew perfectly well who Band was and of his role as Clinton's deputy. The Clinton team, too, knew who the young lady was. They had been briefed on the royal family.

But Band had no such letter on him. No one on the delegation did. They'd only learned while refuelling in Japan (so that the plane could fly straight back to California with the released hostages without having to refuel in Pyongyang) that President Obama, despite agreeing to Kim Jong Il's request, hadn't written any letter.

According to Band, Clinton took the news stoically. Perhaps Kim Jong Il would not make the letter a dealbreaker. But by coming straight to Band, Kim Yo Jong had immediately revealed her father's priority. She also revealed that she spoke English, a fact confirmed to this author by Stephen Biegun, former US Special Representative for North Korea Policy, who met the Kim siblings up close in 2018. During a two-and-a-half-hour negotiation between Kim Jong Un and his sister (and an interpreter) on one hand and Secretary of State Mike Pompeo, Senior CIA Officer Andrew Kim, and Mr Biegun on the other, Kim Yo Jong let out a laugh when the Americans cracked a joke among themselves, while her brother sat stoically and expressionless, apparently because of a lack of English.[6]

Band tried to buy time. He replied that the American delegation first wished to see Lisa and Euna and make sure they were in good physical condition – his brother Roger, Bill Clinton's personal physician, was a member of the party.*

The visitors' wish to go straight to see the detainees was granted. Laura and Euna hadn't been told they were going to meet Bill Clinton, and on seeing the former president standing in front of them were flabbergasted. Roger Band found them in good physical shape, but traumatized. They would have to spend one last night in North Korea, before undergoing a 'judicial procedure' the following morning in front of a judge

---

* Also on the trip was John Podesta, Clinton's former chief of staff, sent by the White House to rein Clinton in if he went off-script and embarked on some freelance diplomacy, as Jimmy Carter had done in 1994, announcing the result of his negotiations with Kim Il Sung to a travelling CNN reporter.

to confirm that they were being released thanks to Kim Jong Il's special pardon.

After meeting the women, the delegation checked in at the Paek Hwa Garden State Guest House, reserved for foreign dignitaries inside a sprawling, fenced-off compound. The guest house had already hosted two South Korean presidents, Jimmy Carter, Japanese Prime Minister Junichiro Koizumi, and Bill Clinton's Secretary of State Madeleine Albright. As was his custom, Kim Jong Il graciously arrived there to greet the foreigners, instead of receiving them in his office or one of his many palatial estates.

With Kim Jong Il having suffered a serious stroke just a year earlier, Dr Band's second priority was to try to assess the Dear Leader's health. Kim walked up to the Americans, looking calm and smiling broadly, and moving quite easily. But it was clear he had not yet shed all the after-effects of the stroke: for one thing he looked markedly less paunchy than in previous photos. But, above all, and as many outsiders had observed, Kim appeared 'very normal' – that is, not one bit weird or crazy. Doug Band, who had visited nearly 140 countries as a White House official and then with Bill Clinton for the Clinton Foundation, and seen underlings visibly shake with fear in the presence of leaders like Vladimir Putin or Muammar Qaddafi, thought the North Korean officials also seemed at ease and professional around the deified leader, although quite clearly deferential.

After a brief exchange of pleasantries, the Americans were asked to pose for a group picture with the Dear Leader. The

Clinton team had been advised to 'control' their facial expression around North Korean photographers and not smile broadly or wear a frown. Against a giant mural of waves crashing on a craggy shore sat Bill Clinton and Kim Jong Il, looking as stiff as ventriloquist's dummies, the six other Americans just as stiff behind them on a carpet of sickly green: an icon of totalitarian kitsch seemingly devoid of live humans.[7]

Later, Doug Band noticed Kim Yo Jong again directing proceedings, acting more as an event manager than Kim Jong Il's beloved princess. She also attended the lavish dinner, a multi-course meal fit for a king, which of course Kim Jong Il was, the heavily marbled steak washed down with Château Latour.

Understandably, the Clinton delegation wondered if they might catch a glimpse of Kim Jong Un. But the young man who would be king, at the time just twenty-five, was nowhere to be seen during the Americans' stay. They had been briefed in Washington on whom to expect, and Kim Jong Un would have been immediately recognizable for his girth if not his youth. But only daddy's 'sweet princess' was there, planning and managing the visit of a US delegation led by a former president, sizing up Clinton as he attempted to remain stone-faced at dinner.

Kim Jong Il was in his element as the witty host. Indeed, Doug Band found him 'even-keeled and pleasant'. Kim clearly understood English. He repeatedly suggested that after dinner his guests attend a concert with him – as usual, the North Korean leader was keen to dazzle the Americans with something only he could offer: his nation's famed mass games, the biggest outdoor spectacle in the world. After all, he had taken Clinton's Secretary of State to one such event in October 2000. Each time this was suggested, Band, only too aware of how the North Korean leader would use the former US president's presence at a night-time extravaganza for propaganda, politely demurred: Clinton was 'too tired'. Kim took it well, but he must have been deflated at the lost opportunity, to say nothing of the disappointment of the tens of thousands of performers who lost the very rare opportunity to perform in the presence of their peerless Dear Leader, the show's grand impresario.

For the US delegation, the visit achieved its ultimate aim: Ling and Lee were released and were able to fly home with Clinton et al. But there was, perhaps, far more gained by the North Korean regime, at little real cost.

The North Korean maestro had shown his children how hostage diplomacy as a prelude to a long-range missile and a nuclear test not only ensures impunity for the kidnapper, but also wins them flattery. Yo Jong had gotten a close-up look at the power dynamics between her father and the Americans on home ground. Several years later, a hapless American college student named Otto Warmbier was to be Jong Un and his sister's hostage. Otto was detained on 2 January 2016 as he was about to depart Pyongyang on a group tour. Four days later, North Korea conducted a nuclear test, its first in three years, followed by a long-range missile blast in February. On the last day of the month, Otto underwent a forced confession 'admitting' that he was guilty of trying to steal a propaganda poster from his hotel. The words that he read out in front of the cameras were a narrative woven from North Korean stock phrases and non-sequiturs as well as containing hidden messages of desperation for his parents back home. The next month he was sentenced to fifteen years of hard labour. By then, March 2016, Kim Yo Jong had already been for several years her nation's chief propagandist. The nature of the forced confession and sentencing had all the marks of her trademark snark and malice, and as we shall see in Chapter 10, for Warmbier there was no safe return home.

CHAPTER 8

Funeral and Rebirth

A young woman, limp and shattered in grief, clad in a traditional black Korean funeral dress, neckline thinly lined in white. From time to time she bowed her head, cheeks hollow, biting her lower lip as she stood, tears rolling down her cheeks, before the closed glass casket mounted on a giant bier of Kimjongilias (a strain of begonias) and chrysanthemums. At an arm's length in front of her, her brother wiped the tears off his face with his handkerchief. The other women allowed a close-up view of the deceased, including the heir's own wife, made no secret of their sorrow. But the look of pain on the young woman's face was visceral.

Outsiders trying to peer through her dynasty's smokescreen might have guessed the young woman was perhaps a family member, by virtue of her physical proximity to Kim Jong Un, by then a familiar visage. But in December 2011 hardly a soul would have been able to identify her as Kim Jong Il's youngest child or Kim Jong Un's younger sister. After all, North Korea's state media had yet to even utter her name. Fewer still could have predicted that she would, in just a few years, rise to become the second most powerful official in the land, even when, just eight days later at her father's funeral ceremony, North Korea's state media would discreetly foreshadow it.

'When beggars die, there are no comets seen,' Calpurnia warns her husband, the man feared as dictator-in-perpetuity, the morning of his last day on earth, in Shakespeare's *Julius Caesar*. '[T]he Heavens themselves blaze forth the death of princes.'[1] Kim Jong Il's death from cardiac arrest (like his father) seemed to set the heavens ablaze. The announcement on state television at noon on 19 December 2011, two days after the fact, brought his nation to a standstill. For the next ten days, hundreds of thousands of Pyongyang residents poured into the streets and plazas to mourn, throwing their bodies to the ground in fits of agony, wailing away their anguished souls and smiting their chests and the ground repeatedly with their fists. Similar scenes erupted across the nation. The sudden demise of its own dictator-in-perpetuity saw North Korea engulfed in delirium and disbelief. Even the elements roared. A 'series of blinding blue flashes accompanied by thunder' was observed near the southern border, reported state media. 'Even the sky seemed to writhe in grief at the demise of the "great saint born of Heaven,"' witnesses declaimed, five days after the Dear Leader's death.[2]

Over the next few days, state television showed Kim Jong Il's embalmed body inside a glass casket, draped in red, head resting on a white cushion, countering the people's raw grief with reassuring solemnity. But the most majestic and lasting scenes would be reserved for the state funeral, the procession led by a young Kim Jong Un with seven older men more than twice his age flanking the US-made Lincoln Continental hearse carrying Kim Jong Il's casket. The controlled goodbye to the great man could never be truly final, though, for the son, embodying the heroic traits of his father, would ensure that even with Kim Jong Il embalmed in the Mount Kumsu Palace of the Sun, the place of his father's eternal rest, the Mount Paektu spirit of greatness would pervade the land. Even in their ineffable sorrow, the people saw faith and future in the fiery eyes of their new Great Leader, guiding the hearse as the snow fell faintly, reverently, on the North Korean gods both living and dead.[3]

Beyond North Korea, the scenes of North Koreans mourning deliriously seemed at once striking and comical. The sudden transition of power inside a nuclear state, however, was not a laughing matter. What comes next? Reform? Regime collapse? A coup?

Pyongyang-ologists around the world scrutinized the seven men not called Kim Jong Un surrounding the Lincoln Continental as it made its way towards the Palace of the Sun. They were immediately identified. Within the first few months, it became quite easy to see who was on their way out – even permanently. By late 2012, five of the seven had been relieved of their positions with varying degrees of severity and permanence. One was relieved of duty within two months of the funeral; another was forcibly disappeared within seven months and has for some time been presumed to have been killed.

In February 2011, one of the seven, U Dong Chuk, the head of the State Security Department, disappeared. In April, another, Kim Yong Chun, Minister of the People's Armed Forces, was demoted but not irreparably punished. By November, Kim Jong Gak, his replacement, had also been purged. In July, state media announced that Ri Yong Ho, Chief of General Staff of the Korean People's Army and considered at the time the most powerful military man in the kingdom, who had been at the front of the hearse across from Kim Jong Un, had been stripped of all his positions due to an unspecified illness. His replacement, General Hyon Yong Chol, was not one of the original seven but was not fated to live much longer than his predecessor. While North Korea has never confirmed Ri's execution, it did confirm Hyon's three years later. Demoted in late 2012, then in 2014 promoted to Minister of the People's Armed Forces, in April 2015 Hyon was executed in public by anti-aircraft machine gun for having dozed off during a meeting convened by Kim Jong Un.[4]

It was Kim Jong Un's own uncle, Jang Song Thaek, for years Kim Jong Il's closest confidant, who met the most gruesome and publicly humiliating fate. North Korea never confirmed how he was killed, but it was originally assumed that he was shot by a ZPU-4, the Russian anti-aircraft artillery gun. After all, in November 2013, Kim Jong Un had his uncle sit in the front row and watch as his two close aides, Ri Ryong Ha and Jang Su Gil, were shredded to bits by the powerful machine gun. But Kim purportedly told Donald Trump in Hanoi that he had had his uncle's head chopped off and the severed head displayed on top of Jang's chest for his junior colleagues' delectation. What remains undisputed is that Jang was killed, most likely sometime between December 2013 and January 2014. Among the many charges made against someone now sentenced to death and vilified as, among other things, 'despicable human scum' and 'worse than a dog', were treason and undermining the personality cult of the Great Leader, not to mention 'womanizing' and 'half-hearted clapping' during Kim Jong Un's speeches.[5] Since December 2013, his name has never again been mentioned by state media.

With the spectacular downfall of the second most powerful man in the land, those looking in were still searching in vain for clues as to the real movers and shakers inside Kim Jong Un's inner circle.

The two men out of the seven who survived and even thrived in the Kim Jong Un era were Kim Ki Nam, the master propagandist mentor to Yo Jong, and Choe Thae Bok, Chairman of the Supreme People's Assembly. Both remained intact in flesh and high posts, and went into voluntary semi-retirement, in 2017 and 2019, respectively. But the fate of the rest – five out of the seven most senior officials picked by Kim Jong Un to escort his father's hearse – was a sobering reminder of standard procedures in the DPRK, even when ruled by an inexperienced, young, Swiss-educated leader: everyone is susceptible to the Great Leader's caprices. Everyone's life is precarious.

Well, almost everyone. In the days following Kim Jong Il's death, the clues as to who had real power besides Kim Jong Un were in plain sight. Granted, after Kim Jong Un, Uncle Jang was the second most powerful *man* in the land. He just wasn't as powerful as the second most powerful *person* in the land.

At her father's funeral, Yo Jong did not flank her father's hearse. Korean funerary customs preclude females from taking centre stage, a relic of past sexism. Indeed, she was not even listed on the 'National Funeral Committee List' of over 200 names. (Though neither was Jong Chol, her older brother.)

At the same time, nothing, not even the most deeply entrenched male-dominated cultural norms, would stop the second most powerful person in North Korea from taking her rightful place on the red carpet at Mount Kumsu Palace of the Sun, where her father would join his own father in embalmed eternity. There she was, three spots from her brother's left, the only woman in the line-up, reviewing her country's goose-stepping regiments march patriotically past. Only Kim Yong Nam and Premier Choe Yong Rim stood in between her and the new Great Leader, both figureheads whose place in the line-up was by then more down to their many years of service than an indicator of power. Uncle Jang stood five places further down the line from her royal personage.

During the eulogy, Kim Yo Jong suddenly left the line-up to walk away, presumably overcome.[6] Had anyone else interrupted such a sacred ceremony, the deadly vengeance would have outstripped even that unleashed for the 'half-hearted clapping'. But from the very first days of her brother's reign, Kim Yo Jong has been untouchable and ambitious.

CHAPTER 9

The Vile Ventriloquist

The death of Kim Jong Il in December 2011 had thrust his youngest son, still only in his late twenties, into the spotlight as the kingdom's new Supreme Leader. Outside North Korea, observers came, by and by, to resignedly accept that the third-generational de facto king of North Korea, and the first to have been educated in Switzerland, despite initial rosy prognostications, would neither flounder nor espouse European cosmopolitanism. There also slowly came the recognition that his sister was gradually increasing her public profile.

She would frequently accompany her brother in a supporting role as he visited government branches, military bases, factories, museums, amusement parks, farms, the newly renovated Pyongyang International Airport, an animation film studio, day care centre, orphanages, upscale stores, a nuclear missile assembly facility, and concert halls. But not once did she issue a statement or give 'on-the-spot guidance' herself. Mundanity seemed her role of choice.

Seven months after her father's death, in July 2012, she was seen enjoying a day out at Rungna People's Pleasure Ground, a new amusement park in Pyongyang complete with a dolphinarium, dressed plainly in a light shirt and black skirt, almost as though in school uniform – just a young person having fun, or so it seemed. Her long hair blew in the wind as she cheerfully waved to friends joyfully screaming on the 360-degree swing ride. The scarf she wore on her right wrist would soon become a popular trend.[1] Even the serious business of the amusement park's formal opening failed to check her carefree manner: walking around by herself, bursting out laughing as she stood a few metres behind her brother and his wife, while the other officials, including her aunt and husband, stood stiffly to attention. She was caught on video hopping over a flowerbed in a belated attempt to get out of the frame and run across the square. The Propaganda and Agitation Department (PAD), charged with editing such untoward scenes out of government newsreels, left them in. It was no oversight. She ran the department, after all.

According to Ri Jong Ho, a top North Korean defector who was among the cognoscenti when it came to the Great Leader's schemes and slush funds,[2] Kim Yo Jong joined the PAD in early 2012 as vice director. In late 2012, upon Uncle Jang Song Thaek's recommendation, she joined a special fifty-person class created for her at Kim Il Sung University's Politics and Economics Department, where her fellow classmates were master's and doctoral students. The special crash course lasted six months. It was intended for Kim Yo Jong to brush up on academics and also a possible way for her to meet candidates for a future husband. A former classmate of Mr Ri's son also enrolled in the special class. He was the grandson of a cousin of Kim Il Sung. Kim Yo Jong, other students and party officials observed, was very good with computers. She used two monitors simultaneously with ease while typing away deftly.[3] Whether the match-making worked or not is, of course, a state secret. There is speculation that Kim Yo Jong is married and has a child or two, but so far it is just speculation.

The following year, when Jang Song Thaek was condemned to death, questions arose. Was Jang seen by Kim Jong Un as such a threat that he had to be purged? Or had Jang not been that powerful after all? As we have seen, in a system like North Korea's, formal rank and even observable informal power, like standing close to the Supreme Leader at events, are not always the correct measure of actual power. North Koreans know that unless you are a core member of the royal family, a direct descendent of the founder of the Mount Paektu clan, then you're expendable. Uncle Jang was a side branch who married into the family. In contrast, Kim Yo Jong, despite her youth, could afford to exude boundless self-confidence and even insouciance in her brother's presence.

Two years later, in March 2014, when she was first mentioned by name in state media after casting a vote for her brother, Kim Yo Jong was still viewed by most outsiders as an 'ordinary', happy-go-lucky young woman in her mid-twenties. State media would mention her twice more that month, both times as attending a concert by the Moranbong Band (Kim Jong Un's favourite) with her brother and his wife – and both times

Kim Yo Jong was mentioned last, of respectively eleven and seventeen attendees, with no indication whatsoever of her blue blood.

Shortly after Kim Yo Jong's discreet introduction by the state media, it seems she got down to work. A sudden and unusual surge of foul language burst forth from the propaganda outlets, articles in the state media in April and May 2014 brimming with profanity, aggressive racism, sexism and homophobia. The KCNA called Michael Kirby, a retired justice of the high court of Australia, who is openly gay, 'a disgusting old lecher with a 40-odd-year-long career of homosexuality.'[4] His 'offence' was to have chaired the United Nations Commission of Inquiry Report on Human Rights in North Korea, a monumental 372-page study released in February 2014 that had found the regime's extreme human rights abuses to be the work of a state 'that does not have any parallel in the contemporary world.'

Concurrently, the KCNA repeatedly maligned South Korea's first female elected leader, President Park Geun Hye, who was single and had never married, as a 'dirty old prostitute'. In a 27 April news article, in reference to President Park's warm reception of President Obama in South Korea two days earlier, North Korean propagandists stated that Park reminded them of 'an indiscreet girl who earnestly begs a gangster to beat someone; of a capricious whore who asks her fancy man to do harm to other person while providing sex to him.' After asserting that Park 'thus laid bare her despicable true colours as a wicked sycophant and traitor, a dirty comfort woman for the US and despicable prostitute selling off the nation,' the article concluded with a reference to her late father, who in 1979 was shot and killed by his trusted aide: 'her fate will be just the same as that of her father Park Chung Hee, who met a miserable death.'[5]

On 29 April, the *Rodong Sinmun*, the party newspaper that primarily caters to domestic readers, characterized the Park–Obama summit as 'nothing but a disgusting kiss between the boss of gangsters asking his political prostitute to serve him before going to war and his partner flattering him.'[6] On 2 May, the state news agency demeaned President Park again as 'no more than an old prostitute coquetting with outside forces.'[7] For the KCNA, the next day she was 'a disgusting old prostitute raising even her skirt, not feeling any shame to bring a stranger [President Obama] into her bedroom.'[8] A 25 May article called for her death: 'Such prostitute, special-class traitor has to be eliminated at an early date.'[9]

North Korea's splenetic rants continued through the autumn, with the KCNA attributing President Park's speech at the United Nations General Assembly calling on North Korea to dismantle its nuclear program to a 'political prostitute . . . venomously swishing her skirt.'[10]

The following year, Pyongyang's propagandists somehow managed to escalate the abuse: 27 May 2015 saw a nine-page diatribe from the KCNA ranting that President Park 'has remained glued to her American master's stinky groin . . . like a whore drunk on spring breeze shaking her tail.' This 'hideous American comfort woman, a dirty prostitute who is a traitor to the Korean nation,' it concluded, 'North Korea will be certain to punish.'[11]

By late 2014, nearly three years into Kim Jong Un's rule, the person in charge of the propaganda department and its endless abuse-mill was none other than his 'ordinary', happy-go-lucky sister. As a mere 'vice director', she was in any case already the de facto chief of the PAD, working under the alias 'Kim Ye Jong'.[12] She was not entirely visible, but her voice was clearly audible.

By then, those who paid attention to North Korean propaganda had perhaps grown immune to such extreme language. With repetition and time, North Korea's vicious verbal attacks on President Park became less shocking. Even the intensification of the vituperation received little coverage in South Korea beyond cursory references to 'unspeakable language'. There was to be no public outcry. Kim Yo Jong's propagandists had, in effect, normalized sexist profanity against the South Korean leader and had conditioned South Koreans to live with it. Silence, in this instance, was not the best expression of scorn. It was tantamount to tacit acceptance. Once again, North Korea had set the tone of the inter-Korean relationship. The abusive ventriloquist in Pyongyang had won each round.

To many Americans, shock and disgust at North Korea's profanity had already been felt in the spring of 2014, when Pyongyang had hurled a vile, racist invective at the first-ever African-American President of the United States of America. North Korea's chief external propaganda outlet called Barack Obama 'a wicked black monkey' who should go back and 'live with a group of monkeys in the world's largest African natural zoo and lick the breadcrumbs thrown by spectators.' Calling President Obama a 'crossbreed with unclear blood', the KCNA stated that he 'still has the figure of a monkey while the human race has evolved through millions of years.'[13]

Such invective could never be broadcast without the approval of the Supreme Leader, so Kim Jong Un, together with his chief propagandist, his sister, who may have actually come up with many of these words, or would at the very least have approved them, owns this particular bit of vileness. The White House's measured rebuke merely noted that, 'While the North Korean government-controlled media are distinguished by their histrionics, these comments are particularly ugly and disrespectful.'[14]

But few were able to connect this peculiarly vulgar voice to the young woman who would have signed off on it. The diatribes were not, of course, necessarily the creation of one person. Rather, they are the collective effort of scores of full-time professional writers in each party department and government ministry, recruited from the nation's top universities for their literary flourish. They make their mark by churning out phrases both repugnant and poetic. All South Korean leaders have at some point borne the indignity of North Korean invective, even those who heartily welcomed the North Korean Supreme Leader and his – at least at the time – polite sister.

CHAPTER 10

The Pyongyang Games

By the beginning of 2018, US–North Korea relations had reached a particularly low ebb. The past year had been marked by relentless missile blasts by the North, punctuated by three progressively more powerful ICBM tests starting on 4 July, US Independence Day, and an unprecedented thermonuclear test in September 2017. Kim Jong Un and President Trump (who was inaugurated in January 2017) had been calling each other unkind names, from 'Rocket Man on a suicide mission' to 'mentally deranged American dotard'. Each had threatened the other with nuclear annihilation. In January 2018, both were talking about their 'nuclear button'. Kim Jong Un, in his New Year's Day speech, made a point of emphasizing that it lay 'always on my desk'. Two days later, Trump tweeted, 'Will someone from his depleted and food starved regime please inform him that I too have a Nuclear Button. But it is a much bigger and more powerful one than his, and my Button works!'[1]

The previous November, President Trump had addressed the South Korean National Assembly and spoken firmly about North

Korea's human rights violations. 'North Korea is a country ruled as a cult,' he said. 'At the centre of this military cult is a deranged belief in the leader's destiny to rule as parent-protector over a conquered Korean peninsula and an enslaved Korean people.' He went on to set out the basic internal dynamic in the Korean peninsula, one that in the long term did not favour North Korea: '[T]he very existence of a thriving South Korean republic threatens the very survival of the North Korean dictatorship.'[2]

In his speech, Trump also mentioned Otto Warmbier, the University of Virginia student who, on a visit to North Korea in late 2015, had been taken hostage, tortured and sentenced to fifteen years of imprisonment and hard labour. By the following April, he had been rendered brain dead, and more than a year later, in June 2017, was released in a persistent vegetative state, and died later the same month. 'The Kim regime,' President Trump – who deserves credit for pushing North Korea to release Warmbier – said, in his speech in Seoul, 'tortured Otto Warmbier, ultimately leading to that fine young man's death.'

During the bluster barrage of the previous two years, the Kim regime had conducted three nuclear tests, three ICBM tests, and dozens of shorter-range ballistic missile blasts. Now, as the US was all too clearly aware, North Korea's typical ploy was to follow up with a charm offensive, and this was definitely the time to change the tune.

It so happened that February 2018 marked the start of the twenty-third Winter Olympics. And where were they going to be held? Pyeongchang, South Korea. Sure enough, on 8 January

2018 came a remarkable announcement: at the eleventh hour, North Korea was going to participate. Even more remarkably, it was going to send a dozen of its female ice hockey players to join the South Korean squad in a 'Unified Team Korea'. They would be accompanied by an official government delegation from the North.

Many South Koreans expressed their disapproval, while the Canadian head coach of the South Korean women's national team was among the voices of concern over fairness and athletes being used as political props. What was the big deal? riposted Prime Minister Lee Nak-Yon: the South Korean team was already 'out of medal range anyway'.[3] (He was later forced to issue an apology for his remarks.)

But though South Korea was the nation that stood to lose the most from a nuclear stand-off with North Korea, it remained in denial even to the extent of building up the Pyeongchang Olympics as the 'Peace Games'. The powerful force of nationalism, the message of unity, the International Olympic Committee's (IOC) business considerations, and President Moon Jae-In's political calculations all converged. The IOC granted a special last-minute exemption to the team roster limit of twenty-two and allowed the united Korean team to have thirty-five players. Special times called for special favours.

In the days leading up to the opening ceremony, North Korea reached out to the White House via the South Koreans. Its message was quite dramatic. Despite more than a year of provocation and hurling unkind statements back and forth, the

North Koreans wished to meet with the US vice president, who would be leading the American Olympic delegation. After much discussion with President Trump and their advisors, Mike Pence eventually agreed to sit down with the North Koreans. The meeting was to take place on 10 February, the morning after the opening ceremony, in the Blue House.

In the run-up to Pence's departure for South Korea, the White House was at pains to declare that he would 'not allow the North Korean regime to hijack the messaging of the Olympics.'[4] President Trump's State of the Union Address in Congress on 30 January kept up the pressure, acknowledging the presence of Otto Warmbier's parents, Fred and Cindy, in the audience, as well as Ji Soeng-Ho, a double amputee North Korean escapee and human rights activist, who in 2020 would become a member of the South Korean parliament. Fred Warmbier was even invited to be part of Pence's delegation to Pyeongchang. During a stopover in Japan, with Japanese Prime Minister Shinzo Abe next to him and just two days before both men would find themselves at a face-to-face meeting with Kim Yo Jong herself, Pence reinforced the president's message. 'An estimated 100,000 North Koreans suffer in gulags,' said the vice president, 'toiling in forced labour, and enduring torture, starvation, rape, and murder on a constant basis.'[5]

To the US government, it was no secret that Kim Yo Jong's flirtation with diplomacy was a ruse to loosen sanctions in order to buy time and money to build more bombs. Japan knew this too. 'Together with Japan, and all our allies,' Pence concluded resolutely, 'we will continue to intensify our maximum pressure campaign until North Korea takes concrete steps toward complete, verifiable and irreversible denuclearization.'[6]

Kim Yo Jong's visit to South Korea for the 2018 Winter Olympics was sensational in itself, but the timing – just a month after Kim Jong Un and Donald Trump had been trading nuclear threats – seemed to make it almost an act of salvation. On her slender shoulders lay the future of humanity!

By the time she arrived in South Korea, the crescendo of warm and fuzzy feelings held sway over common sense. North Korea's glamorous female singers, musicians, and hundreds of cheer-leaders had already jazzed up the hitherto lacklustre Olympics in a city few had heard of and many confused with Pyongyang.[7] Now came Pyongyang's masterstroke: the North Korean princess personally gracing the proceedings. How could Mike Pence – far from the world's most charismatic politician – compete? Already, by the time he arrived in South Korea on the same day as the North Koreans, the Pyeongchang Olympics stood at risk of becoming the 'Pyongyang Games': paid for by the South, and paving the way for Kim Jong Un's image makeover.

While the Pence delegation was meeting with four North Korean defectors on the day of the opening ceremony, and Pence himself going on to the memorial to the forty-six South Korean sailors who died when their ship, the *Cheonan*, was torpedoed by a North Korean submarine in 2010,[8] most South Korean eyes were on Kim Yo Jong, and hearts and minds dreaming of the princess's visit heralding a new era of peace.

At such a historic moment, sober discussions of human rights in general and the North Korean visitor's role in oppressing her people in particular seemed quite out of place. At the opening ceremony, as well as the reception and dinner preceding it, the well-meaning US vice president stood by his principles and did his best to ignore the North Koreans.[9] '[President] Moon's priority,' Pence writes in his memoir, 'was Korean reunification, so he was eager for me to engage with Kim's sister and Kim Young-Nam [*sic*], North Korea's ceremonial head of state . . . It was evident that [Moon] wanted to politely force a meeting between Kim Young-Nam and me . . . No chance.'[10]

But he also made a series of unforced errors.

Pence had made it clear that he would not attend the pre-opening ceremony dinner if he were seated at the same table as Kim Yong Nam. But he turned up at the Olympic village to find out he had been assigned a seat at the head table directly across from him.[11] Exasperated, Pence and his wife, Karen, shook hands with 'every other leader in the room' and left the reception to go and meet American athletes instead.[12] Thus, the impression created was that it was the US, instead of North Korea, that was uninterested in dialogue and diplomacy.

In the VIP box at the opening ceremony itself, Vice President and Second Lady Pence were confronted by an even more disagreeable seating arrangement, and this time they could not walk out. The North Korean delegation had demanded that they be seated one row behind the US delegation – or 'above' them, given the tiered seating – insisting to the South they 'would not attend the opening ceremony if South Korea did

Kim Yo Jong in the row behind Mike Pence at the 2018 Winter Olympics.

not make it happen.'[13] In the end, President Moon caved, and seated Kim Yo Jong above not only Mike Pence but also himself, the face of the host nation. The effect created was that the North Koreans were 'above' them all – both the Americans and South Koreans – in every sense.

Kim Yo Jong clearly took that view. She met President Moon in person for the first time when Moon entered the VIP box. Moon looked up to his very special guest with a sunny smile, and extended his hand. She reached down only halfway to shake his hand, keeping her elbow by her side and her posture erect, tilting forward no further than necessary, as though this young woman were acknowledging a much older, junior officer respectfully looking up at her.

While few, if any, South Koreans would have cheered at such optics had their leader been greeting, say, the prime minister of Japan, or even Kim Jong Un himself, many cheered at this 'historic handshake'. Indeed, the photo of the handshake went viral.[14] The Mount Paektu princess smiling and shaking hands with the South Korean leader somehow neutralized all questions of diplomatic protocol, national image, or even deeply entrenched national pride. Kim Yo Jong had seized the moment. *I am the main draw here*, said her body language. *You should all be grateful I am gracing your opening ceremony.*

As for the American vice president, for the entire evening Kim Yo Jong, chin in the air, would beam her imperious smile over him and his wife as they sat almost directly below.

When the North Korean and South Korean athletes made their joint entrance into the arena, Vice President Pence dug himself into a deeper hole. President Moon and his wife, both wearing matching white parkas with black lines and red-and-blue scarves, the colours of the national flag, stood up to applaud. So did Kim Yo Jong and Kim Yong Nam, the princess much more restrainedly. Moon and his wife turned to reach up to Kim Yo Jong and Kim Yong Nam and shake hands once more. Once again, Kim Yo Jong managed a restrained smile. And Mike and Karen Pence, in matching blue-red-white Team USA parkas, stayed hunched in their seats, not willing to impart even a perfunctory clap or two, let alone cheer, the North Korean athletes. As a result, they ended up not applauding the South Korean athletes, either.

The optics of the VIP box were as unflattering to the South Korean leader as they were to the US vice president, but most South Koreans chose to dwell only on the latter. At the world's biggest sporting event, the top US delegate appeared a poor sport, a dour curmudgeon. Many South Koreans took umbrage at what they saw as Pence's lack of respect for South Korean athletes on South Korean soil and, of course, his sour display of contempt at the historic moment of South and North Korean athletes marching as one at the Olympics – admittedly, now in its tired fourth sequel since the 2000 opener in Sydney (followed by Athens 2004 and Turin 2006).

As Fred Warmbier put it subsequently, it was North Korea that had received the maximum benefit from Moon's actions. Pence, on the other hand, 'wasn't going to kowtow to the North Koreans.'[15] That he showed it was his error: it made him the boorish party-pooper in the eyes of many.

In retrospect, it would have been better for Pence to grit his teeth and sit down at the head table, force his lips into the rictus of a smile, and talk to the Japanese prime minister, the German president and the United Nations Secretary-General, while feigning short-sightedness that made him unable to focus on the North Korean guest across the table. It would have been better to approach Kim Yo Jong and Kim Yong Nam in the VIP box and try to shake hands. If the North Koreans refused, so much the better: one-nil to Team America and an own-goal for North Korea.[16]

As good as Kim Yo Jong was in giving her cold, brutish state a softer, feminine cast, she was not perfect. When the US athletes made their entrance, she in turn stayed in her seat, nose in the air and scowling ever so slightly, and applauded not once, which cost the Moon administration some points. Imagine the excitement had she flashed that heart-melting smile, clapped three or four times and then, with a little gasp, stopped as though catching herself in a forbidden act! 'How adorable!' people would have crooned.

But at least one American saw right through it all. Fred Warmbier wanted to talk to the North Korean delegation. He wanted to ask about his son, Otto. He wanted Otto's medical and legal records during his seventeen months in captivity in North Korea. 'I was still really upset at them killing my son. But the South Koreans wouldn't allow it. The Russian ambassador to North Korea was in attendance. He told me, "I'm really sorry about what North Korea did to your son." I wanted to hear it from the North Koreans.'

'Moon came across as decent,' Mr Warmbier reflected later. 'But I realized he was willing to do whatever North Korea demanded.'

In fairness to President Moon, wanting better relations between the North and South was a laudable aim. His mistake was in thinking that spending the next two days beautifying the North Korean royal family and pleasing Kim Yo Jong would create some kind of reciprocal relationship rather than make him look weak in her eyes. Fred Warmbier had a different view of the young princess from North Korea: 'I looked at her. She is evil, all the way through. She is a murderer, a criminal, a thug. She just happens to be a woman.'[17]

CHAPTER 11

The Blue House Visit

The next day, Kim Yo Jong cancelled the scheduled meeting with the Americans just two hours before it was due to take place.[1] But, as expected, she honoured her engagement with President Moon.

She and her retinue arrived at President Moon's residential-office compound at 10.59 a.m. She wore a black suit with the ubiquitous badge of her father's and grandfather's smiling head-shots against a red backdrop flashing on her left lapel. Although President Moon was prone to wearing the national badge when meeting world leaders like Donald Trump, Shinzo Abe, and Boris Johnson, on this very special inter-Korean occasion he chose tactfully to forgo it – neither the Democratic People's Republic of Korea nor the Republic of Korea recognizes the other as a sovereign state. He would do the same in his meetings with Kim Jong Un later in April, May, and September.

For the first time since her arrival in South Korea, Ms Kim was seen in public without her winter coat. Although it wasn't immediately apparent, she appeared to have a slight bulge around her abdomen. She also seemed slightly heavier than she had in previous photos. Internet sleuths, pundits and even intelligence analysts opined that Kim Yo Jong was probably pregnant.

She may have been in her final trimester, went the speculation, and gone on to give birth in late March or early April, as at the first inter-Korean summit she attended with her brother in late April she would appear visibly thinner.[2] Yet she was observed at public events to take sips of alcohol, a social taboo for an expectant mother in both Koreas.

But she was a powerful princess. She could do virtually what she liked. Perhaps her boldness, like her brother's supposed reform-mindedness,[3] was a product of early exposure to Swiss cosmopolitanism: according to a 2020 Harvard Medical School report, Switzerland recorded the third highest percentage of women imbibing alcohol during pregnancy – 20.9 per cent – after the United Kingdom and Russia, which is twice as high as in the US.[4]

Hers was the first North Korean delegation to the Blue House since 23 August 2009, when Kim Ki Nam, North Korea's 'Godfather of Propaganda' and the long-serving nominal head of the Propaganda and Agitation Department, and Kim Yang Gon, the chief of the Committee for the Peaceful Reunification of the Fatherland, had visited President Lee Myung Bak to pay their respects to former President Kim Dae Jung, who had died several days earlier. President Kim, once again, had been a benefactor extraordinaire to the Kim Jong Il regime, in 2000 having furnished Kim Jong Il with $450 million in cash in the days leading up to his visit to Pyongyang that June, with another $50 million worth of goods to follow: certainly deserving of the North Koreans' homage.

President Moon's privilege of being the first South Korean leader to receive a North Korean royal, on the other hand, and a glamorous young lady at that, entailed a major pledge of future support. In the coming months and years, Moon would persistently call on the US to concede to Kim Jong Un on sanctions enforcement and allow South Korean investment in North Korea in violation of United Nations Security Council Resolutions and US laws. For the Kim siblings, however, he still didn't try hard enough: Kim Yo Jong's later vitriol mocking Moon as a 'scared dog', 'first-class idiot' and 'parrot raised in America' expressed her disappointment at his failure to deliver.

The very special envoy signed the Blue House's guest book. Above her name she wrote, instead of listing a specific title or rank, 'Senior Delegation of the Democratic People's Republic of Korea'. Then, in the famed cursive hand of the Mount Paektu Bloodline, in which the words seem to rise at a forty-five-degree angle, she wrote the following message: 'I wish for Pyongyang and Seoul to come closer together in the hearts of our compatriots and for an accelerated future of reunification and prosperity.'

Kim Yong Nam, as the nominal head of the delegation, also signed the guest book. 'Bearing the efforts of solidarity and conviction in the pursuit of reunification must be the cherished dream of the Korean nation,' he wrote.

At first glance, both messages seem platitudinous. But each was loaded with a vital exhortation. Kim Yo Jong's was essentially fundraising: please would Seoul subsidize her government as previous South Korean governments had. Kim Yong Nam's was more ideological: that 'solidarity' and 'conviction' in the noblest pursuit of national reunification – submission to the North – will set you free.

Moon could barely hide his joy at hosting the first of the Mount Paektu Bloodline to visit the Blue House, but the visiting team held all the cards. Kim Yo Jong had the whip hand to make excessive demands, and even, if she so desired, walk out halfway through, as she had threatened the night before over the opening ceremony's seating arrangements. But today, the special envoy revealed to President Moon that the blue folder she carried bearing the words 'Democratic People's Republic of Korea' contained a formal letter from her brother, and placed it portentously on the table in front of her. Her host may have leaned forward eagerly in anticipation, to the point where he was perched precariously on the edge of his seat, but Kim Yo Jong leaned back and, instead of looking her excited interlocutor straight in the eye, cast her gaze ever so slightly down. Make no mistake: she looked bored.

This iconic snapshot captured Kim Yo Jong's arrogance, and how she viewed the power dynamics inside the room. Many South Koreans and observers around the world remarked on it. 'Nostril eyes', was how they put it in Taiwan: she looked at people not with her eyes, but down her nose.[5] The princess's contempt for the South Korean president was evident even to the layperson.[6] 'Kim Yo Jong put her elbows on the armrest of the chair, which showed she didn't care to show proper [East Asian] decorum to

Kim Yo Jong, President Moon (centre) and Kim Yong Nam at the Blue House, posing in front of the specially commissioned graphic that features the Chinese symbol for tong, meaning 'mutual flow'.

Moon Jae-In at all,' observed the Japanese psychologist Ayako Sato. 'And even her smile toward Moon Jae-In was fake.'[7]

But Moon, unable to mask his elation, was undaunted. Presented with the blue folder, Kim Yo Jong at last gracing him with a pursed-lip smile and a shake of the hand, he dropped his eyes and head slightly – a traditional Korean gesture of respect to an elder or superior. The optics remained, as they had been the night before, unconventional.

But Moon's over-the-top hospitality to Ms Kim peaked in a most thoughtful display. He had a surprise in store: a specially made graphic canvas, in front of which he posed for photos, à deux with Kim Yo Jong, and à trois with Kim Yong Nam. The canvas featured a big Chinese character, *tong*, which means 'mutual flow' or 'mutual communication',* written in black ink in an elaborately cursive calligraphic script. The word is a homophone of another Chinese character, which means 'to possess'.† When the word 'one' is added to the latter *tong*, the two-word formulation means 'reunification'.

To the right of the cursive Chinese character was a picture printed in ink of the Korean peninsula, and under it the following caption:

If 'reunification' is the end state, then 'mutual flow' is the process. Finding a new path at a dead end and the resolve to break a path where there isn't one is desperately needed in order to overcome division and to traverse the path

* 通
† 統

136

toward unification. Communication and dialogue, constant exchange and understanding, are the substance and method of 'mutual flow'. 'Mutual flow' begets 'reunification'. Aspire to achieve 'reunification' through 'mutuality'.*

The Blue House later reported that Moon explained to his special guests the meaning of the special character, 'mutuality', as if the guests didn't already know. He wished for the North and South, he stated, to continue to communicate and cooperate with one another. He went on to tell the visitors how much he admired the calligrapher of the special script, Shin Young-Bok.

In fact, Kim Yong Nam had already heard this from Moon's mouth the night before at the Olympic reception, during the president's speech:

Shin Young-Bok, an esteemed Korean intellectual, once said that huddling together to brave the wintry chill and sharing body heat with the person next to you is primordial friendship. I am certain that the friendship we share among all of us gathered here today from all corners of the world will further be cemented in the cold of Gangwon Province.[8]

Moon continued, 'The little snowball we hold in our hands, now,' – the fragile chance of peace – 'we must roll it together and roll it carefully. I and my people will never forget the friend-

---

* '통(統)이 완성이라면 통(通)은 과정입니다. 막다른 데서 길을 찾고 길 없는 데서 길을 낼 결심이 분단 극복과 통일로 가는 길에서는 더욱 절실합니다. 소통과 대화, 꾸준한 교류와 이해가 通의 내용이 자 방법입니다. 通은 統입니다. 通으로 統을 이루게 되기를.'

ship the world has sent to Pyeongchang. I will repay you very nicely with a peaceful Korean peninsula.'[9]

The meaning may have been lost on just about every foreign guest in attendance, but at least one North Korean visitor, Kim Yong Nam, would have known of Moon's special fondness for Shin Young-Bok, which was common knowledge among the cognoscenti. But who *was* Shin Young-Bok?

Shin was an accomplished artist, intellectual, economist, and university professor whose distinctive penmanship had a wide appeal in South Korea. The 'Shin Young-Bok font' is featured on the label of a very popular brand of *soju*, a low-cost alcoholic beverage called 'Cheo-eum Cheo-reom' ('Just Like the First Time'), ubiquitous in the country's 40,000 convenience stores – by far the highest per capita total in the world at approximately one for every 1,275 persons.

Shin was also convicted, in 1968, of being a spy for the North. He received the death sentence, later commuted to life, and, after spending twenty years behind bars, was released on probation in 1988 upon writing an oath renouncing his allegiance to the North. Years later, he publicly rescinded that conversion oath. 'I never changed my ideology or betrayed my comrades,' he said,[10] lauding North Korea's 'autonomy' while decrying the capitalist South's 'loss of ethnic Korean autonomy' and 'satellization' – that is, having become a satellite of the imperialist United States.[11]

What many outside South Korea don't know, however, is that Moon, along with his closest aides, was once an activist protesting against their authoritarian regimes, while denouncing

US imperialism in the 1980s and extolling Kim Il Sung's anti-imperialist stance. In his memoir, Moon wrote that he felt 'euphoria' on reading a book by Ri Young-Hee, a prominent leftist reporter and pundit, that correctly predicted the US defeat in the Vietnam War.

Even if Kim Yo Jong herself was not familiar with Shin Young-Bok, a throwback to a bygone era, she would certainly have been briefed by Kim Yong Nam on Moon's reference to him the night before, and been pleased to see for herself Moon's affinity for a bona fide pro-Grandpa South Korean intellectual. She would have been especially tickled to learn what Grandpa had thought of Shin. In the wake of the fall of South Vietnam in 1975, the communist victors, Pyongyang's quasi-ally, had taken hostage three South Korean officials stranded in Saigon. Thereafter, Kim Il Sung insisted that Shin be on Seoul's prisoner-swap list; that is, in return for Seoul releasing pro-Pyongyang detainees like Shin, Kim would persuade Hanoi to let go the South Koreans. But Kim never got his wish. In 1980, Vietnam unilaterally released the South Koreans.

Later that day, the Blue House revealed Kim Jong Un's message to Moon. The North Korean leader 'requests President Moon to visit North Korea at a time of his convenience,' Kim Yo Jong had told Moon. 'If you meet Chairman Kim and exchange views on a wide array of issues, North–South relations will be able to leap forward, rendering yesterday old history. I hope you will be a main actor in opening a new chapter of reunification, leaving many traces for posterity'.

'Let's make it happen,' replied Moon, 'by creating the conditions for it.' Starting 'North Korea–US talks early', he added, 'is essential to further developing North–South relations.' Kim Yo Jong would have understood this to mean that for suspending both US and United Nations sanctions that prohibited cash transfers and joint ventures with her government, getting the US on board was essential. Moon said he was very enthusiastic about the idea of holding a summit meeting with Kim Jong Un, which came as a surprise to no one, since he had been calling for it even during North Korea's missile barrage the previous year. Kim Yo Jong's mission was to hook Moon with this offer of a summit meeting with her brother, in order to soften up the Trump administration for eventual sanctions relief. Moon, she knew, would certainly give that his best shot.

Over the course of two hours and forty-five minutes at the presidential Blue House, the parties postured, mingled, posed for photos, dined, and conversed on the theme of Korean peace and reunification. For now, in the Blue House at least, Kim Yo Jong's visit was viewed by both parties as a smashing success.

At quarter to two, the North Koreans left the presidential compound and returned to the waterfront Skybay Hotel, which dominates the skyline as the sole high-rise in the vicinity, its glassy gleam refracted by the East Sea and Gyeongpo Lake.

Later in the day, Kim Yo Jong showed up at the ice rink to cheer on her women's ice hockey squad on the first night of the Games. In the evening, she showed up to dinner in a two-piece ensemble marked by a no-frills maroon jacket, holding a black handbag with gold chain. No rings, bracelets, or necklace – just the badge of her beaming father and grandfather. Her dinner host was a marked downgrade in rank from lunch: Unification Minister Cho Myoung-gyon, who had greeted her at the airport lounge the day before.

After dinner, she attended speed-skating preliminary rounds. Later, seated in the stands behind the 'Army of Beauties' – the North Korean cheerleader contingent – with fellow comrade Kim Yong Nam, IOC President Bach, and President Moon to her right, Kim Yo Jong watched the North–South united women's hockey team's 8-0 drubbing by Switzerland.[12] She had not necessarily made the trip to 'southern Korea', as people say in the North – 'southern' as in the southern region of the entire Korean peninsula that her family purportedly governs and aspires one day to actually govern – to watch North Korean athletes get thrashed, but she put on a brave face and smiled more naturally in the stands than in the VIP box the night before. For many, it was one more reason to adore the 'down-to-earth' princess.

Two weeks later, Kim Yong Chol, North Korea's former spymaster and the mastermind behind the sinking of the *Cheonan* and the massive cyberattack on Sony Pictures in 2014, would, to much controversy, arrive as the head of the North Korean delegation to the Olympics closing ceremony.

Why would Kim Jong Un send such a controversial figure to South Korea after his sister's celebrated visit? It couldn't have been that he had no other capable men available. The reason was simple: to make South Korea yet more dependent on his largesse. The more bitter pills Kim Jong Un forces South Korea to swallow, the more psychologically dependent on the Supreme Leader's next act of beneficence it becomes. Call it 'Seoul Syndrome': the North Korean tyrant's 'bewitching mix of gangsterism and come-ons usually inspires Seoul to pay up.'[13] At the very least, Kim Jong Un's decision, as the Associated Press observed, was a 'careful – and insulting – attempt to gauge just how far Moon is willing to go to accommodate the North in his quest to lower hostility between the rivals.'[14] The siblings' project, of Kim Jong Un playing the 'bad cop' to his sister's 'good cop', was still at an early stage. The time for a wrong-footing role reversal would come later.

On the last evening of her visit, Kim Yo Jong was wined and dined by Im Jong-Seok, President Moon's chief of staff, who was sent to prison for his involvement in violent pro-North Korea protests in the 1980s. They met at a hotel across the street from the National Theatre of Korea, the venue for the final item on Ms Kim's agenda: a feel-good musical performance by the North's Samjiyon Band, with select South Korean musicians joining in, an appropriate finale to her fabulous trip. When she arrived at the show, she'd changed from a plain grey jacket into a cream one over a matching blouse with a gold button: the South Korean press continued to follow her every move, facial expression, and sartorial selection.

By the time she flew back home that night on her brother's plane, it was only the end of the second day of the Olympics. But the Pyeongchang Games, as far as both the South and North Korea were concerned, had already become a great success.

She came, she saw, she smiled, and she set the stage for her brother's international bait-and-switch act to follow.

Two days later, on 13 February, North Korea's state media published a photo of a smiling Kim Yo Jong clutching her brother's left arm with both hands. To Kim Jong Un's right stood Kim Yong Nam, wearing that ubiquitous faint smile, the Great Leader affectionately holding the nonagenarian's wrist. The two other senior officials on the southern trip, Choe Hwi and Ri Son Gwon, stood at either end.

Kim Jong Un was reported to be delighted by the result of his sister's southern sortie, and the picture showed him beaming, too. In a matter of days, without much exertion, they had transformed themselves from pariah brother and sister to sibling king and princess. Now that they had Seoul on a string, it was time to move on to a bigger stage.

CHAPTER 12

A Korean Comedy of Errors

At 9.25 a.m. on 27 April 2018, Kim Jong Un, wearing a handsome smile over his signature black five-button Mao suit, emerged from Phanmun Pavilion, the two-storey building on the northern side of the Military Demarcation Line (MDL) in the inter-Korean border village known as the Joint Security Area. The North Korean dictator-for-life was to hold his first summit meeting with the elected leader of South Korea, President Moon Jae-In.

Millions around the world watched as the portly leader descended the steps with his brisk, rolling gait, arms swinging, flanked by his sister and six other senior officials. A few steps south of the MDL, having stepped out of Freedom House opposite, President Moon Jae-In stood waiting. As the North Korean entourage approached Moon, Kim Yo Jong and the other officials parted to left and right so the two principals from Pyongyang and Seoul could stand as one, with the world looking on, to shake hands across the MDL.

Thus began what must surely have been the single most dramatic twenty-four-hour image makeover of a tyrant in history – had one not seen this movie before. In a few brief hours, Kim Jong Un transformed himself from a weird, pitiless dictator into a thoroughly good chap. But while this may have been the most watched summit meeting attended by any North Korean leader, it was neither unprecedented nor the most dramatic. His father had already set a high bar for sensational inter-Korean summitry. The first had been in 2000, the sequel in 2007. Both times, viewers had gasped to see Kim Jong Il transformed from an eccentric, cruel dictator into an affable statesman. Indeed, in 1972 Grandpa had shown how it's done, coming out of his cocoon to meet, in rapid succession, reporters from *The New York Times* in May, *The Washington Post* in June, a Harvard Law School professor in July, and several Japanese journalists and politicians throughout the year.[1]

The main difference between the magic acts of the past and those starring Kim Jong Un, however, was that he had a sister, and during this day-long summit, which ended after 10 p.m. with a banquet and post-dinner outdoor theatre, Kim Yo Jong shadowed her brother every step of the way, charming both South Korean officials and the millions watching on.

A seventy-minute North Korean documentary on Kim Jong Un's first inter-Korean summit, the usual paean to what it presented as a diplomatic victory that marked (as the narrator reverently announced) a 'dramatic transition in the Korean peninsula', showed his sister's position in the political hierarchy. She was a star in her own right. No other actor besides her brother exuded such an aura of self-confidence, and their southern counterparts were reduced to bit-parts. North Korea's most powerful man and woman apparently had learned well from their father the art of summit performance.

Kim Jong Un beamed as he approached President Moon. He shook Moon's hand. This magical moment, the two Korean leaders' hands clasped together and waving up and down directly over the 5 cm-high brick ledge that represented the actual border, brimmed with bonhomie – though other, more jaded viewers, remembering previous inter-Korean summits, may have merely seen banality. Kim put his left hand over Moon's right hand in a show of extra warmth before good-humouredly inviting President Moon to actually step over the dividing line – to his own side, the North. For a moment Moon looked surprised, clearly unprepared for Kim's coup de théâtre. Forty kilometres south, a collective gasp reverberated around the cavernous Kintex press centre, hung with signs reading 'Peace, a New Beginning', where approximately 3,000 South Korean and foreign reporters were watching on the big screen. Kim led Moon a few steps into his kingdom, to be greeted by the kind of squeals normally emanating from teenage girls when Jungkook of BTS, one the biggest pop groups in the world, lifts up his shirt for an instant. As Kim Jong Un and Moon Jae-In hopped back and forth across the border together, holding hands, the press cheered. It was like that scene in Shakespeare's *The Comedy of Errors* when one of the Dromio clowns, on finding his long-lost twin brother, says, 'We came into the world like brother and brother / And now let's go hand in hand, not one before another.'

Even veteran journalists who had covered such inter-Korean

melodrama before seemed to be sold. 'This time it really feels different,' a reporter for a major American newspaper told BBC Radio.

'Well, each time it seems different,' grumbled another pundit on the same programme (the author of this book).

'Why are you so sceptical and cynical?' asked the anchor.

'If one has repeatedly been pummelled by the tag-team duo of reality and history, one grows a bit disillusioned.'

But sceptics were not welcome at the circus. In the press centre, mouths were open in joyous disbelief. Many were even in tears. Folks watching the spectacle on a big screen in front of Seoul City Hall cheered and applauded. Men and women, young and old, all cheered loudly, visibly moved, wiping the tears from their faces: a new era of peace was dawning. For the despotic, deceitful dynasty, it was all going to plan.

A South Korean boy and a girl presented the special guest from the North with a small bouquet, which Kim Yo Jong stepped forward to retrieve from her brother and hand to a subordinate. Then, led by a military band and flanked by guards garbed in colourful, pre-twentieth century military uniforms and armed with traditional instruments and weapons like spears and arrows, Kim and Moon walked side by side towards Freedom House on the southern side, directly facing the North's Phanmun Pavilion across the MDL. (Having these honour guards wear pre-partition attire was intended to soften the blow of the regular honour guards being reviewed by the Northern tyrant moments later.)

Kim must have sensed the palpable excitement at the sight of him and Moon side by side, jovially chatting, Moon clearly the happier-looking. Every step on South Korean soil seemed to promise a new mirage – of peace, unification, denucleariza-tion, family reunion, tourism, joint ventures, perhaps even the Nobel Peace Prize. Just a few steps off the red carpet, almost alongside her brother, walked Kim Yo Jong.

The procession by the two Korean principals, flanked all the way by the guards in anachronistic garb, ended in front of Peace House, where soldiers of South Korea's three military branches and a military band in contemporary uniform awaited.

Kim Jong Un stood confidently on the platform, as though he'd played this role before. But he was already breathing hard, despite only having walked some 200 metres, or half a lap of a running track. It was the first time he had been seen in public looking out of breath. Both men had their mouths open – Kim to catch his breath; Moon, agape, barely able to contain his delight.

Thus did the 'mad', 'fat', 'Rocket Man on a suicide mission' of Donald Trump's mockery begin his magical metamorphosis into a regular statesman. Despite the high stakes of the summit – preventing nuclear war and forging a permanent peace – it was this moment, more than anything else, that seemed to bring them within grasp. He still had his finger on the nuclear button, he still presided over concentration camps for political prisoners and delighted in gruesome public executions, and over decades his father and grandfather had honed and perfected the family business of strategic deception – but under clear spring skies all such considerations seemed swept aside by his smiling, if laboriously breathing, affability.

The two sides had an equal number of officials in their retinue: nine each. When it was the turn of Kim Yo Jong, second to last in line, to shake Moon's hand she gave him a big smile and murmured, 'It's nice to see you.' The delegations moved on to Peace House for their first sit-down together, Kim Yo Jong walking by herself, the picture of confidence as ever, chin up and occasionally smiling for the cameras.

The meeting room inside Peace House had undergone a last-minute facelift, its rectangular conference table replaced by a softer-toned oval one exactly 2,018 millimetres wide, to mark the auspicious year. A new carpet had been laid, its warm blue reminiscent of the Unification Flag depicting one Korea,[2] and, as backdrop, there was a blueish-purple painting of Mount Kumgang. The mountain was the site of the South's ill-fated Hyundai Corporation tourism investment in the North, where, in July 2008, a fifty-three-year-old South Korean woman, Park Wang-Ja, had been shot in the back and killed by a North Korean guard for straying into a no-entry zone during her early-morning walk.[3] But Moon and his exalted guest posed and clasped hands in front of it all the same.

Kim Yo Jong shadowed her brother throughout the proceedings, bringing him a pen to sign the guest book, in which he wrote, 'A new history begins now. An age of peace, at the starting line of history', in his studied, sloping 'Mount Paektu' script. For the brief chat before the formal talks, Kim Yo Jong sat directly at her brother's side, as she did for the formal talks that followed, of equal ranking with his former spymaster Kim Yong Chol, who sat on his other side. During the few minutes the cameras were allowed in the room, she was the only person to take notes.

Then there was a closed session of talks, selected details of which were released later by the Blue House. 'I heard you attended early morning National Security Council meetings due to our frequent missile tests last year,' Kim Jong Un had apparently told President Moon. 'I made sure you will now not be woken up early any more,' Kim kindly intoned. He also recycled his father's exquisitely self-humanizing patter from the two previous North–South summits, showing empathy for North Korean émigrés in the South: 'I see that displaced persons from the North, North Korean escapees, and Yeonpyeong Island residents who lived in fear of being bombarded with North Korean artillery also have high expectations of our meeting today. I hope our meeting is an occasion for curing the pain of past North–South relations. The demarcation line I see is not even that high. As many more people tread over the line, it shall be erased.'

The Blue House presumably released these precious words of empathy in order to confirm the North Korean leader as a reasonable man at last bent on doing the right thing. But only two years later, Kim Yo Jong would call escapees to South Korea 'human wastes' and 'mongrel dogs'.[4] The reference to the deadly shelling of Yeonpyeong Island was also ironic: after all, it had been Kim Jong Un who, in November 2010, had ordered the shelling, as well as the sinking of the South Korean naval ship the *Cheonan* earlier in the year, according to a former North Korean spy.[5] As experts already knew, deadly operations against the South like these could not have taken place without orders from the top. But in the merriment of the moment, Moon seemed to eat it all up.

To President Moon's expressed wish to visit Mount Paektu, Kim Jong Un replied humbly, 'One concern we have is that due to the poor state of our public transportation infrastructure you might experience discomfort. My folks who've visited Pyeongchang all say the [KTX] high-speed train is very nice. To host you who are used to such amenities I fear may be quite embarrassing. We shall do our best to prepare for your visit so that you are comfortable.' This was actually a passive-aggressive way of spitting back at the South Koreans for their patronizing idea of giving Kim Yo Jong and her team the eye-opening experience of being whisked from Incheon International Airport to Gangneung by high-speed rail. A deified leader sitting on nukes tends not to envy a term-bound leader sitting in a nice train.

The pleasantries inevitably carried over to Kim Yo Jong, whom President Moon pointed out as having become, as a result of her previous visit, 'a big star in the South', which drew a hearty laugh from the room. 'I'm in my first year in office,' Moon went on to say. 'In my remaining time in office, I hope we can maintain the same speed with which we've come this far today from Chairman Kim's New Year's Day Speech.'

'Kim Yo Jong's department came up with "Manlima Speed Battle,"' replied the Great Leader. 'Let us make that the speed under which we achieve North–South reunification.'

'Manlima' is Kim Yo Jong's variation on her grandfather's

1950s slogan calling for rapid industrial development – 'Chonlima speed'. Chonlima is a mythical horse that can gallop 1,000 li per day: 'chon' being 1,000; 'li' being a traditional Chinese measurement of about half a kilometre; and 'ma' meaning horse. 'Man' means 10,000:[6] as the head of her nation's Propaganda and Agitation Department, Ms Kim had come up with a far more ambitious slogan, aiming at 10,000 li a day, or ten times faster. All burst out in approving laughter.

After lunch, during which the two sides had a respite from one another, Kim Jong Un emerged from his Mercedes-Benz 600S Pullman Guard, surrounded by thirteen robust-looking bodyguards, to join a beaming Moon and shake hands again. Kim Yo Jong handed her brother a pair of white gloves and helped him put them on, lest with the world watching he accidentally drop one; President Moon dexterously managed his own. Then the two leaders 'planted' a pine tree, albeit one that had already been planted back in 1953, the year of the signing of the Korean War armistice. Each man spread three spadefuls of soil on the ground by the tree, a mix from the North's Mount Paektu and Mount Halla in Jeju Island, South Korea's southernmost territory. Onlookers clapped; so, briefly, did the two protagonists, and then there were more handshakes. Yo Jong handed her brother a pale-green watering can containing a special cocktail of the Taedong River from Pyongyang and Han River from Seoul, and the two men lovingly watered the tree. Apart from the briefly arduous act of shovelling soil, Kim Jong Un appeared the more at ease, as if he were the host.

After the unveiling of a rock emblazoned with the words, 'Planting Peace and Prosperity' came a choreographed walk along a narrow wooden bridge freshly painted blue, and then tea and private conversation at a picnic table with no aides present, to underscore the trust between the leaders and their common language. What was said during those forty-four minutes has never been fully disclosed, but at one point professional lip readers saw Moon utter the word 'power plant'. Moon later admitted that the USB flash drive he handed Kim Jong Un during the tête-a-tête did contain information on building a power plant and developing a 'new economy' in North Korea, but beyond that, the full contents of the drive have not been revealed.

What subsequently emerged, in January 2021, was that just five days after the 2018 summit, South Korea's Ministry of Trade, Industry, and Energy began drafting plans to build nuclear reactors in North Korea. In December 2019, the night before an audit of his office, a ministry official had deleted all seventeen files kept on the ministry's computers under the file name '*pohjois*',' Finnish for 'north'. After the controversy broke, all of the files were recovered and opened up. Building any industrial plant in North Korea – let alone a nuclear reactor – without the approval of the United Nations Security Council would have been in violation of Security Council Resolution 2375, which prohibits the 'opening, maintenance, and operation of all joint ventures' in the North. A spokesman for the energy ministry said these plans were simply an idea for 'inter-Korean energy cooperation' that was for discussion internally, rather than official policy. He pointed out that one document acknowledged the difficulties of the plan, which would depend on US and North Korean nuclear negotiations.[7]

After some fifty minutes of outdoor theatre, the principals retreated to Peace House to sign a joint statement, the Panmunjom Declaration, and it was Kim Yo Jong who brought her brother the pen once again, before pulling his chair back for him to stand up and shake hands with President Moon and exchange the folders each had signed. At one minute past six, the two men, standing side by side outside Peace House, read their respective statements. 'There will never again be war in the Korean peninsula,' declared President Moon, confirming with Chairman Kim that the 'complete denuclearization of the Korean peninsula is our common goal' and reassuring the world that the hitherto minimalist 'nuclear freeze measures' taken by the North recently had 'very important implications'. He and Kim, he went on, had agreed to pursue an 'end-of-war declaration' that would lead to a 'peace regime' to 'fundamentally change the international order surrounding the Korean peninsula.' Henceforth, he concluded, neither side would ever again engage in 'hostile acts toward the other on land, in the skies, or at sea', and he and Kim would meet on a regular basis and speak frequently through a 'direct phone line'.

No such communication has ever taken place, and was never going to. The North Korean leader may give out his number when the mood is right, but chatting on the phone with foreigners facing term limits is beneath him. Donald Trump's boast in mid-June 2018, just days after meeting Kim Jong Un in Singapore, that he had given Chairman Kim a 'very direct phone number' proved similarly chimerical.[8] But, for now, hope was in the air. 'We will never turn back,' Moon assured the world.

When his turn to speak came, the North Korean visitor spoke of the common bloodline between the people of the North and South, 'who should unite and live happily together, and not act like foreigners whom we must confront and fight.' As to whether this entailed taking over the South or being absorbed by it, granting his own people basic freedoms or depriving Moon's people of theirs, the chairman didn't elaborate. But he and President Moon agreed to 'put our knees together and closely communicate and cooperate with each other, so that the agreement reached today under the eyes of all the people of the North and South and the world does not end up like previous North–South agreements that faltered soon after take-off to become a part of shameful history.' The suddenly drastically more approachable North Korean leader sounded as if he was actually serious about it. Kim Jong Un closed his speech, which was punctuated with his laborious breaths, with rare thanks to the press corps, though in the North Korean definition, 'the press' meant agents of the state who propagate the party line rather than independent journalists. Kim Il Sung had kindly explained the distinction to the two reporters of *The New York Times* with whom he'd had a three-hour meeting in his office on 26 May 1972.[9] The two leaders took no questions.

Kim had good reason to be pleased. Just like the two previous North–South summit agreements his father had signed in 2000 and 2007, the one he had just put his name to was lopsidedly in favour of the Democratic People's Republic of Korea. The old trope of reconnecting the 'blood relations of the nation' and bringing about 'independent reunification led by Koreans' made a prominent return. Since 1995, Kim Jong Il had defined ethnic Koreans as 'Kim Il Sung *minjok*' (Kim Il Sung *nation* or *people*) and the entire Korean peninsula as 'Kim Il Sung Choson' (Kim Il Sung *Korea*). 'We, the Korean ethnic nation' (*minjok*), as the joint statement put it, undeniably meant, for the North, Kim Il Sung-Kim Jong Il *minjok*: a pretext for the North to extend its censorial and, in future, jurisdictional control over the South. As for South Koreans, they, though not unintelligent, consider the formulation an acceptable rhetorical freebie.

The day got even more jovial with the arrival of Ri Sol Ju, Kim Jong Un's wife, in a pink jacket and skirt, a black ribbon on the back of her head, and Kim Jung-Sook, Moon's wife, in a chic light-blue ensemble to accentuate the blue Unification Flag motif. The parties adjourned to the banqueting hall where bonhomie, camaraderie, and goodwill swelled as each side underwent another round of greetings with the principals, who stood to receive them at the entrance of the dining room. Several new South Korean dinner guests appeared and stood in line to shake hands with President Moon, Kim Jong Un, Kim Jung-Sook, and Ri Sol Ju, in that order. When it was her turn, Kim Yo Jong lightly stepped forward to shake Moon's hand, then her brother's hand – casually, for a split second, a faint, insouciant smile on her face. As Kim Jong Un met his sister's gaze, she cast hers down, still smiling, almost as if she was trying to avoid giving away her thoughts – that the day was going swimmingly . . .

As the official North Korean documentary of the banquet approvingly explained, 'The southern side prepared many special-themed dishes, and our side made a deep impression by presenting at the dinner table Pyongyang *naengmyon* (cold noodles served either in cold beef broth or with chili paste) from Okryu-gwan.' Indeed, the odd gesture of the southern host inviting chefs from Pyongyang's famed restaurant to prepare for the special northern guests noodles they could enjoy at home at any time nonetheless resonated with cheery onlookers in the South. Demand for the dish spiked over the next days.

The North Korean narrator did not comment on the special meaning of other delicacies prepared by the hosts. For example, the Koreanized potato rösti, a Swiss potato pancake that Kim Jong Un had developed a liking for while attending school in Bern in the late 1990s.[10] As a further nod to the Kim siblings' Swiss education, Swiss chocolates, macarons, Mont Blanc dessert (chestnut purée and whipped cream), and Gruyère cheese were also on the menu, but again the narrator chose to keep the North Korean people in the dark about the supreme family's privileged life and education abroad.

A Korean banquet without alcoholic beverages would be unthinkable. Besides Champagne and wine, two traditional liquors, Dugyeon-ju, an azalea-infused spirit distilled from rice at a respectable 18 per cent ABV, and Munbae-ju, 'wild pear spirits', named for its pleasing fragrance of the sweet, tart Korean pear, at a more robust 20 per cent, were presented for a proper

Korean shot-downing ritual. The guest of honour found the Munbae-ju, a delicacy first brewed in Pyongyang over a millennium ago, more agreeable, knocking back shot after shot poured happily by the South Koreans. They held the bottle with both hands, the traditional show of respect and hierarchical order, but naturally the Supreme Leader accepted not with two hands together, the traditional show of modesty, but by holding out his glass in one hand. And naturally, each time, Kim Jong Un downed his drink in one. Virtually all of the thirty South Korean attendees poured Kim Jong Un a shot, and not once did the Great Imbiber refuse, until even he was looking flushed in the face. The Supreme Sister, meanwhile, poured a drink for President Moon and his wife, properly, with two hands.

Kim Jong Un had brought along a North Korean magician who, by all accounts, was at the top of his game. His finest hour was the money-laundering trick. He would ask for a 500,000 South Korean won note, worth about $45 at the time, and turn it into a $100 bill, making a very nice profit. This magical reenactment of the North Korean state's actual counterfeiting of US currency (the US Department of the Treasury had long referred to North Korean counterfeit $100 bills as 'Supernotes' – simply, the best in the world) brought the greatest cheers of the night. Kim Yo Jong, seated at the head table, was caught on camera dissolved into unrestrained laughter. By now it was impossible to say who was from the North and who from the South.

The summit was a near-perfect fulfilment of the Aristotelian unities: 'action' – the summit; 'time' – occurring over no more than twenty-four hours; and 'place' – a single venue, the border village. In just one day, the North Korean Supreme Siblings had conned the world, or at least rendered much of it more gullible than ever. The memorable night ended with an outdoor concert that must have been a bit dull for the North Koreans used to grand spectacles featuring 100,000 performers. Kim Yo Jong was the very last person to exit the building and take her seat in the makeshift outdoor seating area. Everyone else, including her brother, was seated while she casually walked over to her seat. In the line for the farewell handshakes after night had fallen, it was the South Koreans who looked on, wistful and smitten, at the First Sister of North Korea as she passed her brother and her Mona Lisa smile momentarily froze into a pregnant gaze. *Well done, brother*, she seemed to be thinking. *On to Washington . . .*

CHAPTER 13

Who Trumped Whom?

On Thursday 8 March 2018, some six weeks before the historic inter-Korean meeting in the border village, two very senior South Korean envoys had come to the White House to bring President Trump some uplifting news. Three days earlier, they had been part of a delegation from their country invited by Kim Jong Un to a rare dinner in his main office compound – the first since the North Korean leader had assumed power in 2011.[1] There, over the almost four-hour-long meal, Kim Jong Un had told his enthralled guests, among whom were South Korea's National Security Council Advisor, Chung Eui-Yong, and the head of the National Intelligence Service, Suh Hoon, that the 'denuclearization of the Korean peninsula was his grandfather's dying wish and dictum.'

Back in Seoul the next day, the South Korean officials announced the marvellous news to the world – but Chung and Suh didn't stop there. They went all the way to Washington to stress to their American counterparts that this had come from none other than Kim Jong Un himself, and . . . that Kim wanted to hold a summit with the US president. Of course, in North Korea, the Supreme Leader's words had to be true and unassailable. In any case, it was hardly likely that Kim Jong Il and Kim Jong Un would so blatantly defy the founder of their nation's 'dying wish', was it? (More than thirty years of them nuking-up notwithstanding.)

Perhaps it was jetlag that saw the envoys fail to spell out to the ingenuous Americans that Kim Jong Un's exact words had been 'denuclearization of the Korean *peninsula*', not 'denuclearization of North Korea', or what this phrase actually meant, above all, to North Korea. To all of North Korea's three rulers, Pyongyang's stock phrase has always meant the complete withdrawal of US nuclear weapons (achieved in 1991), US troops, and all strategic weapons from South Korea and the region, including Japan, and the abrogation of the US–South Korea military alliance treaty. It was Kim Yo Jong herself who made this clear as recently as August 2021: 'For peace to settle on the Korean peninsula, it is imperative for the US to withdraw its aggression troops and war hardware deployed in South Korea.'

Neither did the South Koreans choose to mention that none other than Kim Jong Un's own father, Jong Il, had recycled the tired 'Kim Il Sung's dying wish' trope many times already; in 1994, for example, as Pyongyang was gearing up to enrich uranium while temporarily shutting down its main plutonium reactor in Yongbyon in return for over $1.3 billion worth of food and energy aid from the United States alone; in 2005, as the North was preparing to conduct its first nuclear test the following year; in 2009 too, as it was preparing to bolster Kim Jong Un's credentials by planning to blow up a South Korean navy ship four months later. And in June 2013, by now firmly in the Kim Jong Un era, a senior North Korean official had yet again invoked the founder's dying wish, curiously four months after his state's third nuclear test, followed by a hundred days of making threats about nuclear war.[2]

Never mind: President Donald Trump, on receipt of the great news that the North Korean tyrant was amenable to parting ways with his nukes and keen on meeting him, and apparently oblivious to the ambiguity in Kim Jong Un's amenability to 'denuclearization', said yes on the spot. In fact, the president told the South Koreans, the sooner the better. So a date was set for June – just three months away – for this utterly unprecedented US–North Korea summit.

The official announcement was made, appropriately, in a somewhat unconventional way. Rather than making it himself or through his office, President Trump had one of the South Korean officials, National Security Advisor Chung, announce the news to a gaggle of reporters on the White House lawn, with no US officials present. Mr Chung, reading out his hastily drafted exclusive in English, said he had informed the president that Kim Jong Un had told him *in person* earlier in the week that he is 'committed to denuclearization'.[3] Just who would be denuclearizing whom went unaddressed.

With South Korea and the US thus softened up, the next stop for the Kim siblings was China. On 7 May, Kim Jong Un and Kim Yo Jong flew to the north-eastern Chinese city of

Dalian to meet President Xi Jinping. It was Kim Jong Un's second visit to China in a little over five weeks. After six years of anti-social behaviour since taking power in 2011, refusing to meet with a single world leader or make a single foreign trip, in late March 2018 Kim Jong Un had ridden his personal train to Beijing with his wife, a month before meeting the South Korean leader, and already having booked a meeting with the US leader. Once again, the strategy was straight from his father's playbook: six years of reclusiveness, before Kim Jong Il finally came out in 2000 as the epitome of the convivial cosmopolitan, with an unannounced trip to China in May to meet the Chinese president followed by hosting the South Korean president in June, the Russian president in July, and the US Secretary of State in October, before a further trip to China the following January, making a point of visiting China's Special Economic Zone cities. Unfortunately, the consequent expectations of peace, reform, and the opening-up of North Korea were not, for a variety of reasons, borne out.

It made sense, though, to get China, North Korea's sole treaty ally and its biggest benefactor, on board with Kim Jong Un's plan to use multilateral peace overtures to loosen sanctions against his regime and buy time to build bigger bombs, not least because over the past six years President Xi had been rather displeased with the North Korean leader. In February 2013, during the Lunar New Year's holiday, Kim Jong Un had sent his own brand of congratulatory telegram to Xi for acceding to the top job in the form of a nuclear test, a clear message to China that the young North Korean leader was to be taken seriously. 'I'm going to make that punk pay,' Xi told President Obama soon after. Pay President Xi certainly did, but with the largest annual Sino–North Korean trade figures in history, totalling $6.5 billion that year, confirming the adage that for Pyongyang, it always pays to provoke. Placation rather than punishment has been the preference for both Washington and Beijing when faced with an adventurous North Korean commander-in-chief of a military over 1 million strong. It was telling that by 2018 Xi had yet to visit Pyongyang, even though he had already paid a visit to Seoul in 2014. But the six-year-old frost between Beijing and Pyongyang melted the moment Kim Yo Jong made a splash in Seoul.

In Dalian, the two allies shook hands, exchanged pleasantries, posed for photographs, and sat down for talks and meals. Having already reset the geopolitical table with a date with Trump, both the North Korean leader and the Chinese leader had good reasons to meet again so soon after their first summit meeting in Beijing. Back in March, Kim had been feted by his host with full military honours and a lavish banquet featuring a rare $200,000 bottle of Maotai, a traditional Chinese spirit. In Dalian in May, President Xi and Chairman Kim didn't just dine together. They also took a leisurely stroll along the beach, and President Xi and his wife, Peng Liyuan, hosted Kim Jong Un and his sister at lunch the next day in an exclusive 'family-like' atmosphere, as the North Korean documentary voiceover put it. Now that Kim Jong Un had strengthened his leverage against China with an unprecedented summit with the US leader on the horizon, it made sense for President Xi to extend the utmost hospitality to Kim, and perhaps plan their next moves vis-à-vis the US together.

On Tuesday 22 May, almost a month after the historic meeting of the two Korean leaders in the border town, President Moon of South Korea met Donald Trump in the White House, and told the US president that in his opinion Kim Jong Un could be trusted to give up his nuclear weapons. He returned home with no inkling that Trump, just days later, would flip-flop on the forthcoming summit.

On 24 May, however, in a letter to Kim Jong Un, President Trump cancelled his highly anticipated meeting with the North Korean leader, which had been due to take place in Singapore on 12 June. Trump's ostensible reason, as he explained in a bizarre college rejection-style letter that began, 'We greatly appreciate your time, patience, and effort with respect to our recent discussions and negotiations relative to a summit long sought by both parties,' was the 'tremendous anger and open hostility displayed in your most recent statement.' Trump was referring to North Korea's Vice Foreign Minister Choe Son Hui's statement several hours earlier calling Vice President Mike Pence a 'political dummy'. Ms Choe was expressing disapproval at Mr Pence's recent comments on a US news programme that North Korea should follow Libya's example of a quick, front-loaded dismantlement of its nuclear programmes.

Pence had not meant that Pyongyang should also follow the Libyan model of its tyrannical leader being overthrown and killed in a US-backed uprising, but Choe had seen fit to take umbrage all the same and called Pence's comments 'ignorant and stupid' as well as 'unbridled and impudent'.

The sudden cancellation startled both Kim and Moon. The two men needed to strategize, fast – to continue the spurious quest for peace regardless of where it might lead. So, less than forty-eight hours later, on Saturday 26 May, Kim Yo Jong found herself greeting President Moon for the third time in less than four months, and this time on home turf, on her side of the Military Demarcation Line, as he exited his limo for his last-minute emergency summit with her brother, just twenty-nine days since their first meeting.

The day after his cancellation letter, however, Donald Trump had just as impulsively declared that the Singapore meeting could go ahead on 12 June as scheduled. 'They very much want to do it,' he said. 'We'd like to do it.' However, he did not confirm the meeting. The self-professed artful dealmaker opted for ambiguity, which prompted the two nervous Korean leaders to hold an impromptu meeting.

Trump was right. Kim Jong Un very much wanted to hold the summit and snare the US in an open-ended, protracted process of nuclear negotiations that would nevertheless compel the US and the UN to loosen up on sanctions enforcement. Previous protracted nuclear talks had brought Pyongyang billions of dollars worth of blandishments. So, five days after his ad hoc meeting with President Moon, Kim Jong Un turned even more proactive and signalled his eagerness for the 'denuclearization' talks by sending General Kim Yong Chol to the US to appease Donald Trump. On 1 June, the former spymaster became the first North Korean official in nearly eighteen years to pay a visit to a US president in the White House. He came bearing a cordial letter from the Great Leader, its oversized envelope playing up to the former reality TV show host's ego. Singapore was back on.

Kim Jong Un and his retinue took off for Singapore on the morning of 10 June. The send-off by his senior staff and the crowd gathered was appropriately thunderous, with roaring cheers of 'Manse!' (Hurrah!) – surely, the US president was no match for their peerless Supreme Leader. The Great Leader 'has boarded the Chinese private plane', the state TV announcer said, with no further information provided. Indeed, China had lent Kim Jong Un a private jet, the Air China Boeing 747 used by Chinese premier Li Keqiang.[4] In fact, the unusual flight path south to Singapore was emblematic of China's support for the North Korean leader's campaign. Over half of the flight route took place in Chinese airspace over inland territory instead of over the sea. The plane with the Chinese flag and 'Air China' painted across its fuselage touched down at Changi International Airport at 2.36 p.m. local time. At the airport to receive the special visitors was Singapore's Foreign Minister, Vivian Balakrishnan.[5]

It was not Kim Yo Jong's first visit to the city-state. She had been sighted there with her brother, Jong Chol, at an Eric Clapton concert in February 2011. Kim Jong Un, however, appeared impressed by the city and told his hosts the following day, 'Singapore is clean and beautiful, as it's known to be. Each building has its own architectural distinction. I hope to learn much from Singapore.' He had good reason to be gracious.

The Singaporean government had footed the $15 million bill for the Kim–Trump summit, including the North Korean delegation's luxury hotel stay. Prime Minister Lee Hsien Loong justified the expense as being for a 'good cause' that would enhance his nation's 'reputation'.[6]

As Kim Jong Un's motorcade of over thirty vehicles approached the St Regis Hotel at 3.40 p.m., a familiar scene unfolded against an unfamiliar backdrop. Some twenty or more North Korean bodyguards who had been standing by quickly flanked Kim's Mercedes and jogged alongside the sedan until it came to a stop. Crowds of Singaporeans and foreign visitors who had been waiting to catch a glimpse of the famous North Korean cheered vigorously. At this scene, which the Great Leader himself would have found utterly unremarkable, North Korean TV trilled, 'Even though countless heads of state have visited before, never before have Singapore's streets been lined with waves of welcoming people.' She almost certainly was right.

Inside his spacious suite, Kim Jong Un sat back comfortably, facing his senior-most officials, including his sister, muttering inaudible instructions while twitching his hand. Kim Yong Chol, Ri Su Yong (the Kim children's former chief caretaker in Switzerland), Ri Yong Ho, Choe Son Hui, and General No Kwang Chol all stood stiffly at attention, holding their pens and notebooks, ready to capture the Great Leader's profound thoughts. Yo Jong, on the other hand, stood to listen for a moment, then roamed about the room insouciantly with a smile. No other official in the land could have committed such blasphemy with impunity.

Kim Yo Jong provides a pen for her brother to sign the joint statement with Donald Trump in Singapore, 2018.

The next night, Kim Jong Un and his team went out for a stroll on the Marina Sands SkyPark Observation Deck, fifty-six floors up. Kim Jong Un smiled pleasantly and nodded occasionally at his tour guide's words, as crowds cheered joyfully at the North Korean leader gazing at the night scene. His officials, on the other hand, looked stiff and uncomfortable under the spotlight, perhaps nervous about the momentous summit happening the next day. But Kim Yo Jong acted as she does at home. She often chose to walk by herself, her famous faint smirk on full display, occasionally swinging her arms to and fro, as if she had not a care in the world.

On the morning of the summit, Kim Jong Un arrived at the meeting place, the ritzy Capella Hotel on Sentosa Island, at 8.10 a.m. President Trump, who had arrived in Singapore two nights before, arrived soon thereafter. At 9 a.m., the two leaders, facing each other on the world stage, shook hands for the first time. Trump, the seasoned TV star that he was, placed his left hand on Kim's right shoulder for a second as he visibly led the up-and-down shaking of the hands. Kim, in a momentary lapse of concentration, glanced up to look the taller Trump in the eye with his mouth slightly open, instead of looking straight ahead without tilting his head or eyeballs at all, even if his gaze fell on the American's chin. But he recovered right away. As the two men turned to face the whirring cameras, Kim Jong Un struck his tough-guy pose – chest out, arms straight and slightly forward, and the convivial smile turned into a stern frown.

The historic day ended with a post-lunch joint statement

signing. The agreement was a watered-down version of the wobbly statements of the past. North Korea committed to 'work *toward* [emphasis added] complete denuclearization of the Korean Peninsula', instead of committing to 'abandoning all nuclear weapons and existing nuclear programs' (2005). That the two sides even had the signing 'ceremony' was telling. Both were more interested in the optics of progress than substance. As Kim Yo Jong and Secretary of State Mike Pompeo, her counterpart in this moment, stood waiting, the two principals entered the room side by side. Kim Yo Jong pulled out the chair for her brother to sit on. She placed his pen case on the table. She and Pompeo held two folders each, one that contained the agreement in Korean and the other in English. The US folders were dark blue, the North Korean folders maroon. They handed them to their respective leaders to sign, and swapped them over for counter-signature. With the last piece of paper signed, Trump and Kim Jong Un, still seated, made statements to the press. With the other side's folder still in front of them, they shook hands, smiled for the cameras, got up, picked up the wrong folders, and carried them out of the room and into the hallway unawares. In this historic moment with cameras whirring, neither Kim Yo Jong nor Mike Pompeo felt impelled to risk photo-bombing the dramatic moment of the two leaders projecting peace and gravitas by entering the camera frame to swap folders. Trump and Kim continued to carry the wrong folders in the hallway. It was a fittingly inartful ending to a spectacle that was focused more on stage-management than substance.

* * *

The world may have been excitedly tuning in, but the highly anticipated first-ever US–North Korea summit proved to be a rerun of previous ones with a Great Leader in the starring role; the only novelty was that this time the antagonist was an American. The North Korean leader dominated the show by creating false hopes of genuine peace, reconciliation, reform, and denuclearization – none of which, as conventionally understood by outsiders, he had any intention of following through on. He coaxed Donald Trump to suspend combined military defence drills with South Korea for the next few years, and even to refer to these routine defensive exercises by Pyongyang's phrase of choice, 'war games'. Trump now dismissed them as 'provocative' and 'expensive', and said the US would 'save a fortune' by suspending them.

The summit also became, just like all three earlier North–South summits, an occasion for 'reframing' and even defending North Korea's atrocious human rights violations. As recently as January, in his State of the Union Address, President Trump had been condemning Kim Jong Un as a 'cruel dictator' and 'depraved character'; now, simply by showing up, that same dictator had, by the end of the day, succeeded in getting his fierce critic not only to drop all talk of human rights but, by the time of Trump's lengthy solo post-summit press conference, also praise him as a 'very talented man' and a 'very worthy, very smart man'.[7] Pressed by an American reporter on North Korea's human rights abuses, Trump replied, 'I believe it's a rough situation over there. It's rough in a lot of places, by the way, not just there,' thus drawing a moral equivalence between the gulags-running North Korea and less dictatorial, even free societies beset by their own human rights problems.

On the flight home aboard Air Force One, Trump, in an interview with Bret Baier of Fox News, continued to beautify Kim Jong Un. When Baier put it to him that the North Korean dictator was a 'killer' who was 'executing people', Trump replied that Kim was a 'tough guy'. 'Hey,' he went on, 'when you take over a country, tough country, with tough people, and you take it over from your father, I don't care who you are, what you are, how much of an advantage you have – if you can do that at twenty-seven years old, that's one in 10,000 that could do that.' 'He's a great negotiator,' acknowledged the president approvingly, 'but I think we understand each other.'

'But he's still done some really bad things,' objected Baier.

The president stuck to his guns. 'Yeah, but so have a lot of other people done some really bad things. I could go through a lot of nations where a lot of bad things were done.'[8]

Air Force One touched down on American soil, and soon Trump was tweeting 'Just landed', flushed with success like an excited teenager just back from their first Interrailing trip abroad – 'a long trip, but everybody can now feel much safer than the day I took office. There is no longer a Nuclear Threat from North Korea.' Americans and the rest of the world, a further tweet assured, could 'sleep well tonight.'[9]

The Singapore summit featured other oddities, both sophomoric and solipsistic. The US delegation had prepared a video clip to show the North Korean team, one designed to inspire Kim

Jong Un to seek a better path of denuclearization and economic reforms. As an example of a happier capitalistic future, the video featured scenarios under which Wonsan, a city on the east coast where the Kim family liked to spend time, might be transformed into a tourism hotspot. The Kim siblings had spent much time at their palatial mansion in Wonsan as children as well as adults, and must have had a good laugh when Donald Trump told Kim Jong Un, with his sister within earshot, that he would help develop their nation by building beachfront hotels and condos in Wonsan in exchange for Kim parting ways with his nukes, or as Kim was wont to call them, his 'treasure sword'.

In his eagerness to sell Kim his money-for-missiles scheme and thus make history, Trump then played for Kim a bizarre, four-minute faux movie trailer that his National Security Council had supposedly made on how to make bold decisions and become a great figure in history. He played it again at his post-summit press conference and told the hundreds of reporters gathered that the North Korean leader 'loved it'. The film opened with a snapshot of a North Korean boy and girl running through Kim Il Sung Square followed by split-second flashing images of the Roman Colosseum, Times Square in New York City, Egyptian pyramids, the Great Wall, the Taj Mahal, a night-time shot of Namdaemun ('South Great Gate') in contemporary South Korea, the Lincoln Memorial in Washington, D.C., and a giant North Korean flag – presumably to evoke notions of history and grandeur. 'Seven billion people inhabit planet Earth,' declaims the narrator in a dramatic bari-tone. 'Of those alive today, only a small number will leave a lasting impact. And only the very few will make decisions or take actions that . . . will change the course of history.'[10]

While it might have won cheers as a student summer project shown in a high-school classroom, the film's kitsch visuals and corny 'special effects' are unsettlingly comical. A tired night-time aerial shot shows the southern half of the Korean peninsula illuminated while the North is largely plunged in darkness – only to suddenly and miraculously light up. A brighter future awaits, apparently, if Kim would just listen to Trump. Bold decisions are there for the Supreme Leader to make, is the clip's principal message. The footage of the four medium-range missiles North Korea fired off simultaneously on 5 March 2017 is doctored to presage a happier future in which the projectiles reverse-fly back into their silos. 'The world will be watching, listening, anticipating, hoping,' booms the narrator of this new world transformed by superheroes: 'Will this leader choose to advance his country and be part of a new world? Be the hero of his people? Will he shake the hand of peace and enjoy prosperity like he has never seen? A great life – or more isolation? Which path will be chosen?'

Well, the path chosen by the real-life superhero of North Korea seemed clear from the very beginning, despite the incipient elephant-trap of a follow-up summit.

But at the press conference, President Trump was pressing on with his vision for a happier North Korean future. 'As an example, they have great beaches. You see that whenever they're exploding their cannons into the ocean, right? I said, "Boy, look at the view. Wouldn't that make a great condo behind?" And

I explained, I said, "You know, instead of doing that, you could have the best hotels in the world right there." Think of it from a real estate perspective.'[11]

What the president didn't understand is that the Kim siblings already have world-class facilities in Wonsan, as well as dozens of other mansions dispersed throughout their decrepit kingdom, and are not prone to lose sleep over the vast majority of their subjects living in extreme deprivation. In fact, they already had a plan to build a 400 km^2 international tourist zone centred in Wonsan, stretching more than 100 kilometres south-east to Mount Kumgang, although construction would not commence in earnest until later and the project remains very much unfinished. Whatever Trump's rationale, the Kim siblings would have been quite certain that exchanging nukes for handouts would be a poor deal. Why bargain away nukes and missiles for some construction materials and financial support when nuclear extortion had enabled their regime to extort tens of billions of dollars worth of cash, food, and fuel? It would be an insult to Daddy's legacy. *Mr President*, the royal brother and sister listening to Trump in Singapore might have thought, *what you're suggesting is unpatriotic; indeed, downright unfilial.*

During the summit meetings with President Moon and then President Trump, Kim Jong Un morphed into a reasonable leader trying to do the right thing. The young North Korean leader stood tall, wore affable smiles, and signed pleasant-sounding statements. Kim Yo Jong's supporting role, meanwhile, affirmed both closeness to her brother and, quite simply, her clout.

But her role, and the nature of her relationship to her brother, have often been misunderstood. Nimbly shadowing her more slowly moving, statuesque brother as the cameras stayed on him, the sister stepped in and out of view, pulling her brother's chair out for him as he took his seat at the signing table, placing his Mont Blanc pen case before him to sign guest books and joint statements, often walking from one venue to the next right behind him, she was his shadow and dutiful aide.

But by picking up the folder containing the statement once Kim Jong Un had signed it and exchanging it with her South Korean and American counterparts, she was equating herself with people who, in reality, are not her equals. The US Secretary of State, Mike Pompeo, with whom she exchanged folders containing copies of the joint statement her brother and Donald Trump signed, was certainly not her equal. No matter how high the rank, they, like her brother's head-of-state counterparts, are in the end functionaries confined by term limits. Even Chinese President Xi, dominant as he is within the Chinese Communist Party and aspiring to extend his term into the indefinite future, is bound by some semblance of institutional checks and balances. But the Kim siblings' hold on power is unconstrained, all-powerful, inviolable. As small a country as it is, compared to Xi's or Trump's, only the Kims rule it forever. They don't just run their country: they own it.

There was more drama three months later. When President Moon visited Pyongyang in mid-September 2018, the Kim siblings went all out on hospitality. At Pyongyang International

Airport the two leaders hugged each other cheerfully. Kim Yo Jong escorted the South Korean first couple across the tarmac amid Pyongyang residents wildly cheering, 'Unification!'

South Korea's large delegation, which included the heads of seventeen of its biggest conglomerates – like Samsung, Hyundai, and LG – as well as religious leaders and pro-Moon politicians, spent the afternoon visiting a children's hospital, theatre, and conservatoire in Pyongyang, and by the end of that evening's banquet Kim Jong Un, obviously pleased with how the dinner conversation had gone and red in the face from copious drinking, exited the hall with arms swinging jovially.

The product of the talks was the 19 September Pyongyang Declaration and an inter-Korean military agreement, essentially a rehash of the 2007 joint statement Kim Jong Il had signed with Roh Moo Hyun. Years later, unsurprisingly, not a single item has come to pass. Aspirations of turning the area of the Northern Limit Line, the de facto maritime border in the West Sea, into a 'maritime peace zone' that permits peaceful joint fishing activities between the North and South, for example, seem as distant as they were in 2007. Two years later, in 2020, North Korean guards shot and killed a South Korean government official adrift in the West Sea, then burned his body.

But the real surprise was saved to the very end of the document.

The North and South agreed to cease 'military hostility in regions of confrontation' such as the border; engage in 'constant communication and close consultation'; reopen two defunct inter-Korean joint ventures, the Kaesong Industrial Complex

President Moon and Kim Jong Un holding the Pyongyang Declaration.

and Mount Kumgang tourism project; connect 'east-coast and west-coast rail and road'; cooperate on North–South environmental and public health initiatives; open a 'permanent facility for family reunion meetings' and hold 'video meetings and exchange of video messages among the separated families'; deepen cultural exchange, with a North Korean art troupe visiting Seoul the next month; participate together in future Olympics; 'jointly commemorate the 100th anniversary of the March First Independence Movement Day'; 'cooperate closely in the process of pursuing the complete denuclearization of the Korean peninsula' – the ardent wish of North Korean leaders both living and deceased; and, finally, that Chairman Kim Jong Un would 'visit Seoul at an early date.'*[12] Just like all previous North–South agreements, none of this has come to pass, because Pyongyang violates agreements at will and Seoul has no way to compel Pyongyang to enforce them.

In the copy to be kept by the northern side, President Moon's signature to all this appears, per protocol, to the right of Kim Jong Un's. But Moon has imitated Kim Jong Un's 'Mount Paektu-style' penmanship, signing his name at a rising forty-five-degree angle (he did not do this in the copy he would take home). If this was an attempt to ingratiate himself

---

*   On 1 March 1919, the Koreans launched a peaceful protest against Colonial Japan, declaring Korea's independence. The Japanese authorities responded with a brutal crackdown, killing thousands of protestors, and the movement failed to gain recognition from any sovereign state. But the event is celebrated as a national holiday in South Korea, for it engendered the Korean Provisional Government in China and symbolizes the spirit of Korean resistance. In North Korea, the movement does not gain much attention.

to Kim, it will have backfired. The Great Leader would not have looked favourably on a southern leader, both temporary and inferior, encroaching on the distinct style of the sacred Mount Paektu royalty.

In the evening, President Moon and his top officials were treated to the mass games, as President Roh had been in October 2007. But Kim Jong Un went much further in his hospitality. On 19 September, Moon Jae-In became the first president of the Republic of Korea to be offered the chance to give a speech in North Korea, and to a massive audience of 150,000 in Pyongyang. With Kim Jong Un seated next to him, Moon stood up to speak. It was a night for posterity. Kim Yo Jong stood close behind Moon throughout his speech, her steely gaze focused on the back of his head.

Introducing himself to the crowd as the 'president of the southern side' instead of 'the Republic of Korea', his country's formal name, Moon paid tribute to his counterpart's 'indomitable courage' in defending 'the pride of the ethnic Korean nation even in the face of hard times.' If that was a problematic choice of words, implying that the current Supreme Leader was presiding over an era no more paradisal for his citizens than his father's, the rest of Moon's speech was more emollient.

The next morning, the southern delegation was treated to a visit to the fabled Mount Paektu. During President Roh Moo Hyun's meeting with Kim Jong Il in 2007, the North Korean leader had unexpectedly asked, 'Why should people from the south need to fly to Pyongyang and then take off again on a flight to Mount Paektu? Why not fly directly from Seoul to

Paektu?' A flickering vision of a brighter future was born: direct flights between Seoul and Samjiyeon, the main city at the foot of Mount Paektu equipped with an airport, developing it into a tourist hub for South Koreans. It sounded too good to be true. But how tantalizing! South Koreans with cash to spend would finally get to see the mountain with their own eyes. North Korea would bank the revenue. Ordinary North Koreans would see free South Korean tourists and be inspired to become more like them, and slowly – South Korea's long-held fancy – through its generous aid and investment the North would open up . . . It was a short while before the South Koreans realized the North Korean leader had not meant it. He refused to discuss the matter again.

But the son, young and Swiss-educated, was different, perhaps. On 20 September 2018, he actually led President Moon and his entourage to the hallowed mountain. When the South Koreans touched down at Samjiyeon Airport at 8.15 a.m., the Chairman and his wife were courteously waiting, both wearing long black coats. The South Koreans, coatless, were unprepared for the colder air in Samjiyeon in mid-September. Mrs Moon was shivering. The Mount Paektu visit was a last-minute surprise treat for the Moon delegation, a once-in-a-lifetime experience the southerners would not forget. Just as his father had unexpectedly suggested opening an air route between Seoul and Samjiyeon, so Kim Jong Un had suddenly suggested a group visit to the mountain, the 'Cradle of the Revolution', as North Koreans put it. The difference was that the son was not just talking about a future visit. He was actually taking the southerners on a climb. Winter coats for the South Koreans were flown over from the south.

In the North Korean documentary of the visit, the South Koreans were giddy with euphoria, smiling and laughing as they survey their majestic surroundings. One by one, they crouched down at a creek and tasted the cold water. First to crouch down and scoop a handful of water to his lips was the nation's spy chief. Moon and others filled their plastic water bottles with the precious Mount Paektu water. The first couples posed for photographs. Moon tapped Kim Jong Un's left hand and held his arm up high, and the Great Leader did not resist. Foreign Minister Kang Kyung-wha showed Kim Jong Un how to do the finger-heart, a hand gesture seen as emblematic of the global rise of South Korean popular culture in recent years. The North Korean leader smiled broadly and tried it. Barely able to contain their excitement, the South Koreans asked the North Korean leader to take photos with them, until a long line had formed and an irritated Kim Jong Un said, 'Enough.' And all the while, looking on, just out of frame and content not to join the finger-hearted revelry, stood Kim Yo Jong, gazing at the giddy South Koreans with her trademark Mona Lisa smirk.

Once lunch was finished, the South Korean delegation were seen off at Samjiyeon Airport, after a visit during which Kim Jong Un had at all times extended Moon full courtesy. When the president landed in Seoul two hours later, he wore a broad grin, while his waiting officials hollered and fist-pumped. It was a hero's triumphant return home.

Very few could then have foreseen the dark clouds that would gather. The second Kim Jong Un–Donald Trump summit in Hanoi, Vietnam the following February would end in deadlock, and set back both North Korea's and South Korea's common interest of persuading the United States to lift sanctions against the Kim regime.

But while the sanctions stayed in place, their enforcement had already been rendered sluggish since Kim Yo Jong's visit to South Korea. Pyongyang had made some token gestures in the first half of 2018, like detonating the entrance of an old underground nuclear facility, temporarily freezing a nuclear site and partially closing a missile launch site in order to entice President Trump to meet Kim for the first time in Singapore. But the three weapons facilities gradually reopened. What did not open again was the North Korean siblings' hearts. After all the stops they had pulled out for Moon in Pyongyang and Mount Paektu, they were clearly disgruntled. No matter how hard Moon tried to flatter and reach out to them, they would soon openly mock and insult him. From March 2020 to March 2023, Moon, his successor, and the US would be the target for Kim Yo Jong's vituperation on average every six weeks. The frequency of the official statements and the severity of insults indicated a plan rather than a tantrum. For the time being, she would cook up a storm for her adversaries, both South Korean and American.

CHAPTER 14

The Ascent: Mounted Paektu Princess

Like her brother, Kim Yo Jong has often been misunderstood. Solely by virtue of having attended school in Switzerland, the brother was initially viewed by many as a potential reformer. In 2018, his coming out, with beaming smiles and shaking hands with world leaders, triggered similar forecasts. Perhaps, just perhaps, this time was different?

Similar fancies have swirled around the sister, with 2018 a banner year for both Kim siblings. First, she brought glamour and gossip to the Pyeongchang Olympics. Then she shadowed her brother as he met Moon Jae-In in April, Xi Jinping in May, Moon again later in May, Donald Trump in June, and Moon in Pyongyang in September.

Once again, all this, many observers mused, may suggest Kim Yo Jong's role as essentially 'secretarial'.[1] During Kim Jong Un's sixty-nine-hour train ride from Pyongyang to Hanoi in February 2019 for his second meeting with Donald Trump, for example – a distance of over 4,500 km – the Kim siblings were caught on film at a rest stop in the middle of the night, standing by themselves beside the train in the Chinese city of Nanning, Guangxi Province, a little over 200 km from the border with Vietnam. The North Korean leader was having a smoke, his sister holding up a crystal ashtray for him with both hands. 'Subservient,' some said of this vignette.

But what Yo Jong was doing was anything but subservient. She was being herself: the only person in Kim Jong Un's entourage who had his complete trust, able to approach him at any time without being summoned. Hers was the role not of a fawning secretary but the self-assured, attentive, doting mother-figure. She was making sure her brother would leave no cigarette butts bearing traces of his DNA for foreign intelligence agencies to examine. No one else, aside from his wife, has such intimate access to the Supreme Leader – but North Korea's First Lady is not a political figure. On matters of statecraft, no other person has such ease of access to the Great Leader as his dear little sister.

Once the train arrived in Hanoi around noon on 26 February, Kim Yo Jong, in high heels and a black two-piece suit, was the first to alight. She looked around, 'cleared the grounds', got back on the train and ushered her brother out. When her brother was given flowers, she half-sprinted forward and shoved aside General Kim Yong Chol to relieve her brother of the burdensome bouquet. In Hanoi later that day, she was spotted surveilling the Sofitel Legend Metropolitan Hotel, the venue for her brother's summit meeting and dinner with Donald Trump. She was also photographed visiting the North Korean embassy in advance of her brother's visit.

The sight of the First Sister of North Korea busily inspecting meeting places and attending to her brother might categorize her as an 'event planner' or 'protocol officer' – which, were she not a member of the Mount Paektu family, is exactly what she would be. But Kim Yo Jong is much more. After all, Kim Jong Un's state affairs, including foreign visits, are a family business, and she was overseeing and advancing them with the full confidence of the boss.

In Hanoi, the Kim siblings suffered an unexpected setback. Their well-honed family practice of 'bait-and-overload' hit a wall. They had come all the way by train, expecting Donald Trump to give away the farm – to agree to the lifting of all US and UN sanctions in return for the usual North Korean charade of shutting down the main Yongbyon nuclear reactor – and then to sit back and enjoy a pleasant if not positively triumphant train ride home. The same old trick had worked a treat for their father, namely in 1994, 2005, 2007, and 2008: in return for North Korea simply freezing the reactor for a few years or even months, President Trump's predecessors had given generously: over $1.3 billion worth of fuel and food – while South Korea had come in with ten times that. Food aid had resumed, financial sanctions had been lifted, and, in 2008, North Korea was removed from the US State Department's list of state sponsors of terrorism (though it was put back on by President Trump in 2017 in the aftermath of Otto Warmbier's death).

When North Korea had been found to be cheating, for example, enriching uranium after the 1994 denuclearization deal or proliferating nuclear material to Libya and Syria amidst the Six-Party denuclearization talks in the mid-2000s, the Americans had soldiered on with gifts rather than spark an adverse reaction that might, for example, see Pyongyang escalating with small-scale but deadly attacks on the South. Even when North Korea was found to have built a nuclear reactor in Syria almost identical to the one in Yongbyon, they had blinked. Politically hobbled by the invasion of Iraq in 2003, the Bush administration had decided not to support Israel in a military operation against the reactor, and in the end, after months of internal deliberation, Israel had gone it alone. On 6 September 2007, eight Israeli Air Force jets completely destroyed the reactor.[2] Syria, as a signatory to the Treaty on the Non-Proliferation of Nuclear Weapons (NPT), chose not to protest, lest the serious breach of nuclear cooperation with North Korea invite further scrutiny.

In Hanoi, surely, Donald Trump would follow the same path of aid and appeasement – perhaps even go further? After all, he was the first and only US president to have basked in the spotlight of shaking hands with the North Korean leader. Such spectacles raised expectations of lasting peace. There had even been loose talk of Trump winning the Nobel Peace Prize. Trump seemed particularly vulnerable to flattery and, like the Japanese and South Korean leaders, Kim Jong Un himself had laid it on with a trowel, to the extent that just months earlier President Trump had even spoken of how he 'fell in love' with the North Korean leader.[3]

'The perfect love affair,' said George Bernard Shaw, 'is one which is conducted entirely by post', and by early 2019 Kim Jong Un and Donald Trump had been sealing their relationship for months through several adulatory letters. In a 20 September 2018 letter to Trump, Kim remarked on Moon's 'excessive interest' in the matter of 'denuclearization', which he regrettably found 'unnecessary'. He stoked Trump's ego by writing that the subject was 'our matter' on which he wished to deal directly with the US president.[4] Granted, triangular relations among nations, just like those among individuals, are a complex affair. But to demean Moon like this to Trump, just one day after having so graciously taken him and his wife up Mount Paektu, suggests that the splendid courtesy rendered was just that, a mere formality, and that Kim's real object of desire was Trump. The US president might even go all the way and agree to sign a peace treaty with North Korea that saw all American troops withdrawn from South Korea.

In the way, however, stood Trump's National Security Advisor, John Bolton, the occasional focus of North Korea's distaste since early 2001.[5] Notorious for his hawkish stance on North Korea and Iran, Bolton had urged Trump to walk away if Kim Jong Un refused to disclose and shut down all his nuclear facilities. Kim, in his talks with Trump, refused, while demanding that the US president lift all sanctions imposed on his regime since 2016, which accounted for 90 per cent of the sanctions in place. Bolton wrote in his 2020 memoir that he and his national security team had repeatedly warned Trump of the pitfalls of buying the same Yongbyon horse thrice. At a prep session in the White House Situation Room on 12 February, Bolton, thinking hard 'about how to prevent a debacle', showed Trump a film that opened with 'news clips of Carter, Clinton, Bush, and Obama all saying they had achieved great deals with North Korea.'[6] Three days later, at a second briefing, Bolton showed his boss a 'North

Korean propaganda film showing them still engaged in robust war games', even as the US and South Korea had halted their routine outdoor defensive drills following the first meeting with Kim Jong Un in Singapore. Trump asked for a copy of the video.[7] Walking away from a faulty deal, Bolton repeatedly impressed on the president, was the least bad option.

By the time Trump got to Hanoi at the month's end, his state of mind was far from placid. Back in Washington, Michael Cohen, his long-time former lawyer and fixer, who had just been sentenced to three years in prison for campaign finance violations, tax evasion, and lying to Congress, was about to give damaging testimony against his former boss at a congressional hearing on the same day Trump was due to meet Kim in Vietnam. Cohen's opening remarks set the tone: 'I am ashamed because I know what Mr Trump is. He is a racist. He is a con man. He is a cheat.'[8] The hearing was the talk of the nation. After a short dinner with Kim Jong Un, the US president 'stayed up well into the night' watching the hearing. In the morning, Bolton recalled, he 'cancelled the preparatory briefings.'[9]

Trump's one-on-one with Kim Jong Un started at 9 a.m., and forty minutes later, as Bolton describes in his memoir, Trump and Kim were joined by their respective foreign policy deputies, Secretary of State Mike Pompeo and General Kim Yong Chol. 'Kim Jong Un did not like the heat and humidity, so they went inside a greenhouse-type structure in the inner courtyard used as a café, undoubtedly air-conditioned . . . His sister stood stoically outside in the heat and humidity, while the Americans, needless to say, went inside nearby where it was air-conditioned.'[10]

Michael Cohen may unwittingly have deprived Kim of a victory. His testimony certainly had Trump distracted and eager to leave Hanoi.

In the end, neither Donald Trump nor Kim Jong Un yielded. The two sides were not even able to issue a bland joint statement, since not even optical progress had been made since Singapore. President Trump, apparently tired and frustrated, cancelled the scheduled signing ceremony. He even cancelled the scheduled lunch. After his press conference, he got on his plane and took off for home, effectively walking out on Kim Jong Un, whose Vietnam itinerary had him staying for longer. Trump may not have intended it, but his abrupt take-off left the Supreme Leader looking as if he had time on his hands. It was almost certainly the greatest public humiliation the North Korean leader had ever suffered.

So the long train ride home wasn't joyous. It certainly could not have been triumphant. For all the officials not of the Mount Paektu blood it must have been almost seventy hours of treading back and forth on thin ice, if not worse. Once he returned home, Kim Jong Un did what Great Leaders do when things don't go as expected: punish underlings. (His grandfather blamed his foreign minister, Pak Hon Yong, a widely respected native Korean Communist, for the Korean War ending in a split instead of a victory, branded him a US spy and had him executed.) Reports surfaced in South Korean papers a month later that General Kim Yong Chol had been sent off to do a few months' hard labour. Kim Hyok Chol, the junior point-man on US negotiations, who had visited President Trump in the White House together with Kim Yong Chol on 17 January, was reported to have been executed, along with four other officials of the United Front Department, which specializes in counterintelligence and propaganda operations vis-à-vis the South, although no source or confirmation was presented. For her failure to convey to Trump Kim Jong Un's 'last-minute offer' as Trump was about to walk out on him, even the humiliated Great Leader's interpreter was reportedly packed off to a prison camp.[11]

Even Kim Yo Jong kept out of public view for a couple of months. Notably, she did not accompany her brother to the Russian Far East, where in late April 2019 he held his first summit meeting with President Vladimir Putin, again travelling by train, this time to the Far Eastern Federal University in Vladivostok – a manageable 700 km trip compared with the 4,500 km to Hanoi.

But unlike in Vietnam, on this trip Kim didn't seem quite the full ticket. Not only did he look heavier but, after getting out of his car and slowly walking just a few steps to the waiting Putin shortly past 2 p.m. on 25 April, his breathing was already stertorous. Video footage showed the tails of his black Mao suit creased and pulled up. No one on the North Korean delegation dared approach the Great Leader and lay a hand on him to straighten his clothes. Just when he needed his sister, she was not there.

To make matters much worse, Putin, while treating his guest to a proper meal, pulled on him a Trump-in-Hanoi variation. After bidding Kim farewell and sending him off when it was still light outside, Putin thereafter made himself unavailable. He had places to go – namely Beijing, the very next day, for China's Belt and Road Forum for International Cooperation. The next morning, Kim was expected to show up to a wreath-laying ceremony at the headquarters of the Pacific Fleet without the Russian president by his side. In a disgruntled Great Leader move, Kim was over two hours late, possibly due to a hangover. As for the aquarium visit in the afternoon and the evening ballet on the itinerary (while the Russian leader would be mingling with Xi Jinping and other world leaders some 800 miles away), Kim cancelled both and got back on his train for home.[12] The ride back must not have been a merry one for all on board.

In June, Kim Jong Un and Kim Yo Jong showed up for a brief, last-minute meeting with President Trump at Panmunjom, the site of Kim's triumph over Moon the year before, Kim Yo Jong reprising her customary role of shadowing her brother. Kim graciously led Trump to step over the Military Demarcation Line into his domain, so that Trump could later boast of being the first US president in history to 'visit' North Korea. The previous day, on a visit to Japan, Trump had floated the idea of meeting Kim in a tweet: 'While there [South Korea], if Chairman Kim of North Korea sees this, I would meet him at the Border/DMZ just to shake his hand and say Hello(?)!'[13] Kim took the bait, having nothing to lose by coming across once more as a peace-loving statesman. Before the formal talks, Trump introduced his daughter, Ivanka, who was travelling with him, to the North Koreans. It was the first time the two women, the First Sister of North Korea and the First Daughter of the US, met.

The meeting produced nothing substantive, and the North Korean leader followed this made-for-TV photo-op by resuming his reclusive, missile-shooting lifestyle in earnest. From 4 May to 28 November the North unleashed short-range missiles on thirteen different days, five in the month of August alone. While the world stayed focused on the flying missiles, in October, atop a snow-capped Mount Paektu, Kim Jong Un elevated his sister still higher, with an outing heavy with symbolism and family emblems. The visit intimated an even greater formal role in government for her, but went almost unnoticed outside North Korea.

Several years earlier, in late November 2013, on a visit to the Samjiyeon Revolutionary Battlefield Monument, a sacred site of national pilgrimage situated at the foot of Mount Paektu straddling the border with China, Kim Jong Un had uttered these immortal words:

> In order to inherit and complete across generations the great tasks of the Juche [autonomous] revolution and the Songun [Military-First] revolution, we must keep alive eternally the life of our party and revolution by the Paektu Bloodline, and ceaselessly inherit and develop the tradition of the revolution, and thoroughly adhere to its purity.

But what does it mean? In plain English, that the state and the party 'must be kept alive by the Paektu Bloodline', and no one else.[14]

This convoluted exhortation came several months after Kim Jong Un had revised the Ten Principles for the Establishment of the Monolithic Ideology System.[15] The highest written authority of the land is neither the constitution nor the Charter to the Workers' Party of Korea, but these 'Ten Principles'. Established by Kim Jong Il for his father in 1974, transcending all laws on the statute books, they yield only to the personal directives, written or oral, of the Supreme Leader. Setting aside the irony of a regime so committed to the persecution of Christianity unabashedly appropriating the idea of the ten commandments, as originally crafted, the principles were all about the personality cult of Kim Il Sung. In 2013, Kim Jong Un had them revised and unveiled under the modified title of 'Ten Principles for the Establishment of the Monolithic Leadership System'. Like the original, the amended version boils down to the single message: 'We must give our all to the Great Leader and his progeny.' The addition of his father's name next to his grandfather's as an eternal co-leader further bolstered Kim Jong Un's own legitimacy, and the names of founder and son appeared next to each other in eight of the ten commandments and copiously throughout. Above all, in the revamped version came the pregnant passage about the uncompleted revolution having to be completed by the 'Paektu Bloodline':

We must pass down the great achievement of the *Juche* revolution and the *Songun* revolution, pioneered by the great Comrade Kim Il Sung and led by Comrades Kim Il Sung and Kim Jong Il, from generation to generation, inheriting and completing it to the end.

The designation of Kim Yo Jong, from this very Mount Paektu Bloodline, as Kim Jong Un's surrogate and heir was a process begun back in 2019, a few months before the world descended into pandemic. It commenced as grand theatre: an outdoor pageant on a white horse atop the famed mountain itself.

On 16 October 2019, the KCNA reported that the previous day Kim Jong Un had ridden a white horse to the top of Mount Paektu, 'in the first snow' of the season: 'a great event of weighty importance,' intoned KCNA, 'in the history of the Korean revolution.' That pronouncement may, in time, indeed prove portentous.

The visually arresting tableau of the North Korean leader, convention-defying as ever, galloping up the hallowed mountain on a white horse, clad in long, double-breasted winter coat, drew international attention, much of it mocking. Lost among the sneers at the rotund horseman, however, was the fact that he was not alone. Accompanying him on horseback was his sister: this was her symbolic elevation to bearer of the mantle of the Mount Paektu Bloodline. Across the lower slopes of Mount Paektu galloped the Kim siblings – Yo Jong, as she had shown herself at diplomatic summits, right behind her brother – before they ascended further up the mountainside in the company of a handful of senior officials. In the state TV coverage, Kim Yo Jong's unique status in the dynasty was repeatedly emphasized, if only visually.

It was further accentuated just seven weeks later when, on 3

December, the Great Leader returned to Mount Paektu on horseback with his wife, Ri Sol Ju, and a much bigger contingent. They visited the revolutionary 'battlefields', monuments, and log cabins at the base of the mountain, studiously soaking up the exaggerated history of the original Great Leader's resistance against imperial Japan. This time, however, Kim Yo Jong was nowhere to be seen. But her brother's second visit in less than two months, *without* his sister, only reaffirmed her destiny – for what if he, for some reason, should one day fail?

Before that first public pilgrimage to the mountain on horses, the two siblings riding side by side, or the sister covering her brother's back, the North Korean state had not publicly acknowledged the two as even related by blood.

Of the twenty-five official photographs released of the pilgrimage, Kim Yo Jong appears in six. In two of them, brother and sister are the only ones in the shot. In both, she is galloping directly behind her brother while casually holding the reins in her right hand.[16]

In the state television footage, there is a frame showing a single-file procession with Kim Jong Un at the head and his sister, looking straight at the camera with a smile, right behind him.[17] In another photo, the sister is all smiles as she rides up a wooded hill directly behind her brother,[18] her olive-green military-style outfit and beret looking more appropriate to the occasion than her brother's double-breasted, fur-collared coat. Like her brother, she appears at ease in the subalpine surrounding with the cameras flashing around her. These photos show Yo Jong as the closest individual to Kim Jong Un not only in her literal proximity to the Supreme

Leader, but also, and more tellingly, by the apparent comfort and affinity between the royal siblings.

But one picture stands above the rest in significance. It informally, but unmistakably, elevated Kim Yo Jong to a class of one. It is a shot of the Kim siblings from the front, direct descendants of Kim Il Sung and carriers of the 'Mount Paektu Bloodline', astride their stately horses, making a slow gait on a bed of soft, white snow atop the 'Sacred Mountain of the Revolution', as the state TV announcer declaimed. 'On sacred Mount Paektu,' Ri Chun Hi, the most celebrated of North Korean news anchors, said, her voice holding a reverent quiver,

> which majestically rises up, carrying the proud spirit of our fatherland that dashes forward tempestuously while accomplishing extraordinary achievements that the world watches in astonishment, the legendary canvases and special marks engraved so meaningfully by the great man of unsurpassed greatness shook heaven and earth.[19]

Why was this scenic picture more significant than the rest? Because it makes clear that both horses carrying North Korea's supreme siblings are wearing a five-pointed silver star on their headstalls, the central symbol of the dynasty and national flag. No one else in the ensemble was accorded the privilege – not even Kim Jong Un's wife, Ri Sol Ju, on her climb the following month. Also captured is Yo Jong's trademark imperious, closed-lipped smile. The image of Kim Yo Jong on horseback, wearing the dynasty insignia, next to the Supreme Leader atop the sacred revolutionary

Kim Yo Jong on Mount Paektu with her brother. The five-pointed star on her horse's headstall makes clear her significance.

mountain, carried revolutionary meaning. As the last photo in the news segment was aired, showing Kim Jong Un striking a heroic pose as he pulls up his horse's front legs, Ri Chun Hi's narrative went further still. This pilgrimage will, the anchor said, 'remain immortal as a historic undertaking that accelerates the complete victory of our revolution.' It tacitly incorporated Kim Yo Jong into the official Mount Paektu narrative of heroic leadership:

> The profound meaning and holy marks engraved by the Great Comrade Kim Jong Un when he rode to the peak of Mount Paektu on a white horse in person will shine with great splendour that will cast North Korea higher as a most powerful socialist state that is the envy of the world and shall remain immortal as a historic undertaking that accelerates the *complete victory of our revolution* [emphasis added].[20]

As of the time of writing no North Korean government agency has yet referred to Kim Yo Jong as the Supreme Leader's sister. The elites in Pyongyang, of course, know. And even the common people can read between the lines; that is, many would have picked up on the symbolism of these and other images, to say nothing of her nearly thirty potent written statements. Kim Jong Un's power and privileges are sacred and inviolable. And his divine right, in the quest for the victory of the revolution, may be passed on to his sister, for she, too, by virtue of her holy Mount Paektu Bloodline, was born with the divine right to become, if necessary, queen.

CHAPTER 15

Weaponizing Food: A Family Practice

Late-nineteenth-century Western travellers to the Far East found Korea a perplexing 'hermit nation'. With the exception of its traditional relations with its more powerful neighbour, China, Korea tried, in vain, to pursue a policy of self-isolation. Thus, Korea stood markedly apart from Japan, which in the mid-nineteenth century had been 'opened' by the United States through a mix of threats and diplomacy. Some two decades later, Japan appeared, to the delight of many Americans and Europeans, to embrace the alien customs of the West, even in fashion and hairstyles. Korea, on the other hand, mired in its outdated mores and resistance to change, seemed hopeless.

Both Korea and Japan drew lessons from the onslaught of the Atlantic world on China's coastal cities as, from the mid-century on, Western nations raced to carve out a sphere of influence for themselves, following the imposition of inequality on China by Britain, then the most powerful state in the world. For much of its history, China had been the world's most advanced nation, the Middle Kingdom surrounded by lesser peripheral states that paid tribute to China's material and presumed moral superiority, but in the nineteenth century China had descended into prolonged internal chaos and foreign exploitation. Unnerved, Korea sought to resist being pulled into the Western-dominated diplomatic arena. Japan, on the other hand, though also unnerved, chose to adapt to the foreign wave and adopt Western knowledge and practices. While Japan sought to strengthen itself, Korea, believing itself to be the last bastion of the traditional Chinese world order – a regional order based on the Confucian precepts of hierarchy among states – tried to shun the outside world.

Americans and other foreign travellers to North-East Asia came to admire Japan, in particular, for its distinctly chaste and asymmetric aesthetic. The term '*Japonisme*' came to denote the thirst for Japanese art in Europe. Korea, though, was another matter. Like China, Korea seemed regressive. Its leadership was embroiled in factionalism while much of the land lay engulfed in a series of peasant uprisings. Korea's hapless ruling elite appeared torn between change and aversion to it. To many outsiders, it was unclear if Korea, quasi-isolated and inward-looking, was an independent state or a mere vassal of China. What was clear, however, was the stark contrast between Korea and Japan in their respective national mentality and policy. Hence, the unflattering moniker 'hermit nation' became Korea's epithet.[1]

It has since become North Korea's. For much of its history, North Korea has been called by outsiders, condescendingly, the 'hermit kingdom'. Like the Korean kingdom, which dissolved into a colony of Japan in 1910, the dynasty founded by Kim Il Sung in 1948 has shown a proclivity towards relative

isolation and disinterest towards the world beyond its neigh-
bouring countries, at least until the early 1970s. Such
perceptions of Korean isolation, both in the case of North
Korea and its predecessor, are born of facts as well as a heavy
dose of fancy. In fact, the hermit nation characterization is far
less applicable to North Korea than the Yi dynasty (1392–1910),
since the former maintains diplomatic relations with over 160
states. At the same time, North Korea has shown, among all
the industrialized nations of the world, the most contrived
scorn for conventional diplomatic intercourse. Whether in
mundane matters like maintaining open lines of communication
with other states, abiding by international norms and agreements, or desisting from state-sponsored crimes like using its
accredited diplomats to traffic illicit narcotics, North Korea
has behaved in an unorthodox, solipsistic manner that might
indeed be described as hermit-like. No other country with
comparable military power, regional influence, and territorial-
and-population size is more deserving of the 'hermit' distinction
than the Democratic People's Republic of Korea.

And if the Mount Paektu clan deems it crucial to surround
itself with moats of mystery – the North Korean people need
not know about the royal family's extravagant lifestyle or the
regime's depravity – that is because North Korea is a land of
misery as well as mystery, and both the miserable conditions
the vast majority of the people face and the extreme opacity
of the regime are entirely deliberate. For the North Korean
people, near-total dependence on the state while harbouring
hopes of even temporary relief from daily hardship is their lot.

The state decides who lives and who dies. Thus it has always been: rule by malice and deception, tempered by the occasional relief from tension. The state assiduously screens the people's suffering from the outside world ('We have nothing to envy' is a much-touted slogan), systematically falsifies facts and history, and falsely projects to audiences both domestic and foreign that happier days of full bellies and denuclearization lie on the horizon.

To Kim Jong Il, the great North Korean famine of the mid- to late-1990s, which may have killed more than 10 per cent of North Korea's population – perhaps more than 3 million people – was but a minor inconvenience. The cause was not flooding and US sanctions (as the regime claims), but the ending of subsidies from the USSR (after its collapse in December 1991) and China, which normalized its relations with South Korea in August 1992. Rather than using his own money to import food, Kim Jong Il preferred to spend it on developing weapons of mass destruction, buying fighter jets, and building the world's most expensive mausoleum for his father. The famine is officially referred to in North Korea as 'Gonan-ui haeng-gun': the 'Marching through Suffering', which, as Professor Sandra Fahy, a leading expert on North Korean human rights, observes, invokes patriotic resistance in the face of hardship.[2] But for the Kim family and their cronies, it became a useful tool of crooked statecraft, even a financial windfall. None of the privileged in Pyongyang starved, but when the piles of corpses in the provinces grew bigger by the day, Kim Jong Il actually saw in the mass deaths of his people a business opportunity – a chance to grow richer himself.

Unabashed at blaming others for his crimes, Kim Jong Il used food as a weapon against the outside world. While committing against his own people what the United Nations in 2014 would call 'the inhumane act of knowingly causing prolonged starvation',[3] he wrung out of the international community as much food aid as he could. Naturally, he diverted the food aid to the most invulnerable: his government and the military. In a speech he gave at Kim Il Sung University in December 1996, at the height of the famine, Kim Jong Il said:

> In a socialist society, the food problem should be solved by socialist means. If the Party lets the people solve the food problem themselves, then only the farmers and merchants will prosper, giving rise to egotism and collapsing the social order of a classless society. The Party will then lose its popular base and will experience meltdown, as in Poland and Czechoslovakia.[4]

Kim Jong Il's criminal scheme continued in the post-famine years. Food shortages and pervasive hunger became for Kim Jong Il a means to lucrative fundraising. Over the next decade, hundreds of millions of dollars worth of free food poured in from South Korea, the United States, and the United Nations. However, despite aid, United Nations agencies found each year approximately one-third to half of the North Korean population – about 8–12 million people – to be suffering from undernourishment. In the late 2010s, more than two decades after the onset of the famine in the mid-1990s, United Nations food agencies still found

North Korea's annual grain shortage to be consistent, at approximately 1.36 million tons.[5] It's as though North Korean officials, in planning their annual national budget each year, purposely left this constant food deficit aside for others to fill.[6] For fear of upsetting the North Korean leadership, which in the past has led to North Korea imposing even more restrictions on the aid agencies, donor nations have seldom called the regime out on this bizarre, recurring phenomenon. Neither UN agencies nor sovereign states have forcefully exhorted the Kim regime to change its expenditure priorities and import more food. Instead, they have largely fallen into compliance with these abnormal norms set by Kim Jong Il and subsequently continued by his son.

The pervasive hunger, which according to the UN annually affects well over 40 per cent of a population of 25 million, places the Democratic People's Republic of Korea among the five nations in the world with the highest prevalence of undernourishment as a percentage of the total population. The latest United Nations report on *The State of Food Security and Nutrition in the World* (2022), which does not formally 'rank' or 'list' states in any order of food insecurity, does reveal North Korea at number four in the world with 41.6 per cent of the population undernourished. The Central African Republic tops all nations (52.2 per cent), followed by Madagascar (48.5 per cent), and Haiti (47.2 per cent).[7] The 2019 report, the last before the pandemic, also revealed North Korea at number four in the world, with even a higher percentage of undernourishment of 47.8 per cent, after the Central African Republic (59.6), Zimbabwe (51.3), and Haiti (49.3).[8] Among those on this dismal 'top ten' list compiled by this author, North Korea stands alone as an industrialized, urbanized, and completely literate society not beleaguered by insurgence and civil strife. No other nation in the top ten – or indeed top fifty – enjoys the economic advantages of being an industrialized, urbanized, literate, and de facto peacetime economy. No other is armed with prohibitively expensive military hardware like nuclear weapons and intercontinental ballistic missiles.

The North Korean nation may be poor, but the regime is rich. Filling the annual food gap of 1.36 million tons would require an annual expenditure of between $200 million and $400 million, depending on the type of grain purchased and the international market price of corn, rice, wheat, etc. The Kim Jong Un regime spends well over $1.3 billion a year on its ballistic missile programmes alone.[9] It uses the chronic hunger of its people as both a spear and shield; that is, a means with which to both extort the international community for free food and defend its leaders against criticism from abroad.

The North Korean government and its foreign defenders claim that US and UN sanctions, as well as bad weather and climate change, are what have caused the perennial hunger. It's a narrative that even resonates in Pyongyang-friendly South Korean administrations going back to the early 2000s. But it wholly discounts the facts: that there were no UN sanctions against North Korea until 2006, more than a decade *after* the start of the famine; that US sanctions against North Korea did not become biting until North Korea-specific US sanctions legislation was finally created in 2016, over *two decades* after the onset of the famine; and that, by some marvel of nature, climate-change-induced bad harvests stop each year, without fail, right at North Korea's northern and southern borders, beyond which hardly anyone goes to bed hungry.

The famine, which killed at least 600,000 and perhaps upwards of 3 million people, was man-made and man-sustained: the direct result of Kim Jong Il's policy of 'deliberate starvation', as the 2014 United Nations study forcefully and repeatedly alleges.[10] The report found that the North Korean government, at the highest level, had committed 'crimes against humanity . . . against starving populations, particularly during the 1990s. These crimes arose from decisions and policies violating the right to food, which were applied for the purposes of sustaining the present political system, in full awareness that such decisions would exacerbate starvation and related deaths of much of the population.'[11]

During the famine years, from 1996 to 2000, Kim Jong Un, his brother and sister were all at school in Switzerland. They frequently travelled abroad on fake foreign passports with bundles of cash. They went home regularly and spent time in their father's numerous secluded, luxurious palaces. They have no first-hand experience of anything less than extreme luxury and the highest privileges, teetering on cringe-making cult worship. While their fellow North Koreans starve, condemned to a life of extreme deprivation and state terror, they have had no reason to fear hunger, poverty, rebellion, or even the faintest criticism from their own people. Theirs is, after all, the most successful – the most perfected – totalitarian state in history.

Moreover, the Kim rulers have never had any real concern about an imminent US attack, despite playing this up for both domestic and foreign consumption to justify oppression and nuclearization. Once again, there has not been a single first shot by Pyongyang's adversaries since the armistice of 1953, despite over 2,000 North Korean attacks, raids, and infiltrations on South Korea, many of which claimed dozens of American as well as hundreds of South Korean lives.

But then came a hitherto unseen, credible, and lethal threat: the Covid-19 pandemic.

It was the greatest threat Kim Jong Un had ever faced – indeed, the most lethal threat to North Korea's supreme ruler since the Korean War Kim Il Sung had started. In May 2022, Kim Jong Un acknowledged for the first time the spread of the coronavirus in his nation, which he called a historic 'great upheaval'.[12] Whereas kings and noblemen never succumb to a famine, even a deified dictator could unexpectedly fall to the rapidly spreading virus. And in truth, Kim Jong Un had good reason to be concerned about the pandemic. In the first week of March 2020, South Korea led the world, after only China, in the number of daily confirmed cases.[13] Caught between these two high-contagion neighbours, the morbidly obese ruler turned insular while (as we will see in the next chapter) rapidly elevating his sister's position in government.

North Korea's public healthcare system was dilapidated, and paranoia surrounded the well-being of its royal family, or 'living Gods', as the Kims sell themselves to their information-deprived population. As early as 22 January 2020, Kim Jong Un revived an old family tradition: sealing his nation in hermetic lockdown. The country's northern borders with China and Russia were closed as, calling disease containment a matter of 'national survival', Kim tried his best to ensure the preservation of himself and his Pyongyang cohorts, doubling down on existing measures to keep unauthorized people out of the capital.

Even if the people suffered or starved, the imperative of protecting his own health required that the borders stayed closed, and the state entered a period of hibernation from regular diplomatic intercourse. Weeks later, Kim Jong Un issued a shoot-on-sight order against any border-crossers. The order was eventually extended to include even mammals and birds.[14]

Kim's fear of infection far outweighed concerns for the well-being of his people. The country's southern border with South Korea was relatively secure; indeed, the most fortified land border in the world. The northern border with China was not. At the cost of his own people's welfare, in May 2020 Kim Jong Un put a stop to imports of commercial goods from China. After all, the regime could not rule out the risk of a Covid outbreak also being imported and making it all the way to Pyongyang.

There were even reasons to believe that the Kim regime would emerge from its hermetic isolation all the better, in spite of – or thanks to – the people's suffering. Turning its back on the outside world and shunning all imports and offers of aid would create humanitarian misgivings abroad, which as we have seen tend to morph eventually into an influx of aid to replenish the North Korean state's coffers.

So Kim Jong Un and his sister turned to their father's playbook of misery and mystery. The borders were closed and the people left to fend for themselves. Kim refused foreign aid, both food and medical, including free Covid-19 vaccines. It would not be until September 2022, nearly three years after the outbreak of the pandemic, that he hinted that he might approve foreign vaccines for his people.[15]

According to various reports from within North Korea, famine-like conditions returned during the Covid-19 era and persisted through 2023 in cities near both South Korea and China, where food is abundant but made inaccessible by Pyongyang.[16] In April 2021, Kim Jong Un invoked the old phrase his father had shrewdly coined, 'Marching through Suffering', and warned of 'many obstacles and difficulties ahead of us.'[17] Later in the year, he told his people to 'tighten their belts' and eat less for the next four years – until 2025.[18]

In early 2023, reports surfaced from Kaesong, a relatively well-off city just across the North–South border, suggesting that each day dozens of people were dying in the streets from starvation.[19] On a cold, clear day in late January, this author, together with several colleagues, stood at the Joint Security Area border and peered into the barren landscape that is Kaesong and its surroundings. Sir John Scarlett, former Chief of the British Secret Intelligence Service, asked what was going through this author's mind: 'People in North Korea, just by the sheer misfortune of having been born north of the border, inherit hunger, misery, and oppression, while those, like I, born south of the wretched border, live in comfort and with freedom. It's not just power and privileges that are hereditary in North Korea, but also the starvation, discrimination, and enslavement, across multiple generations'.

Like his father, in hard times Kim Jong Un considers certain segments of his own population, the lowest 'Hostile Class', expendable. The strict enforcement of border closure also inevitably led to a significant drop in the number of North Korean escapees making their way to South Korea: from 1,047 in 2019 to just 229 in 2020, by far the smallest number in over two decades. The next year, it dipped even further to sixty-three.[20] In remained about the same in 2022, with forty-two recorded as of September, and sixty-nine at the year's end. King Jong Il, too, had targeted border-crossing during the famine years, but not nearly as obsessively and efficiently.

In spite of the dire situation or, rather, in an attempt to maximize it, the *Rodong Sinmun*, in a 22 February commentary, warned against receiving aid from 'imperialists' who, it claimed, use aid as a 'trap to plunder and subjugate' recipient nations.[21] Describing economic aid as 'poisoned candy', the party's newspaper called for self-reliance, the nutrition-less, fantastical state ideology dating from the 1950s. The message, in exhorting the hungry people of North Korea to tighten their belts once again, reinforces the rules of aid-giving to donor nations and agencies: *Do as you're told once we grant you the privilege of providing aid.*

Through these years, in both cracking down on border-crossers and doubling down on nuclear missiles development, the son and daughter may be said to have outperformed the master, their father.

CHAPTER 16

Twisted Sister

By March 2020, the days of cordiality and summitry were a closed chapter. It was time for the Kim siblings to co-write a new script for their elaborate scheme of taming the South. All the face-to-face meetings, meals, drinks, and laughs shared over such a compressed sixteen-month schedule – from Kim Yo Jong's visit to South Korea in February 2018 to June 2019's brief meeting with Donald Trump at Panmunjom – now meant something only to one side, which still clung on to the hope that those sunny days would return. Indeed, the North Korean royal family have nothing but scorn for their ardent South Korean suitors. They use them for their sport, and once their utility expires, belittle them and, ultimately, discard them.

By early 2020, North Korea's chief propagandist was just waiting for an excuse to start lashing out at President Moon, who would be the most common target of her ire. Her 3 March 2020 statement, the first under her own name, was hurled at both Seoul and Washington, but personalized for Moon. While the tone was not as shrill as some of the more vulgar invective later unleashed, it established what would become a characteristic mix of sardonic wit tinged with sadism.

The pretext for Kim Yo Jong's ire was the Blue House's expression of 'strong regret' at the North Korean army's live-strike artillery drills the previous day. The president's statement was dismissed as 'perfectly foolish'; the work of a 'three-year-old'. The last sentence of Kim's statement, as translated into English by the Korean Central News Agency, read, 'It could be a little awful comparison, but it is a frightened dog barking noisier just like someone.' The translation is not only unidiomatic and grammatically incorrect, but also misses the sarcasm mark. She was, in fact, jeering, 'I'm so sorry to make this comparison, but they say a frightened dog barks more noisily than one that's unafraid. Just like someone I know . . .'[1] The original last sentence in Korean ended with the ellipses, as if any doubt existed as to whom she referred.

Considering that her response came just twenty-four hours after Moon's 'strong regret' had been expressed, it was probably something she had prepared earlier to be wheeled out as soon as such impertinent criticism was received. But the aim will have been to drive a stake into Moon's heart: to stress that, as a result of all those cordial and even celebratory meetings, at which Moon's eagerness to be civil spilled over into servility, she knows just how to torment him.

Three months later, in one of her three statements that June, Kim Yo Jong announced (in the stilted English translation of her agency) that, '[B]y exercising my power authorized by the Supreme Leader, our Party and the state, I gave an instruction to the arms of the department in charge of the affairs with enemy to decisively carry out the next action.'[2] The very next sentence clarified what she meant by that 'next action', as well as who the enemy, in this instance, was – South Korea. She would order the blowing-up of the North–South Joint Liaison Building located just north of the border in Kaesong, built and maintained entirely with South Korean funds of over $15 million.

'Before long, a tragic scene of the useless north–south joint liaison office completely collapsed would be seen,' threatened her mangled syntax. Three days later, on 16 June, she followed through on her threat: down came the four-storey building, taking with it part of an even taller building nearby that had also been built by South Korea, in a theatrical explosion recorded on video. This was a woman to be feared – and obeyed.

Although only thirty-three, Kim Yo Jong was showing that she had already mastered the dark arts of psychological manipulation, strategic deception, fake peace overtures, hostage-taking, torture, and ad hominem name-calling, all in the advancement of her family's own interests. The day after having the joint liaison tower blown up, she hurled an epic diatribe at the South Korean president: 'Brazen, shameless, fake, unrepentant, hideous, flatterer, superficial, foolish, unforgivable, sophist, pretends to be deaf and dumb, impudent, flunky beggar, servile, submissive, numb, pathetic, pro-US lackey, floundering, sewer, squalid, idiot, looks mentally ill, child, faker, revolting traitor.'

Ironically, the effect of what she obscurely defined, at the end of nearly 2,000 words of tirade, as this 'bomb or words' tactic, was to make governments more likely to be dismissive of her, viewing her not as the crafty, supremely self-confident under-boss she was, but merely as potty-mouthed and risible. That she was a young woman made some also more likely to forgive and forget. All this worked to her advantage: to patronize the North Korean leadership was fatally to underestimate it, but because the torrent of abuse came from her, less import would be attached to it than had they been her brother's words.

Even more impressive – in an ominous way – and symptomatic of the power dynamics between Pyongyang and Seoul, had been Kim Yo Jong's written statement on 4 June, when she demanded that South Korea come up with a law to criminalize the sending of propaganda leaflets across the border. (She was referring to the North Korean émigrés who, once resettled in the South, had become activists launching balloons across the border filled with anti-Pyongyang propaganda. As she put it, these activists were 'human scum hardly worth their value as human beings'.) The threat was worthy of a terrorist's ransom demand: South Korea 'had better do what they should do if they do not want to face the worst phase.'[3] This was the first of her written statements to be published in the *Rodong Sinmun*, the party newspaper intended mainly for a domestic audience. It presaged Kim Jong Un's intention to impress on the people his sister's rapidly increasing clout. Her 13 June statement, which invoked her 'power authorized by the Supreme Leader, our Party and the state', was also published in the party newspaper, with more articles on her warnings to the South to come that month.

The balloons were only a minor nuisance to the regime, typically filled with anti-North Korea leaflets, Bibles, toothbrushes, toothpaste, soap, socks, cash, rice, face masks, and other items in short supply in the North. But here was a perfect pretext to project to the world just how paranoid Pyongyang's supreme deity is. More importantly, they enabled Kim Yo Jong to remind South Korea that in the two 2018 joint statements President Moon had signed with her brother, the Panmunjom Declaration in April and the military agreement annex to the Pyongyang Declaration in September, 'both sides agreed to ban all hostile acts including leaflet-scattering in the areas along the Military Demarcation Line' – an egregious error by the South Korean president.

Three days after calling on Seoul to criminalize the exercise of free speech, she had mobilized the masses and riled up the crowd. Large-scale rallies erupted across her nation to denounce South Korea and defectors from the North. Student groups in neat white shirts came together in their thousands, waving banners calling for 'Guns Barrage' and 'Just Give Us the Order!' Young boys and girls waved their fists and brandished placards demanding, 'Let us tear to shreds so-called "defectors", traitors to the nation and human scum!' Middle-aged women pumping their fists in the air opted for 'Let us burn to death wholesale all traitor groups who hasten their own self-destruction!' 'Let us pummel to death the puppet group that has committed an eternally unforgivable sin!' was another, and it was clear that the 'puppet group' everyone had in mind was South Korea. 'If you dare bark indiscriminately, we will pummel you to death!' was blazoned in white letters across red banners, against the blue skies of early summer.

Within days of Kim Yo Jong's nationwide campaign, North Korea, the world's most mass-mobilized nation, seemed itching for war and waiting on her command to strike. After all, on 13 June, she had already threatened it: 'If I drop a hint of our next plan the South Korean authorities are anxious about, the right to taking the next action against the enemy will be entrusted to the General Staff of our army.'

In a land where the word of the Supreme Leader is the word of God, where 'not all the water in the rough rude sea can wash the balm off from an anointed king',[4] the words of Kim Yo Jong, surrogate for her brother, were the words of the Lord, the Supreme Leader, and thereby inviolable. No other high official could have galvanized the entire nation in a matter of days.

The battle lines had been drawn by the sister: over now to the brother.[5] On 24 June, the KCNA announced that the Great Leader had decided, for the time being, to 'suspend' the military action he and his sister had in mind. 'Bad Cop' brother had reined in his 'Even Worse Cop' sister: thus did the Kim siblings toy with the South. Peace, for now, would be preserved. Without officially declaring it, Kim Jong Un had raised his sister's standing to 'Deputy Dear Leader'. Hereafter, her words were his words, vetoable only by him.

Kim Yo Jong's diktat to the South on 4 June was released at 6.14 a.m. At 10.30 a.m., the Blue House gave an unscheduled briefing. 'We remain steadfast in the view that the 27 April

Panmunjom Declaration and the 19 September South–North military agreements must be observed.' The Ministry of Unification went a step further. At 10.40 a.m., its chief spokesman announced, 'We are considering measures that will fundamentally correct activities that create tensions in the border area. We are preparing a plan to overhaul our laws.' With alarming alacrity, South Korea's ministry in charge of managing relations with North Korea had, in the space of a few hours, effectively replied to Kim Yo Jong that, *Yes, ma'am. Your wish is our command. We will work on the law and muzzle our own citizens.*

At 2 p.m., South Korea's Ministry of National Defence declared that 'Leaflet launches by civic groups are acts that endanger the lives and property of border area residents and therefore must stop.' Thirty minutes later, the Blue House warned fellow South Koreans that 'Sending leaflets into North Korea are acts that do all harm and no good', and that, 'The government will respond firmly to acts that harm security.'[6]

The very next day, sponsorship and drafting of new legislation began. By mid-December 2020, the bill had been passed by the pro-Moon party and its allies, who held a three-fifths supermajority in the national assembly. The bill was passed by 187 votes to none, with opposition lawmakers abstaining in protest.[7] Pro-Moon lawmakers congratulated themselves in the national assembly with fist bumps. Just hours later the same day, 14 December, US Congressman Michael McCaul issued a statement: 'The South Korean National Assembly's anti-leafleting law is cause for concern . . . A bright future for the

Korean Peninsula rests on North Korea becoming more like South Korea – not the other way around.'[8]

The new law has been misleadingly labelled the 'Anti-Leaflet Law' by critics and supporters alike – an unfortunate misnomer. Banning leaflets was what Kim Yo Jong had called for. But South Korea, in its zeal to please her, went much further.

The law ostensibly targets the activists sending balloon-borne leaflets across the North–South border into the North, with a maximum punishment of three years in prison and 30 million won (approximately $27,000) in fines. But its reach is far broader and its intent stealthily insidious. In reality, the new law banned the sending of any item with even a minimum exchange value, including the typical items activists fill the balloons with, from copies of the Bible to toothpaste or dollar bills. In effect, it outlawed everything except items that are not easily monetized, like pebbles from the beach or cigarette butts. As the British parliamentarian Lord Alton remarked, it should have been called 'the Republic of Korea's Gag Law'.[9]

The backlash was fierce and global. The United Nations as well as human rights organizations, politicians, and pundits from sixteen countries all voiced their concern and implored President Moon and his party not to go ahead with the law. Once it was passed, they called on South Korea to repeal it. The US Congressman Chris Smith called the new law 'inane' and South Korea's ruling party 'illiberal'. In April 2021, Congressman Smith convened a congressional hearing on the controversial Gag Law. A rare hearing it was, indeed, with the US Congress publicly expressing concerns about human rights violations in the *other* Korean state. Yet Moon and his party (seemingly still prioritizing the cementing of better relations with their northern neighbour) remained committed to obeying Kim Yo Jong's command.

Since acceding to power in 2017, the Moon administration had cut funding to non-governmental organizations (NGOs) that conduct research on the North Korean state's human rights abuses. In 2020, the administration started conducting audits of those groups, revoking the operating licences of two prominent North Korean-émigré-run organizations – Fighters for Free North Korea and KuenSaem, operated, respectively, by the brothers Park Sang-Hak and Park Jung-Oh. Park Sang-Hak has been a favourite target for Moon's supporters in government and the press. A prominent, outspoken activist, Park is the survivor of at least one North Korean assassination attempt and has been under police protection since September 2011, when he narrowly escaped murder with a poisoned needle. South Korean intelligence officers intercepted Park at the subway station where he was to meet his would-be assassin, a former member of North Korea's special forces who had defected to the South in 1995.[10] An Hak-Young, upon arrest, stated that he had been recruited for the task by North Korean agents with an offer of 'money and a better life for his family members who still lived in the North'.[11] The blood money offered by the DPRK was $10,000.[12]

The next year, on 31 July, a major North Korean government agency threatened to kill Sang-Hak; calling him and three other prominent critics of the Kim regime by name, North Korea threatened to mete out 'merciless punishment' on them. In the same statement, Pyongyang called on South Korea and the United States to 'make an official apology for the hideous, politically motivated, state-sponsored terrorism against the dignity of its Supreme Leader and sternly punish the prime movers.'[13] The administrations in Seoul and Washington, D.C. at the time had the good sense not to comply with North Korea's demand. The situation in the Gag Law era, however, was very different. Park Sang-Hak soon became a target of his own government as well as the oppressive one he had left behind.

In late April 2021, Park announced that he had just launched balloons filled with 500,000 leaflets, 5,000 dollar bills, and 500 booklets on South Korea's economic development across the border into North Korea. It was the first deliberate violation of the Gag Law.

As expected, Kim Yo Jong went on the warpath once more. On 2 May, she announced:

> We regard the manoeuvres committed by the human wastes in the south as a serious provocation against our state and will look into corresponding action. Whatever decision we make and whatever actions we take, the responsibility for the consequences thereof will entirely rest with the south Korean authorities who stopped short of holding proper control of the dirty human scum.[14]

The *Rodong Sinmun* dutifully published her missive, conveying to her people once again who was in charge of running their nation's policy towards the South.

Her threat triggered a series of actions by the 'south Korean authorities'. That same day, the chief of South Korea's National Police Agency publicly called for a 'swift and strict investigation' into Park's recent balloon launches. Four days later, the police raided Park's office with a search and seizure warrant.[15] On 10 May, at 11 a.m., President Moon, in his fourth-anniversary inaugural speech, declared that 'It is never desirable to pour cold water on inter-Korean relations while violating inter-Korean agreements and current laws. I can only stress that government cannot but strictly enforce the law.' Two hours later, Park Sang-Hak was summoned by the national police and interrogated for the next six hours. On 28 January 2022, he was indicted for the crime of sending leaflets, dollar bills, and booklets to his compatriots in the North, some of the most downtrodden people on earth.[16]

Back in 2012, North Korea had actually threatened to shell the downtown Seoul offices of newspapers and televisions stations that offended the Kim regime. Ten years later, perhaps memories of Pyongyang's terrorist threat had moved the Moon administration to refuse to rule out shutting down the private radio stations that broadcast to the North. South Korea's continued kowtowing would embolden Kim Yo Jong to issue further threats of violence against South Korean citizens who printed or broadcast any criticism of her despotic family.

The year 2020 marked the dawn of a new brave world in Korea, one in which North Korea's First Sister had achieved what none of her de jure predecessors had managed: to casually extend her repressive nation's censorship across the entire Korean peninsula. The Gag Law was a major victory for North Korea and, personally, for Kim Yo Jong herself, and her standing increased commensurately.

Had it been Kim Jong Un who had issued the order to criminalize free speech across the border from the North, it is doubtful South Korea would have responded with such alacrity. South Koreans had grown accustomed to North Korean leaders – who, to date, have been all men – making threats and unreasonable demands. But the domineering princess had only to snap her fingers and the South's rulers complied with a vigour and a sophistry, not to mention human rights violations the likes of which shall seldom, if ever, be observed in another advanced democracy. They had won the victory – not of the total sort, but still meaningful – over themselves, and learned to love the sister even more.

CHAPTER 17

They Call Her 'Devil Woman'

While extending her censorial reach over South Korea, Kim Yo Jong also set about laying into the United States.

In her longest written statement so far, on 10 July 2020 (2,843 words in the official English translation), she declared that while 'denuclearization' was not impossible, bilateral talks would now be conditional on US 'withdrawal of hostility' – North Korean code for the withdrawal of US troops and weapons from South Korea and the region.[1] Though still leaving the door open for negotiations, she stated that further 'summit talks' would not take place for the rest of the year. Various reasons were tossed about: election year in the US meant such high-profile diplomacy would 'only be needed for the US' while 'unprofitable' to her nation; the DPRK would 'only end up losing time again' in talks, since the US 'does not even have the courage to dare a new challenge' (i.e. pulling US forces out of South Korea and letting North Korea have nukes). And oh, yes – another reason why her brother should not meet Trump again that year: 'because it was foretold by [National Security Advisor John] Bolton who is a human scum.'

Having thus raised the bar some considerable distance for future bilateral talks and summits, she closed her missive with a parting shot. Referring to the US Independence Day celebrations she had 'seen on TV a few days ago', she asked President Trump if he could send her a DVD of future 4 July celebrations. She had, she added, received 'permission from Comrade Chairman', no less, to 'personally obtain' such recordings. While the foreign cognoscenti somehow managed to read an olive branch into this, as though in an age of live-streamed blockbuster movies the royal siblings enjoyed nothing better than to curl up in front of a video of crowds waving their little Star-Spangled Banners, it was of course her own distinctive blend of sarcasm and rudeness.

Her statement came just six days after her government's official newspaper, *Rodong Sinmun*, had anointed 4 July 2017, when North Korea had fired its first-ever intercontinental ballistic missile, as, pointedly, the 'July Fourth Revolution'. On that glorious day three years earlier, Kim Jong Un had celebrated the landmark blast by generously dubbing it a 'gift package' for 'American bastards'.[2] So the precedent had long been set for dissing the US celebration, and by invoking videos of American Independence Day, Kim Yo Jong was reopening the wounds caused when Trump patronized her brother in Singapore by showing him the video clip on how to rebuild North Korea by getting rid of his nukes.

Just six days before her missive, Vice Foreign Minister

Choe Son Hui, a veteran American-handler who spoke English fluently (and who nearly derailed the Singapore summit by upsetting Trump with her diatribe against the vice president), had made it clear that her nation had 'already worked out a detailed strategic timetable for putting under control the long-term threat from the US' and saw no need to fall again for any new 'shallow trick' by a US that 'persists in the hostile policy toward the DPRK.'[3] As far as the Kim siblings were concerned, it was a way of saying that, the presidential election in November notwithstanding, they were, for now, done with Donald Trump.

The sister's sardonic wit, which pervades all her written statements to date, is a new phenomenon in North Korean propaganda. Certainly on her watch there has been no aversion to racist, sexist, and homophobic slurs – but foul language delivered with a sneer, and coming direct from a top leader, was Kim Yo Jong's own USP. In it there were clues to her personality and ambition: to humiliate, deceive, and be taken seriously.

In North Korea, 2021 began with a major party congress, the nation's eighth, and the second that Kim Jong Un had presided over himself. During the multi-day event, Kim Jong Un gave himself the title of General Secretary, which he had reserved for his father upon ascending to his nation's official top leadership in April 2012.

He did himself another personal favour. Ever the loyal family man, often choosing, unlike his father and grandfather, to be seen in public with his wife, the newly self-anointed

General Secretary also created the position of 'First Secretary of the Party', who would be his senior-most deputy. This would be someone who, in the event he himself became incapacitated, or, God forbid, suffered a premature death, could ease into his role and consolidate power. In effect, he was taking out a life insurance policy for himself and his family. From the ascent of Mount Paektu in late 2019 to her numerous edicts and actions throughout 2020 (when she had also headed the powerful Department for Organization and Guidance, with the power to hire, fire, and disappear key state officials, including military commanders), it was clear there was only one candidate for this Great Leader-in-waiting, this unnamed surrogate who might inherit the party, state and, perhaps one fine day, the entire Korean peninsula: the First Sister.

After a lull in the second half of 2020, in 2021 the name-calling and personal attacks against South Korea returned with a vengeance. In January, Kim Yo Jong called President Moon and his officials 'a truly weird group' who were 'hard to under-stand' – indeed, 'first-class idiots' bent on inviting 'world laughter' on themselves.[4] The pretext was the remark by the South Korean Joint Chiefs of Staff – 'craning their neck,' as she put it, 'to follow what's happening in the north' – that, following the conclusion of the week-long Eighth Party Congress, there had been signs of North Korea preparing for a big military parade. But the real target was President Moon, who on 11 January had said in his New Year's address that he would make a 'final effort to achieve a major breakthrough in the stalled North Korea–US talks and inter-Korean dialogue.'[5]

But Moon wasn't ready to give up quite yet. On 18 January, at a rare press conference – practically an annual event for his administration – he said ruefully that although Kim Jong Un had agreed to visit him in Seoul this had not happened, and there were no signs of a southern sojourn or any meeting on the horizon. Moon said he hoped that 'it will happen some day' before he left office in May 2022.[6] 'Chairman Kim,' he maintained, as though the sister had never uttered a word, 'is firmly determined to seek peace, dialogue, and denucleariza-tion.' And this after Kim Jong Un, during an eight-hour-long birthday speech on 8 January at his party congress, had called for developing an 'advanced capability for making a pre-emptive and retaliatory nuclear strike by further raising the rate of precision, good enough to strike and annihilate any strategic targets within a range of 15,000 kilometres with pinpoint accuracy'; and for waging 'offensive diplomacy to smash the attempts of the hostile forces to violate our sover-eignty'; and, once again, for 'prevailing over and subjugating the US, the fundamental obstacle to the development of our revolution and our principal enemy.'[7]

For Moon to disregard such strongly stated positions by none other than the Supreme Leader himself would, to the Kim siblings, have been at least a mild annoyance. But in late January Moon's deputy, Prime Minister Chung Sye-Kyun, chimed in with his hopes of yet another inter-Korean summit, and Seoul leaned heavily on the new administration of Joe Biden, who had defeated Donald Trump in November's US election, to resume dialogue with North Korea.[8]

By mid-March, Kim Yo Jong had had enough. The South Korean leader was 'born with stupidity', had become 'dumb and deaf, bereft of judgment'. Whatever Moon and his men 'may do in the future under their master's [the US] instructions,' she warned, 'those warm spring days three years ago, which they desire so much, won't come easily again.'[9] Later in the month, this time under her official title of 'Vice Director of the Publicity and Information Department' (aka the Propaganda and Agitation Department), she branded President Moon's expression of 'concern' over North Korea's recent tactical guided missile tests the 'height of effrontery'. Calling him a 'parrot raised by America', she advised Moon he should 'think about how he is viewed by the world'.[10]

During the 15 April ceremony to commemorate Kim Il Sung's birthday, the most important national holiday, Kim Yo Jong wore a very different look, one of solemnity and resolve. At the Kumsus Palace of the Sun, where both her father and grandfather lay embalmed in state, an uncommon scene unfolded. Whereas in previous years Kim Jong Un had led rows and columns of officials to the grand mausoleum to pay their respects to his predecessors, in 2021 the Supreme Leader came with the barest contingent. The previous April, he had not shown up at all for this most symbolic of all national holidays, presumably because of concerns over catching Covid-19. But skipping two years in a row would have been unmannerly. Besides the soldiers carrying an oversized floral arrangement inside a silver vessel and officers from different branches of the armed forces lining the wall standing guard, just six people, the core members of the nation's top leadership, stood in line facing the oversized effigies of Kim Il Sung and Kim Jong Il. To Kim Jong Un's left stood Marshal Pak Jong Chon. To Kim's right stood, in order, his wife Ri Sol Ju, deputy party chief Jo Yong Won, Kim Yo Jong, and Hyon Song Wol, who had been lead delegate to South Korea on the eve of the 2018 Winter Olympics and was also Kim Jong Un's former girlfriend.[11]

In unison, the six made the traditional deep Asian bow, the lower the better. Kim Jong Un, his wife, and Jo Yong Won tilted their torsos to about forty-five degrees. Kim Yo Jong, on the other hand, bowed with such excessive reverence that her back bent forward the full ninety degrees, arms pulled back with fists clenched and battle-ready, and her head dropped lower still, her hair cascading towards the floor. She would repeat this histrionic bow three months later at the same venue, on the occasion of the twenty-seventh anniversary of her grandfather's death.

Ms Kim's gesture was down to neither lack of confidence nor awkward social skills. Rather, it showed her resolve to carry out faithfully her grave duties in the service of the dynasty, which of course invariably involved serious, systematic, and widespread human rights violations. Calculated ruthlessness must guide her work as Kim Jong Un's chief of staff, national security advisor, chief propagandist and, for the foreseeable future, heir-apparent. Reckless boldness must also be projected occasionally, but cautiously. The clenched fists revealed her confident commitment to her task; no longer the timidity and carelessness of giddily hopping over a flowerbed in 2012 as her brother was speaking at the opening of the Rungra People's Pleasure Ground, or taking a peek at her brother from behind a pillar at the Military Foundation Day parade on the eve of her historic visit to Seoul in February 2018. In the brief seconds of that ceremonial bow to the founding North Korean leader and his son – her own father – Kim Yo Jong, the sole viable inheritor of the Juche Revolution, was summoning the spirits of her forefathers for guidance. It was a pledge of allegiance to her ancestors, the source of her power and, perhaps one day, her own legitimacy as Supreme Leader.

Even as the new Biden administration called throughout the year for talks without preconditions, the North Korean leadership showed little interest in being engaged. On 22 June 2021, Kim Yo Jong derided the US National Security Advisor Jake Sullivan as clueless. Mentioning a Korean proverb, she effectively called him a daydreamer. What was the occasion? On 18 June, her brother had issued his first statement on the new US administration, calling on his nation to 'prepare for both dialogue and confrontation, especially to get fully prepared for confrontation, in order to protect the dignity of our state and its interests for independent development'. Two days later, responding to a reporter's question, Sullivan called this an 'interesting signal'.[12] Two days later, Kim Yo Jong issued a short statement mocking Sullivan's rather plain comment. Americans' 'expectations' of talks with her nation, the haughty princess said, 'would plunge them into a greater disappointment.' Her discourteous message was: 'Dream on.' She may as well have been addressing simultaneously leaders in Washington and Seoul. For the foreseeable future, North Korea was committed to turning its back on both Washington and Seoul and strengthening its nuclear arsenal.

On 1 August 2021, Yo Jong issued another statement, calling on the South to cancel the annual summer combined military exercises with the US. Since Kim Jong Un's first summit meeting with Donald Trump, South Korea had insisted on radically scaling down the drills that President Trump, once again echoing Kim Jong Un, had called 'war games', and by 2021, they were a shell of their former selves, reduced almost entirely to computer simulations. But still Kim Yo Jong could not be appeased. 'We have never discussed the scale or form of the joint military exercises,' she fulminated. Choose wisely, she warned the South, between 'hope and despair'.[13]

So they did. Within seventy-two hours, fifty-eight lawmakers in Moon's party had signed a petition calling for the military exercises to be cancelled. While the Blue House, mindful of the Biden administration's scepticism on North Korea, dithered, the number of signatories grew to over seventy overnight. The ruling party's rationale was that the two Koreas stood on the cusp of rapprochement once again, as during the past week, on 27 July 'Victory Day' in the Korean War as claimed by the Kim dynasty, North Korea had restored the military and civilian lines of communication between the two sides that Kim Yo Jong had unilaterally broken off in June 2020. Why irk Pyongyang now?

On 10 August, under pressure from Washington, the Moon administration reluctantly started the defence exercises. They may have been simulated, but Kim Yo Jong reiterated her disappointment and upped the ante. 'For peace to settle on the peninsula,' she stated, 'it is imperative for the US to withdraw its aggression troops and war hardware deployed in south [sic] Korea'. As long as the US forces stay in South Korea, she warned, in the tone of a stern parent admonishing a petulant child, 'the root cause for the periodic aggravation of the situation on the Korean peninsula will never vanish.'[14] Once again, to underscore to the North Korean people who was running North Korea's policy towards both South Korea and the US, the party newspaper published her statement in full.

On 11 September, the twentieth anniversary of the terrorist attacks on the US, her nation resumed missile tests, the first since the two ballistic missiles launched towards the East Sea on 25 March. The next day, Pyongyang fired another cruise missile. More were to follow.

On 15 September, North Korea launched two ballistic missiles at approximately noon. Hours later, President Moon attended a pre-scheduled submarine-launched ballistic missile test. 'Our missile test today,' he subsequently explained, 'was conducted according to schedule . . . and was not meant as a response to the North Korean provocation. But strengthening our missile force,' Moon went on, 'will provide us with a firm deterrent against North Korean provocations.'[15] On this occasion, President Moon apparently made the 'mistake' of using the word 'provocation' not just once but twice.

The inevitable rebuke came that evening. Expressing 'very great regret over [Moon's] thoughtless utterance of the word "provocation" which might be fitting for hack journalists,' mourned Kim Yo Jong, 'We can not [sic] but voice our great regret at south Korea's illogical and stupid habit of describing its act as a just one supporting peace and describing our act of similar nature as the one threatening peace. This raises our concern about the future development of the north–south relations.'[16]

She issued another statement on 25 September, the eve of her thirty-fourth birthday. Would South Korea kindly not characterize the North's missiles as 'provocations', when they were actually 'actions of self-defensive dimension to cope with the military circumstances and possible military threats existing on the Korean peninsula'? South Korea's military exercises, on the other hand, were 'a blunt disregard of and challenge to the sovereignty of the DPRK.'[17] Never mind that her nation was prohibited by nine United Nations Security Council Resolutions – all previously supported by both China and Russia – from developing or testing any ballistic missiles, whereas South Korea and the US were under no such restrictions.

Thereafter, and throughout the rest of President Moon's term, which ended on 9 May 2022, all branches of the South Korean government ceased using the word 'provocation' to refer to North Korea's missile tests.

On 28 September, North Korea conducted its first-ever hypersonic missile test. Hypersonic missiles fly at a lower altitude than ballistic missiles and are more manoeuvrable, making them harder to track and defend against, which posed a new threat to South Korea. Kim Jong Un had stated in the January party congress that his nation would be developing them.

On 19 October, North Korea fired a submarine-launched ballistic missile. The next year, in January alone, North Korea conducted seven different missile tests, including a Hwasong-14 intermediate-range ballistic missile (IRBM), which had previously been tested three times in 2017. By the time President Moon left office, North Korea had fired missiles on fifteen separate days, including four ICBM or ICBM component tests. No one in the South Korean government was allowed to call any of them a 'provocation'. The official response fluctuated from 'concern' to 'deep regret'.

Kim Yo Jong had won yet another battle without exerting herself beyond some heavy-handed statements. After coercing the Moon administration into criminalizing freedom of speech and sharing information across the border, she had now got Seoul to censor itself on North Korea's deadly missiles, which of course were primarily trained on none other than South Korea itself. President Moon may have been on his way out, and a new, more forceful leader in Yoon Suk Yeol, a former top prosecutor and political novice, about to take office on 10 May, but no matter who was at the helm in Seoul, she had already conditioned many South Koreans to be controlled by her gaslighting ways.

In April 2022, Kim Yo Jong issued a nuclear threat on the South, her first. It was aimed ostensibly at the outgoing Moon administration, but in fact was intended for the incoming Yoon administration. During the campaign, Mr Yoon had openly talked about a pre-emptive missile attack option on the North in the event of clear signs of an imminent nuclear-tipped missile attack on the South.[18] Calling the South's Defence Minister a 'senseless and scum-like guy' for having spoken two days earlier of a 'pre-emptive strike' on North Korea's missile launch site if an imminent attack on the South was detected, she issued, 'by her authority', as she said, a 'serious warning' against South Korea. How could the 'confrontation maniac' dare mention a pre-emptive strike 'at a nuclear weapons state', she sallied.[19]

Just forty-eight hours later, she reinforced the threat, lest they forget: 'Two days ago, we solemnly warned that the south Korean army will face an unimaginably terrible disaster, the worst-ever, if it violates even an inch of our territory.' Once again, she threatened a pre-emptive nuclear attack on South Korea. '[O]ur nuclear combat force will have to inevitably carry out its duty,' she stated, which, again, would bring about a 'miserable fate little short of total destruction and ruin.' Never a laggard when it comes to mockery, she closed with a typical sneer. Calling the South Koreans 'frightened', she remarked: 'I pray that such morbid symptom as feeling threat for no ground would be cured as early as possible.'[20] The *Rodong Sinmun* published both her statements, conveying once again that she was her nation's top nuclear threat-issuing executive, even though the final authority rested with her brother.

In fact, her brother soon drove home the message. At a big, night-time military parade later that month, on the occasion of the ninetieth anniversary of the founding of the Korean People's Revolutionary Army, Kim Jong Un announced, 'If any forces try to violate the fundamental interests of our state, our nuclear forces will have to decisively accomplish their unexpected second mission.'[21] The second mission of the North's nuclear forces was the one Kim Yo Jong had outlined: if South Korea 'violated even an inch' of the North's territory even with conventional weapons (South Korea does not have any nuclear weapons), nuclear bombs would come its way.

In mid-May 2022, none other than Kim Jong Un himself acknowledged for the first time the spread of Covid-19 in his nation, including in the capital. Again calling the situation a 'great upheaval' to befall North Korea, he declared war on the virus. For the very first time, Kim Jong Un was shown in photos donning a mask, at times even two layers. Perhaps he felt even his own greatness may be no match for the invisible enemy.[22] But, in just three months, great leadership did prevail, and the virus was vanquished.

At a political gathering in August 2022, during which Kim Jong Un triumphantly declared 'brilliant victory' over Covid-19,[23] his sister gave a fiery speech that in phases was lachrymose, bellicose, and profane. It was the very first time that North Korean state TV had aired her voice. Brimming with love and reverence for her brother, she said that her 'country and people brought about an epoch-making miracle of defusing the unprecedented health crisis within the shortest period', thanks, naturally, to her brother's 'energetic and meticulous', indeed 'outstanding' leadership.[24] An appropriate tremor entering her voice, she revealed that her hard-working brother had himself fallen ill during this arduous task, gravely suffering from a 'high

Kim Yo Jong's first speech broadcast on North Korean television, at a party gathering where she revealed her brother had recently had a very high fever and also threatened to 'exterminate' the 'South Korean authority bastards'.

fever'. Yet the Great Leader had soldiered on, refusing to take to his bed 'even for one second', so committed was he to taking care of his people 'to the end'.

At this revelation of the Great Leader's susceptibility, moving and alarming at the same time, the audience – men and women of all ages – broke down, some heaving with shock and pain as they wiped away the tears streaming down their faces. The shock reverberating through the cavernous auditorium was genuine, since the health of the royal family, let alone that of the deified Supreme Leader, was a closely guarded secret that should be revealed with only the greatest discretion. No one else in the room could have mentioned it, reverently or other-wise. Only Kim Yo Jong, as Kim Jong Un's supreme deputy, could have brought it off, in a touching moment of sincerity further humanizing the devoted leader.

But Kim Yo Jong had more. The coronavirus, she raged, had been deliberately transmitted to her nation by South Korean 'human trash' and 'scumbags' (i.e. North Korean escapees turned human rights activists), who were 'worse than beasts'. The first traces of this 'malicious virus' in her kingdom were the coronavirus-contaminated 'leaflets, cash, and dirty booklets' such activists had put inside balloons and launched across the inter-Korean border, she informed the audience. Those who had dispatched such 'leaflets and dirty shit' into her country were guilty of a 'crime against humanity' and she promised a 'deadly retaliatory response'. The audience rose into cheers when she pledged that, should the 'enemies continue to do dangerous shit' that reintroduced the virus into her nation, she would 'exterminate' not only the virus but also 'the south Korean authority bastards'.

Later in the month, just to make her position on the 'south Korean authority bastards' even clearer, Kim Yo Jong issued her first diatribe against South Korea's new president, Yoon Suk Yeol, who had taken office just three months earlier. Once again, the *Rodong Sinmun* published her full statement. Three days earlier, in a major speech, the new South Korean leader had proposed an 'audacious initiative' of aid for denuclearization. If North Korea were to cease building up its nuclear programmes and turn to a 'genuine and substantive process for denuclearization', President Yoon had said, Seoul would not only provide 'large-scale' food aid but also wholly revamp the North's infrastructure – from building power plants, ports, hospitals, and airports to facilitating international financial investment in North Korea.[25] An 'absurd dream', was Kim Yo Jong's summary verdict. He would do better to 'shut his mouth, rather than talking nonsense.'[26]

She was taking no prisoners. Yoon's offer of aid in return for her nation turning towards denuclearization was 'most repulsive', 'ridiculous', and 'the height of absurdity' – about as much use as a dog's bark, and as practical as planting 'mulberry fields in the dark blue ocean'. Now she was on a roll, as she had been with his predecessor, President Moon, against whom she'd never passed up the chance to hurl insults. Moon's past 'pretensions' to be the 'driver' in inter-Korean relations were comical enough, she ranted, but this new president was 'excessively ignorant', 'foolish', 'miserable', and 'really simple and childish';

she actively disliked him as a human being, she said. 'No one barters its destiny for corn cake,' she chided the unlikable Yoon. As a parting shot, she made fun of both South Korea and the US for incorrectly identifying the time and place of her nation's missile launch the previous day.

The Kim siblings' bluster – both the ballistic and broadside kinds – swelled into a crescendo in the last quarter of the year. In September, Kim Jong Un promulgated the 'law on the state policy on the nuclear forces'. He set the conditions under which North Korea would resort to a nuclear strike in such broad and vague terms as 'taking an upper hand in a war' (Article 6 [4]) and 'inevitably compelled and cannot help but use nuclear weapons' (Article 6 [5]).[27] By conditioning his adversaries to the idea that he will nuke them whenever he deems it necessary, Kim Jong Un did his best to instil in them the belief that his nuclear weapons are here to stay and then some. And by posing for photos in mid-November with his young daughter after firing his nation's most powerful ICBM, the Hwasong-17 with a range of 15,000 kilometres, Kim intimated that the nuclear weapons he has built will certainly be passed on to the next generation.

The build-up to this climactic moment of theatre was just as dramatic. From late September to early October, Kim Jong Un carried out an unprecedented fifteen-day field guidance of his nation's tactical nuclear operation units, during which he oversaw seven nuclear-capable missile launches that, according to the state news agency, displayed the capacity to 'hit and wipe out the set of objects at any location and any time'. North Korea set a record for the year, with over seventy missiles fired.[28] On 2 November, it set a daily record with twenty-five missile flights, the previous highest tally for a single day having been eight, set back in June (and seven before that, way back in 2006). North Korea capped the year off by firing three ballistic missiles on New Year's Eve and rang in 2023 with one missile shot on New Year's Day. Then Kim Jong Un gloated, stating that the three on 31 December were nuclear-capable and could hit any part of South Korea. He also vowed to 'exponentially' increase the number of his nuclear warheads, launch a military satellite into space, and further enhance his ICBMs.

As in the past, his sister was with him every step of the way, playing the role of 'Even Worse Cop'. On 21 November, the United Nations Security Council (UNSC) convened a meeting to address North Korea's ICBM test in open breach of multiple Security Council resolutions. In a written statement the next day, Kim Yo Jong averred that the:

> Great irony is that as soon as the UNSC opening meeting was over, the US vented its anger on failure in realizing its sinister intention [passing a resolution punishing North Korea] while making public a disgusting joint statement together with such rabbles as Britain, France, Australia, Japan and south Korea, not concealing its bad mood. It reminds one of a barking dog seized with fear.[29]

Despite her nation's record-setting violations of UNSC bans on ballistic missile tests in 2022, the US had not been able to

galvanize Russia and China to sign off on even a single resolution. Putin's war in Ukraine and the atavistic resumption of
the Cold War dynamics of Moscow–Beijing–Pyongyang vs
Washington–Seoul–Tokyo meant that North Korea could go
on aiming for the heavens with impunity.

Days later, she took fiery exception to the South Korean
foreign ministry's invocation of the word 'provocation' and called
President Yoon 'stupid'. Calling South Korea a 'faithful dog'
and 'stooge of the US', she warned 'the impudent and stupid'
– the US and South Korea – to adhere to silence, or else.[30]

She saved the best for last in what had been an epic year.
On 19 November, her state news agency announced the first
successful launch of a spy satellite into space the previous day.
Quoting the nation's Aerospace Development Administration's
assessment of the test as 'an important success which has gone
through the final gateway process of the launch of a reconnais-
sance satellite', the news agency released low-resolution,
black-and-white photos of Seoul and Incheon taken from
space.[31] Analysts in South Korea and beyond remarked on the
poor resolution, to which the sister did not take kindly. In a
lengthy diatribe released the next day, she repeated the canine
cliché ('bark of the South Korean puppets', 'they can't actually
be dogs but . . . keep barking'), threw in a new avian metaphor
('As always, they were like a kind of chattering sparrow'),
expressed her concerns that South Korean analysts may soon
be out of work for doing such a poor job, called the South's
military experts 'military hooligans' and 'gangsters', and, just
to make it even more pungent, unleashed the following

sentence, which the state news agency utterly failed to translate properly: 'Well before their malicious criticism registers in my ear I smell their stinky breath emanating from their bawling traps' [this author's translation].

She sneered at South Korea's propensity to misidentify her nation's missile types and test-site locations. She scoffed at the South Korean military's boilerplate statements on 'carrying out precision tracking'. She took particular umbrage at the South Korean authorities' frequent statements that her nation's 'ICBM's atmospheric re-entry has not been recognized and verified'. She surmised this was a ploy 'just to comfort themselves'. The South had also detected 'high-angle' launches of ICBMs – instead of launches on a normal trajectory, but if they saw this as due to a lack of 'strategic weaponry capability', Kim Yo Jong insisted North Korea's enemies would 'immediately recognize' what her missiles were truly capable of if they were fired at a 'real angle'. With a serious warning comes, just to soften the blow, a disarming jeer. She described South Korea's missiles as having a range of just 'tens of metres'.

Thus, after having threatened earlier in the year to nuke South Korea, Kim Yo Jong capped off 2022 with a serious threat of an ICBM launch over the Pacific; that is, towards the United States. She made it clear that she would not be averse to waging war and killing South Koreans and Americans, should her 'more restrained' (at least on paper) brother support it.

In 2023, she issued two statements over consecutive days following her nation's first intercontinental ballistic missile launch of the year, on 18 February. Jeering at South Korean analysts as 'idiots' whom she felt 'an impulse to scoff at', and calling their analyses of her nation's missile technology 'very disgusting' and 'really stupid', she ended her 20 February riposte by warning that the 'frequency of using the Pacific as our firing range depends upon' the nature of 'US forces' action'.[32] This warning followed another from the previous day: 'By the power vested in me, I issue the following warning: We will watch closely every move by the enemy and take corresponding, very powerful, and overwhelming counteraction against its every hostile move against us' [this author's translation].[33] The next month she escalated still further. In a 7 March statement reminding her 'principal enemy' that the 'Pacific Ocean does not belong to the dominion of the US or Japan', any US attempt to shoot down her dynasty's intercontinental ballistic missiles screaming across the skies over the Pacific she will regard as a 'clear declaration of war.'[34] Thus she foreshadowed more powerful weapons tests, including an ICBM over the Pacific Ocean and a nuclear detonation to come and, in a typical North Korean move, created a pretext for them.

Over the past three years, Kim Yo Jong has remained her despotic nation's chief censor, spokeswoman, mocker, and threat-and-malice dispenser. All this makes Kim Yo Jong one of the most powerful leaders in the contemporary world, her nation's foreign policy at her fingertips, and with unfettered access to her nuclear button-controlling brother. At home, meanwhile, it is rumoured that she has gone beyond merely issuing threats to life.

* * *

In 2021, she was said to have gained the ultimate power of the cruel dictator; the power to play God and decide who lives and who is killed. She reportedly ordered several executions of high-ranking government officials for merely 'getting on her nerves'.[35] She banished those less disagreeable and their hapless families to detention camps and gulags, where a life of gruelling forced labour, beatings, torture, and starvation rations awaited. Rumours of her impulse to purge and kill individuals she found disagreeable became so widespread that top North Korean officials held their breath in her presence. When she drew near, they averted their gaze and stared at the floor. All tried assiduously to avoid falling out of grace with her, or even winning her praise, since just being recognized by her might in due course lead to a fall from favour and a brush with death. Repulsed by her cruelty, they called her a 'bloodthirsty demon' and 'devil woman' behind her back. Ordinary North Koreans also started referring to her as Empress Dowager Cixi, the ruthless de facto ruler of China's last imperial dynasty, in power for nearly fifty years.[36]

Yet the office she holds is not that of the head of state or even of a figurehead monarch. Nor is it even that of a cabinet minister. Since 2020, her formal rank in government is Vice Director of the Korean Workers' Party Central Committee, which falls somewhere in the top forty in the government hierarchy. Nonetheless, every one of her nominal superiors, except for one, her brother, bows down to her. They fear her.

In this family-owned absolute monarchy, it has been the king's prerogative to promote, demote, rehabilitate, and condemn anyone. The king's unassailable power encompasses all, including parents, siblings, brothers-in-law, cousins, nephews, uncles, aunts, and certainly in-laws. Cruelty on such a grand scale is the hallmark of the Kim dynasty. Its three generations have collectively committed homicide, fratricide, nepoticide, avunculicide, geronticide, pedicide, infanticide, neonaticide and, arguably, genocide.

That a female leader in the traditional dictator mould would emerge in a male-dominated country like North Korea is an oddity in itself. But Kim Yo Jong has risen to run her government's policy towards the United States and South Korea, while making men twice her age tremble and grovel before her. She is unparalleled in the contemporary world. As her power grows and tales of her ruthlessness spread, she will increasingly come to be viewed through the prism of being a 'bad woman': an 'un-womanish' character who has usurped the traditional male role of the strongman. But when she decides to put on a more pleasant face and reaches out to the world, as she and her brother did in 2018, it seems likely that many will once again naively place trust in her for no other reason than that she is a woman, and a young one at that. Any new overtures after the storm will become even more intoxicating than those that have come before. Just as governments have routinely underestimated the evil designs of the formerly unlikable North Korean despot, this time they will only be tempted to overestimate the goodwill of the formerly unlikable Mount Paektu despotess.

Her brother willing, she will wield this unique power for decades to come, as his deputy or, the spirits of her deceased predecessor Gods willing, even as the first female Supreme Leader in her nation's history.

ACKNOWLEDGEMENTS

I dedicate this book to John Curtis Perry, my teacher and dissertation advisor at the Fletcher School of Law and Diplomacy, Tufts University, and mentor for life. An inspiring teacher, demanding professor, and a most gifted orator, Professor Perry touched so many lives so deeply during the thirty-five years he taught at the Fletcher School. I am most privileged to have had such a mentor and friend in my life over the past three decades. Without you, John, this book would not have been conceived.

I am grateful to my Research Assistants who supported me, my brilliant former students at the Fletcher School: Donghe Liu, Gina Standard, Evan Tsao, Taehee Lee, Mina Kim, Daniel Choi and Joseph Lim.

Special thanks go to my literary agent, Barbara J. Zitwer, who has done so much to globalize Korean literature by representing South Korean authors, many of them gifted novelists with bestseller English translations, for example Han Kang (*The Vegetarian*). Barbara took a chance on me, encouraged me to write this book and guided me through its full course with trenchant advice and good cheer.

I cannot thank enough Ingrid for her sage advice and keen

attention to detail. Thank you, Ingrid, also for kindly connecting me with Graham, a masterful storyteller. I am also grateful to Rebecca and Fraser, who read my manuscript so carefully and offered such great advice.

My mother and father, from as far back as I can recall clearly – as a little boy, having just moved to London and struggling mightily to learn to speak English – have been my guiding stars. Without their boundless love, and without the warm support of my dear sister, this manuscript would have taken a longer and far more tortuous road in reaching its destination.

Finally, I thank my son, Russell, for putting up with extended silence from his dad as he sat motionlessly staring at the screen, and by whom I am humbled and occasionally inspired. At age six, looking at a cartoon of Kim Jong Un appearing emaciated and surrounded by walls, he asked, 'Daddy, is Kim Jong Un in jail? Does it mean we can now go to North Korea and the people aren't hungry any more?' No, son. But I pray for the day when the people of North Korea are no longer hungry and, at long last, free.

NOTES

CHAPTER I: THE PRINCESS COMETH

1   Treasury Sanctions Additional North Korean Officials and Entities in Response to the North Korean Regime's Serious Human Rights Abuses and Censorship Activities', United States Department of the Treasury Press Center, 11 January 2017. <https://www.treasury.gov/press-center/press-releases/Pages/jl0699.aspx>.

2   Anna Fifield, 'The "Ivanka Trump of North Korea" Captivates People in the South at the Olympics", *The Washington Post*, 10 February 2018. <https://www.washingtonpost.com/world/the-ivanka-trump-of-north-korea-captivates-people-in-the-south/2018/02/10/d56119fc-0e65-11e8-baf5-e629fc1cd21e_story.html>.

CHAPTER 2: THE MOUNT PAEKTU BLOODLINE

1   Zhihua Shen and Xia Yafeng, 'Contested Border: A Historical Investigation into the Sino–Korean Border Issue, 1950–64', *Asian Perspective*, Vol. 37, No. 1 (January–March 2013), 21.

2   'Kim Jong Il's Birth (1941.2.16)', *Daily NK*, 16 February 2005. <https://www.dailynk.com/%EA%B9%80%EC%A0%95%EC%9D%BC-%EC%B6%9C%EC%83%9D1941216/>.

3   'Kim Jong Il, North Korean Political Leader', *Encyclopedia Britannica* (last updated 13 December 2021). <https://www.britannica.com/biography/Kim-Jong-Il>.

4   Donald S. Zagoria and Young Kun Kim, 'North Korea and

the Major Powers,' *Asian Survey*, Vol. 15, No. 12 (University of California Press, December 1975), 1019.

5   Hannah Fischer, 'North Korean Actions, 1950–2007: Controversy and Issues,' *Congressional Research Service*, 20 April 2007. <https://www.everycrsreport.com/reports/RL30004.html>.

6   'Respected Comrade Kim Jong Un Has Photo Session with Contributors to Successful Test-fire of New-type ICBM Hwasongpho-17', Korean Central News Agency, 27 November 2022. <https://kcnawatch.org/newstream/1669504036-323166561/respected-comrade-kim-jong-un-has-photo-session-with-contributors-to-successful-test-fire-of-new-type-icbm-hwasongpho-17/>.

7   A term coined by my colleague Joshua Stanton, the principal drafter of the first US sanctions legislation on North Korea, the North Korea Sanctions and Policy Enhancement Act of 2016, and other North Korea sanctions acts that followed.

8   Robert Collins, *North Korea's Organization and Guidance Department: The Control Tower of Human Rights Denial* (Washington, D.C.: Committee for Human Rights in North Korea, 2019).

9   'First Vice Department Director of WPK Central Committee Issues Statement', Korean Central News Agency, 13 June 2020.

10   Kim Yo Jong, 'Vice-Director of Information and Publicity Department of WPK Central Committee Kim Yo Jong Releases Statement', Korean Central News Agency, 30 March 2021.

11   Jung Da-Min, 'What does Kim Yo-jong's SAC appointment mean?', *The Korea Times*, 1 October 2021. <https://www.koreatimes.co.kr/www/nation/2021/10/103_316335.html>.

12   Timothy W. Martin, 'Kim Jong Un Gets a Promotion, Gives His Sister a Demotion', *The Wall Street Journal*, 11 January 2021. <https://www.wsj.com/articles/kim-jong-un-gets-a-promotion-gives-his-sister-a-demotion-11610360602>.

13 'Press Statement of Vice Department Director of C.C., WPK Kim Yo Jong', Korean Central News Agency, 5 April 2022.

14 Sung-Yoon Lee, 'The Boy Who Would Be King: Can Kim III Last?' The National Bureau of Asian Research, 28 December 2011. <https://www.nbr.org/publication/the-boy-who-would-be-king-can-kim-iii-last/>.

15 Kim Yo Jong, 'Press Statement of Kim Yo Jong, Vice-Department Director of CC, WPK', Korean Central News Agency, 27 January 2023.

CHAPTER 3: PENINSULAR PREDOMINANCE

1 'Socialist Constitution of the Democratic People's Republic of Korea' (Pyongyang: 2014), 2.

2 Judith Munro-Leighton, 'The Tokyo Surrender: A Diplomatic Marathon in Washington, August 10–14, 1945', *Pacific Historical Review*, Vol. 65, No. 3 (August 1996), 460–1.

3 Michael Fry, '*National Geographic*, Korea, and the Thirty-Eighth Parallel: How a *National Geographic* map helped divide Korea', *National Geographic*, 14 August 2013. <https://www.nationalgeographic.com/science/article/130805-korean-war-dmz-armistice-38-parallel-geography>.

4 Michael Fry, '*National Geographic*, Korea, and the Thirty-Eighth Parallel'. Dean Rusk mis-recollects the events that led to the proposal to divide Korea at the thirty-eighth parallel, confusing the date on which the plan was conceived as 'August 14'.

5 Judith Munro-Leighton, 'The Tokyo Surrender', 462–4.

6 Wolfgang Saxon, 'Brig. Gen. George Lincoln Dies; Top Military Planner was 67', *The New York Times*, 26 May 1975. <https://www.nytimes.com/1975/05/26/archives/brig-gen-george-lincoln-dies-top-military-planner-was-67-strategist.html>.

7 David P. Fields, 'How Korea was divided and why the aftershocks still haunt us today', *The Washington Post*, 31 May 2019. <https://www.washingtonpost.com/outlook/2019/05/31/how-korea-was-divided-why-aftershocks-still-haunt-us-today/>

8   Baik Bong, *Kim Il Sung: Biography [I]: From Birth to Triumphant Return to Homeland* (Beirut, Lebanon: Dar Al-Talia, 1973), 529.

9   Andrew G. Walder and Yang Su, 'The Cultural Revolution in the Countryside: Scope, Timing and Human Impact', *The China Quarterly*, No. 173 (March 2003), 76–7. <https://www-jstor-org.ezproxy.library.tufts.edu/stable/pdf/20058959.pdf?ref reqid=excelsior%3A73aed758631a62f790381a49ce1c4ba0>.

10   For a portrayal of Jiang Qing, Mao's vindictive fourth wife, see Ross Terrill, *Madame Mao: The White-Boned Demon* (Stanford: Stanford University Press, 1999).

11   Valerie Strauss and Daniel Southerl, 'How Many Died? New Evidence Suggests Far Higher Numbers for the Victims of Mao Zedong's Era', *The Washington Post*, 17 July 1994. <https://www.washingtonpost.com/archive/politics/1994/07/17/how-many-died-new-evidence-suggests-far-higher-numbers-for-the-victims-of-mao-zedongs-era/01044df5-03dd-49f4-a453-a033c5287bce/>.

12   'The DPRK Attitude Toward The So-Called "Cultural Revolution" in China', Wilson Center Digital Archive, International History Declassified, 6 March 1967. <https://digitalarchive.wilsoncenter.org/document/114570>. Cited in Harry Kim, 'Mythbuster: Beijing's Relationship with Pyongyang', Wilson Center History and Policy Forum Blog Post, 12 July 2017. <https://www.wilsoncenter.org/blog-post/mythbuster-beijings-relationship-pyongyang>.

13   'Quarterly Chronicle and Documentation', *The China Quarterly*, No. 30 (April–June 1967), Cambridge University Press on behalf of the School of Oriental and African Studies, University of London, 195–249, 247. <http://www.jstor.org/stable/651878>.

14   David Rees, 'The New Pressure from North Korea', *Conflict Studies* (February–March 1970). Cited in Donald S. Zagoria and Young Kun Kim, 'North Korea and the Major Powers', *Asian Survey*, Vol. 15, No. 12 (University of California Press, December 1975), 1031.

15 Baik Bong, *Kim Il Sung: Biography [I]*, 560–1.
16 United Nations Peacemaker, Department of Political and Peacebuilding Affairs, 'Korean War Armistice Agreement Text'. <https://peacemaker.un.org/sites/peacemaker.un.org/files/KP%2BKR_530727_AgreementConcerningMilitaryArmistice.pdf>.

CHAPTER 4: ALL IN THE FAMILY

1 Lee Han-Young, *Kim Jong Il's Royal Family* [in Korean] (Seoul: Sidae Jeongshin, 2004), 81.
2 Anna Fifield, 'The secret life of Kim Jong Un's aunt, who has lived in the U.S. since 1998', *The Washington Post*, 27 May 2016. <https://www.washingtonpost.com/world/asia_pacific/the-secret-life-of-kim-jong-uns-aunt-who-has-lived-in-the-us-since-1998/2016/05/26/522e4ec8-12d7-11e6-a9b5-bf703a5a7191_story.html>.
3 Lee Han-Young, *Kim Jong Il's Royal Family* (Seoul: Sidae Jeongshin, 2004), 37.
4 Oh Dong-Ryong, 'Kenji Fujimoto, Kim Jong Il's Chef – An Exclusive Interview: The Kim Jong Un I Know', *The Monthly Chosun*, November 2010. <http://monthly.chosun.com/client/news/viw.asp?nNewsNumb=201011100010>.
5 Telephone interview with Ri Jong Ho, a former top North Korean official, 25 September 2022. In the 1980s, Mr Ri's wife worked on the *Man Gyong Bong* and saw the very important family travel to and from Japan several times.
6 Kenji Fujimoto, *Why Is It Kim Jong Un, North Korea's Successor?* tr. from Japanese to Korean by Han Yu-Hee (Seoul: Maksmedia, 2010), 111.
7 Kenji Fujimoto, *Why Is It Kim Jong Un, North Korea's Successor?*, 135.
8 Lee Young-Jong, *The Women of the House of Kim Jong Il* [in Korean] (Seoul: Neulpum Plus, 2013), 78–80.
9 Konstantin Pulikovsky, *Orient Express: Across Russia with Kim Jong Il* (Gorodetz, 2002), tr. Jong-Hwan Sung, *Dongbang Teukgeup Yeolcha* [Orient Express] (Seoul: Jungsim, 2003), 128–9.

10 Pulikovsky, the Russian special envoy, recounts Kim Jong Il telling a female Russian reporter at a dinner party in Pyongyang in 2002 that his best friend in life was his mother. Konstantin Pulikovsky, *Orient Express: Across Russia with Kim Jong Il*, tr. Jong-Hwan Sung, 224.

11 Lee Han-Young, *Kim Jong Il's Royal Family* (Seoul: Sidae Jeongshin, 2004), 99–104.

12 Joo Sung-Han, 'The Death of Kim Il Sung's Bastard Son, Kim Hyon' [in Korean], *The Donga Ilbo*, 26 May 2022. <https://www.donga.com/news/article/all/20220526/113623778/1>.

CHAPTER 5: THE NARCISSISTIC PSYCHOPATH FATHER

1 Lee Han-Young, *Kim Jong Il's Royal Family*, 191–7.

2 Bradley K. Martin, *Under the Loving Care of the Fatherly Leader: North Korea and the Kim Dynasty* (New York: Thomas Dunne Books, 2004), 208–9; 22–3.

3 John M. Glionna and Barbara Demick, 'Kim Jong Il visits China with his youngest son, South Korea says', *Los Angeles Times*, 26 August 2010. <https://www.latimes.com/archives/la-xpm-2010-aug-26-la-fg-0827-north-korea-china-20100827-story.html>.

4 'Kim Jong Il Pays Unofficial Visit to China', Korean Central News Agency, 30 August 2010. <https://kcnawatch.org/newstream/1451888777-102865159/kim-jong-il-pays-unofficial-visit-to-china/?t=1667595747486>.

5 'Kim Jong Il Pays Unofficial Visit to China', Korean Central News Agency, 30 August 2010.

6 Kim Chi-Gwan, 'Kim Jŏng Il: "I Once Lived Here"', *Tongil News*, 3 September 2010. <http://www.tongilnews.com/news/articleView.html?idxno=91656>.

7 'Kim Jong Il Pays Unofficial Visit to China', Korean Central News Agency, 30 August 2010.

8 'Report on Jimmy Carter's Visit to DPRK', Korean Central News Agency, 27 August 2010. <https://kcnawatch.org/

newstream/1451888728-806016173/report-on-jimmy-carters-visit-to-dprk/?t=1667596644182>.

9   Curtis Melvin, 'Kim Jong-il's only speech in North Korea', YouTube, 2 May 2011. <https://www.youtube.com/watch?v=v02nlU_ZATk>.

10 Lee Han-Young, *Kim Jong Il's Royal Family*,198–9.

11 Jang Jin-Sung, *Dear Leader: My Escape from North Korea* (New York: Atria, 2014), 132–41.

12 Lee Han-Young, *Kim Jong Il's Royal Family*, 200–2.

13 Delroy L. Paulhus and Kevin M Williams, 'The Dark Triad of Personality: Narcissism, Machiavellianism, and psychopathy', *Journal of Research in Personality* (Vol. 36, No. 6, 2002), 556–63. <https://doi.org/10.1016/s0092-6566(02)00505-6>. Special thanks to Han Sung Joseph Lim, my Tufts University student, for his final paper on the subject in Fall 2021.

14 'The 50 Countries Where It's Most Dangerous to Follow Jesus in 2021', *Christianity Today*, 13 January 2021. <https://www.christianitytoday.com/news/2021/january/christian-persecution-2021-countries-open-doors-watch-list.html>. Ryan Hamm, 'Why is Taliban No. 1 on the 2022 World Watch List?', Open Doors, 26 January 2022. <https://www.opendoorsusa.org/christian-persecution/stories/why-is-afghanistan-no-1-on-the-2022-world-watch-list/>.

15 Sandra Fahy, *Dying for Rights: Putting North Korea's Human Rights Abuses on the Record* (New York: Columbia University Press, 2019), 64–5.

16 David Hawk, 'Thank You Father Kim Il Sung: Eyewitness Accounts of Severe Violations of Freedom of Thought, Conscience, and Religion in North Korea', U.S. Commission on International Religious Freedom (November 2005), 44–5. <https://www.uscirf.gov/sites/default/files/Thank%20You%20Father%20Kim%20Il%20Sung%20-%20Nov2005.pdf>.

17   'You Cry at Night but Don't Know Why: Sexual Violence against Women in North Korea', Human Rights Watch, 1 November 2018. <https://www.hrw.org/report/2018/11/02/you-cry-night-dont-know-why/sexual-violence-against-women-north-korea#>.

18   'Rumors Appear with South Korean Couple', *The New York Times*, 23 March 1986. <https://www.nytimes.com/1986/03/23/world/rumors-reappear-with-south-korean-couple.html>.

19   Bradley K. Martin, *Under the Loving Care of the Fatherly Leader*, 208–9; 326–35.

20   'Victims abducted by North Korea throughout the world (2)', Victims of Japanese nationals abducted by North Korea. <http://www.sukuukai.jp/English/Victims2.html>.

21   Sung-Yoon Lee, *United States v. Christopher P. Ahn*, 14 May 2021. Statement Supplemental Exhibit A, Case 2:19-cv-05397-FLA-JPR Document 197-1, entered as expert witness testimony, 25 May 2021. Melanie Kirkpatrick, 'Did North Korea Abduct an American? David Sneddon may have been forced to teach Kim Jong Un', *The Wall Street Journal*, 29 September 2016. <https://www.wsj.com/articles/did-north-korea-kidnap-an-american-1475191557>.

22   'Missiles of North Korea', Center for Strategic International Studies, 24 March 2022. <https://missilethreat.csis.org/country/dprk/>.

23   Kim Jong Il, *The Complete Collection of Kim Jong Il's Works, Vol. 1* (Pyongyang: Workers' Party of Korea Publishing House, 2012). <https://web.archive.org/web/20191124051822/http://www.kcna.co.jp/item/2012/201202/news15/20120215-13ee.html>.

24   'The Time a Fishing Boat Disabled a North Korean Submarine', Sandboxx News, 6 August 2021. <https://www.sandboxx.us/blog/the-a-fishing-boat-helped-capture-a-north-korean-sub/>.

25   Yukyoung Lee, 'South Korea's Moon Becomes Kim Jong Un's Top Spokesman at UN', Bloomberg, 26 September 2018.

CHAPTER 6: STATE SECRETS

1   Anna Fifield, 'Who is Kim Yo Jong? Here's what we know about the North Korean "princess"', *The Washington Post*, 8 February 2018. <https://www.washingtonpost.com/news/worldviews/wp/2018/02/08/who-is-kim-yo-jong-heres-what-we-know-about-the-north-korean-princess/>.

2   Becky Branford, 'North Korea and the Brazil passports: Why were they used by the Kims?', BBC News, 1 March 2018. <https://www.bbc.com/news/world-asia-43242596>.

3   Lee Han-Young, *Kim Jong Il's Royal Family* (Seoul: Sidae Jeongshin, 2004), 180.

4   Conversation with Hyunseung Lee, a former member of the Workers' Party of Korea, in Cambridge, Massachusetts, 17 November 2022.

5   Robert Collins, *Marked for Life: Songbun, North Korea's Social Classification System* (Washington, D.C.: The Committee for Human Rights in North Korea, 2012). <https://www.hrnk.org/uploads/pdfs/HRNK_Songbun_Web.pdf>.

6   Robert Collins, *South Africa's Apartheid & North Korea's Songbun: Parallels in Crimes Against Humanity* (Washington, D.C.: The Committee for Human Rights in North Korea, 2021), 15.

7   Anna Fifield, 'The secret life of Kim Jong Un's aunt, who has lived in the U.S. since 1998', *The Washington Post*, 27 May 2016. <https://www.washingtonpost.com/world/asia_pacific/the-secret-life-of-kim-jong-uns-aunt-who-has-lived-in-the-us-since-1998/2016/05/26/522e4ec8-12d7-11e6-a9b5-bf703a5a7191_story.html>.

8   Lee Han-Young, *Kim Jong Il's Royal Family* (Seoul: Sidae Jeongsin, 2004), 105–14.

9   'In search of the grave of Song Hye Rim, mother of North Korean, Kim jong Nam', *Yonhap News*, 28 July 2009. <https://news.naver.com/main/read.naver?mode=LPOD&mid=sec&sid1=001&sid2=140&oid=001&aid=0002786216&isYeonhapFlash=Y>.

CHAPTER 7: THE APPRENTICE YEARS: 2007–2009

1   Kim Soe-jung, 'Roh comes North bearing gifts for Kim', *Korea JoongAng Daily*, 3 October 2007. <https://koreajoongangdaily. joins.com/news/article/article.aspx?aid=2881105>. Kim Sue-young, 'Dramas Introduce South's Culture to North', *The Korea Times*, 4 October 2007. <https://www.koreatimes.co.kr/www/nation/2021/08/113_11335.html>.

2   Dong-ju Yang, 'Yeokdae Jonggweonbyeol Daebuk Jiweongeum Byeoncheonsa' [역대 정권별 대북지원금 변천사]; History of Past Administrations' Financial Aid to North Korea], *Ilyo Sisa*, 22 February 2016. <https://www.ilyosisa.co.kr/news/article.html?no=96241>.

3   Madeleine Albright, *Fascism: A Warning* (New York: HarperCollins, 2018), 199–200.

4   As recounted to author by Laura Ling at Brewster Public Library, Brewster, Cape Cod, Massachusetts. 18 October 2014.

5   Telephone interview with Doug Band, 16 February 2021.

6   Personal conversation with Stephen Biegun in Seoul, 26 January 2023, during a visit for a series of meetings with top South Korean policymakers.

7   Eric Gibson, 'Why Dictators Love Kitsch Art: Kim Jong Il–Clinton photo op spotlights a style that's long glorified tyrants', *The Wall Street Journal*, 10 August 2009. <https://www.wsj.com/articles/SB10001424052970204908604574336383324209824>.

CHAPTER 8: FUNERAL AND REBIRTH

1   William Shakespeare, *Julius Caesar*, 2:2:31–3, *The Folger Shakespeare*. <https://shakespeare.folger.edu/shakespeares-works/julius-caesar/act-2-scene-2/>.

2   'Even Nature Seems to Mourn the Demise of Great Man', Korean Central News Agency, 22 December 2011. <https://kcnawatch. org/newstream/1451890319-111972249/even-nature-seems-to-mourn-demise-of-great-man/?t=1658235793730>.

3   Borrowing from the graceful last lines of 'The Dead', the last short story among fifteen by James Joyce, *Dubliners* (1914).

4   Elizabeth Shim, 'North Korea officially confirms Hyon Yong Chol's execution', *UPI*, 15 June 2015. <https://www.upi.com/Top_News/World-News/2015/06/15/North-Korea-officially-confirms-Hyon-Yong-Chols-execution/3271434354542/?ur3=1>.

5   'Traitor Jang Song Thaek Executed', Korean Central News Agency, 13 December 2013. <https://kcnawatch.org/newstream/1451900820-902618004/traitor-jang-song-thaek-executed/?t=1658245931014>.

6   'South Korean Media: Kim Jong Un's Younger Sister Replaces Her Aunt as North Korea's "No. 2 Figure"', *China Daily*, 14 March 2014.

CHAPTER 9: THE VILE VENTRILOQUIST

1   'Demystifying Kim Jong Un's Younger Sister Kim Yo Jong [Jin Yu Zheng]: She Has Entered the Core Leadership Circle in Her Twenties', *People's Daily Online*, 29 October 2014.

2   Brian Todd, Dugall McConnell and Joshua Berlinger, 'North Korean money man reveals smuggling operations', CNN, 3 August 2017. <https://www.cnn.com/2017/08/03/politics/north-korea-defector-ri-jong-ho/index.html>.

3   Telephone interviews with Ri Jong Ho, 28 June and 25 September 2022.

4   Adam Taylor, 'North Korea slams U.N. human rights report because it was led by gay man', *The Washington Post*, 22 April 2014. <https://www.washingtonpost.com/news/worldviews/wp/2014/04/22/north-korean-state-media-slams-u-n-human-rights-report-because-it-was-led-by-a-gay-man/>.

5   'Challengers to DPRK Will Never Be Pardoned: CPRK Spokesman', Korean Central News Agency, 27 April 2014. <https://kcnawatch.org/newstream/1546470894-98310727/challengers-to-dprk-will-never-be-pardoned-cprk-spokesman/?t=1659972950935>.

6   'Park Geun Hye Will Have To Pay Price For Treachery', *Rodong Sinmun*, 29 April 2014. <https://kcnawatch.org/newstream/1451903843-325704912/park-geun-hye-will-have-to-pay-price-for-treachery-rodong-sinmun/?t=1659973985317>.

7   'Park Geun Hye Censured as Root Cause of Disasters of Nation', Korean Central News Agency, 2 May 2014. <https://kcnawatch.org/newstream/1451896542-349676148/park-geun-hye-censured-as-root-cause-of-disasters-of-nation/?t=1659971899893>.

8   'Park Geun Hye Accused of Plan to Re-postpone Transfer of OPECON [sic]', Korean Central News Agency, 3 May 2014. <https://kcnawatch.org/newstream/1546470586-183586398/park-geun-hye-accused-of-move-to-re-postpone-transfer-of-opecon/?t=1659971899893>.

9   'Judgment of Park Geun Hye Demanded', Korean Central News Agency, 25 May 2014. <https://kcnawatch.org/newstream/1451896533-569827037/judgment-of-park-geun-hye-demanded/?t=1659973782076>.

10   'CPRK Slams Park Geun Hye's Reckless Remarks', Korean Central News Agency, 26 September 2014. <https://kcnawatch.org/newstream/1451896955-709931410/cprk-slams-park-geun-hyes-reckless-remarks/?t=1659972642046>.

11   'National Reunification Institute White Paper: Reporting Park Geun Hye's Crimes of Inter-Korean Confrontation' (조국통일연구원 백서 박근혜의 동족대결죄악 고발), National Reunification Institute (조국통일연구원), 27 May 2015. <https://tinyurl.com/zeh6zfrd>. Author's translation. KCNA left out all the vile invective in its abridged English translation, 'National Reunification Institute Indicts Park Geun Hye for Her Thrice-Cursed Treachery', Korean Central News Agency, 27 May 2015. <https://kcnawatch.org/newstream/1451904001-391538262/national-reunification-institute-indicts-park-geun-hye-for-her-thrice-cursed-treachery/?t=1660171975057>.

12   Lee Young-Jong, 'Kim Jong Un's Peculiar Sister Gains Prominence', *Korea JoongAng Daily*, 13 March 2014. <https://

koreajoongangdaily.joins.com/2014/03/13/politics/Kim-Jonguns-peculiar-sister-gains-prominence/2986358.html>.

13 Jonathan Capehart, 'North Korea's racist rant against "wicked black monkey" Obama', *The Washington Post*, 8 May 2014. <https://www.washingtonpost.com/blogs/post-partisan/wp/2014/05/08/north-koreas-racist-rant-against-wicked-black-monkey-obama/>.

14 Leon Watson, '"Wicked black monkey": White House furious over North Korea's racist Obama slur, in inexplicable rant from rogue regime's mouthpiece', *Daily Mail*, 9 May 2014. <https://www.dailymail.co.uk/news/article-2624059/Wicked-black-monkey-White-House-furious-North-Koreas-racist-Obama-slur-inexplicable-rant-rogue-states-mouthpiece.html>.

CHAPTER 10: THE PYONGYANG GAMES

1 'Trump to Kim: My nuclear button is "bigger and more powerful"', BBC News, 3 January 2018. <https://www.bbc.com/news/world-asia-42549687>.

2 Donald J. Trump, Address to the National Assembly of the Republic of Korea, 7 November 2017. Full transcript published by CNN. <https://www.cnn.com/2017/11/07/politics/south-korea-trump-speech-full/index.html>.

3 Kim Tong-Hyung, 'Not all South Koreans are happy about unified hockey team', Associated Press, 21 January 2018. <https://apnews.com/article/570d50b836754eb9ae408d24c4027941>.

4 Charlie May, 'Mike Pence won't allow North Korea to "hijack" messaging at Winter Olympics', Salon, 4 February 2018. <https://www.salon.com/2018/02/04/mike-pence-wont-allow-north-korea-to-hijack-messaging-at-winter-olympics/>.

5 Joshua Berlinger, 'US to impose "toughest ever" sanctions on North Korea, Pence warns', CNN, 7 February 2018. <https://www.cnn.com/2018/02/07/politics/pence-tokyo-north-korea-intl/index.html>.

6 Joshua Berlinger, 'US to impose "toughest ever" sanctions on North Korea, Pence warns'.

7   Jonathan Cheng, 'Heading to the 2018 Olympics? Choose your Korea carefully', *The Wall Street Journal*, 23 April 2015. <https://www.wsj.com/articles/heading-to-the-2018-olympic-games-choose-your-korea-carefully-1429830011>.

8   'Remarks by Vice President Pence in Press Gaggle at Cheonan Memorial', U.S. Embassy and Consulate in the Republic of Korea, 9 February 2018. <https://kr.usembassy.gov/020918-remarks-vice-president-pence-press-gaggle-cheonan-memorial/>.

9   Mike Pence, *So Help Me God* (New York: Simon & Schuster, 2022), 282–3.

10   Mike Pence, *So Help Me God*, 282.

11   Soyoung Kim, 'At Games reception, a hopeful dessert and a hasty exit', Reuters, 9 February 2018. <https://www.reuters.com/article/us-olympics-2018-opening-reception/at-games-reception-a-hopeful-dessert-and-a-hasty-exit-idUSKBN1FT20M>.

12   Mike Pence, *So Help Me God*, 282.

13   Telephone interview with Fred Warmbier, member of the Pence delegation, 26 March 2021.

14   Anna Fifield, 'Photo of historic handshake between North and South Korea goes viral', *The Washington Post*, 9 February 2018. <https://www.washingtonpost.com/news/worldviews/wp/2018/02/09/photo-of-historic-handshake-between-north-and-south-korea-goes-viral/>.

15   Telephone interview with Fred Warmbier, member of the Pence delegation, 26 March 2021.

16   Richard Knight, 'Are North Koreans really three inches shorter than South Koreans?', BBC News, 23 April 2012. <https://www.bbc.com/news/magazine-17774210>.

17   Telephone interview with Fred Warmbier, member of the Pence delegation, 26 March 2021.

CHAPTER 11: THE BLUE HOUSE VISIT

1   Ashley Parker, 'Pence was set to meet with North Korean officials during the Olympics before last minute cancellation',

NOTES

The Washington Post, 20 February 2018. <https://www.washingtonpost.com/politics/pence-was-set-to-meet-with-north-korean-officials-during-the-olympics-before-last-minute-cancellation/2018/02/20/89392dfe-1684-11e8-942d-16a950029788_story.html>.

2 Jung Woo-sang, 'Kim Yo Jong was in her final trimester when she visited Pyeongchang' ('Kim Yo Jong mansakdde Pyeongchang watda'; '김여정 만삭때 평창 왔다'), *The Chosun Ilbo*, 16 May 2018. <https://www.chosun.com/site/data/html_dir/2018/05/16/2018051600300.html>.

3 Michael Bassett, 'Kim Jong-un is Liberating North Korea', Fair Observer, 27 November 2015: 'Swiss-educated reformer Kim Jong-un is liberating North Korea by proliferating a capitalist, knowledge-based economy'. <https://www.fairobserver.com/region/asia_pacific/kim-jong-un-liberating-north-korea-32305/>.

4 Ruta Nonacs, M.D., 'Alcohol and Pregnancy: Attitudes and Patterns of Drinking Vary Around the Globe', Massachusetts General Hospital Center for Women's Health, 6 February 2020. <https://womensmentalhealth.org/posts/alcohol-pregnancy-attitudes-around-globe/>.

5 'Media Interpretation of the Arrogance Behind Kim Yo Jong's Fake Smile', TVBS, 23 February 2018. <https://tinyurl.com/5ewm2dbb>.

6 'Young Jin Moon, a nineteen-year-old South Korean student, said: "I think she is really beautiful, but she doesn't look friendly. Her chin is often raised and it looks like she often looks down on people." In the photo, when KYJ was waiting to meet with Moon Jae-in, her head was raised from time to time, and her eyes even had a trace of contempt.' Kao Zhi-En, 'What's Left Unsaid in Kim Yo Jong's Set of Facial Expressions?', HK01, 11 February 2018. <https://tinyurl.com/6vfckdcw>.

7 Kao Hua-Yuan, 'Kim Yo Jong's Smile Offensive Strategy Exposed by Japan Psychologist', HK01, 11 February 2018. <https://tinyurl.com/4emub58a>.

8 'Moon's visit to spy headquarters brings with it pro-North

symbol', One Korea Network, 5 June 2021. <https://onekoreanetwork.com/2021/06/05/moons-visit-to-spy-headquarters-brings-with-it-pro-north-symbol/>.

9   Park Minji, 'President Moon, utilizing the "Shin Young-Bok" word and painting, sends message to North Korea' ('문대통령, '신영복' 글화 서화 활용해 대북 메시지 전달'), *Kookmin Ilbo*, 10 February 2018. <http://news.kmib.co.kr/article/view.asp?arcid=0012121575&code=61111211&cp=nv>.

10   Kim Sung-Hoon, 'Who is Shin Young-Bok, whom President Moon told the North's Kim Young Nam he Admires?' ('문 대통령이 北 김영남 앞에서 존경한다 말한 신영복은 누구?'), *The Monthly Chosun*, 11 February 2018. <http://monthly.chosun.com/client/mdaily/daily_view.asp?idx=2860&Newsnumb=2018022860>.

11   Kim Sung-Hoon, 'Who is Shin Young-Bok, whom President Moon told the North's Kim Young Nam he Admires?'

12   Motoko Rich, 'United, They Fall: Korean Hockey Team Loses, 8–0, in Olympic Debut', *The New York Times*, 10 February 2018. <https://www.nytimes.com/2018/02/10/sports/unified-korean-hockey-team-.html>.

13   Sung-Yoon Lee, 'Sex and the City: The "Pyongyang Games"', The Hill, 13 January 2018. In this op-ed, the author adumbrated Kim Yo Jong's visit to South Korea: 'Should Kim [Jong Un] jazz it up further and send his own sister, Kim Yo Jong, the Pyeongchang Olympics will essentially become the North Korean Games, hosted and paid for by the South.' <https://thehill.com/opinion/international/370140-sex-and-the-city-the-pyongyang-games>.

14   Foster Klug, 'AP Explains: What's N. Korea up to with provocative visit?', Associated Press, 23 February 2018. <https://apnews.com/article/donald-trump-asia-pacific-ap-top-news-michael-pence-olympic-games-3d9f796d4b454d1298b64d40ac49cd6a>.

NOTES

CHAPTER 12: A KOREAN COMEDY OF ERRORS

1   *Juche! Towards a united, independent Korea: Fifteen historical and contemporary interviews with Kim Il Sung, President of the Democratic People's Republic of Korea* (Melbourne: New Democratic Publications, 1973).

2   Joshua Berlinger, Nick Thompson, and Euan McKirdy, 'North and South Korean leaders hold historic summit: Highlights', CNN, [updated] 5 June 2018. <https://www.cnn.com/asia/live-news/north-korea-south-korea-summit-intl/h_958d746fd25f03526d81451f7117c764>.

3   Yang Jung A, 'Park Wang Ja Shot from Behind', *Daily NK*, 1 August 2008. <https://www.dailynk.com/english/park-wang-ja-shot-from-behind/>.

4   'Statement of Kim Yo Jong, Vice Department Director of Workers' Party of Korea Central Committee', Korea Central News Agency, 2 May 2021. <https://kcnawatch.org/newstream/1620270980-652382873/statement-of-kim-yo-jong-vice-department-director-of-wpk-central-committee/?t=1628780928032>.

5   Laura Bicker, 'Drugs, arms, and terror: A high-profile defector on Kim's North Korea', BBC News, 11 October 2021. <https://www.bbc.com/news/world-asia-58838834>.

6   Han Ki-Ho, 'The Panmunjom Moon Jae In–Kim Jong Un Summit: Morning and Afternoon' ('판문점에서 문재인–김정은 정상회담'), *Pen and Mike*, 29 April 2018. <http://www.pennmike.com/news/articleView.html?idxno=5001>.

7   Hyonhee Shin, 'South Korea says North Korea nuclear plant documents were "just an idea"', Reuters, 31 January 2021. <https://www.reuters.com/article/us-southkorea-politics-northkorea/south-korea-says-north-korea-nuclear-plant-documents-were-just-an-idea-idUSKBN2A00CG>.

8   'Call me any time: Trump says he gave North Korea's Kim direct number', Reuters, 15 June 2018. <https://www.reuters.com/article/us-northkorea-usa-trump/call-me-any-time-trump-says-he-gave-north-koreas-kim-direct-number-idUSKBN1JB1R5>.

9   Kim Il Sung, *Juche! Towards a United, Independent Korea:*
      Fifteen historical and contemporary interviews with Kim Il Sung,
      President of the Democratic People's Republic of Korea
      (Melbourne: New Democratic Publications, 1973), 140.
10   Joshua Berlinger, Stella Ko and Jungeun Kim, 'North Korea
      to send special noodle-making machine (and chef) to DMZ
      for summit', CNN, 24 April 2018. <https://www.cnn.
      com/2018/04/24/asia/inter-korea-summit-dinner-menu-intl/>.

CHAPTER 13: WHO TRUMPED WHOM?

1   Bruce Harrison, 'Kim Jong Un welcomes South Korean
      envoys to dinner', NBC News, 5 March 2018. <https://www.
      nbcnews.com/news/north-korea/kim-jong-un-welcomes-
      south-korean-envoys-dinner-n853546>.
2   Lee Yong-Su, 'The "Denuclearization Dying Wish" Kim Jong
      Un Mentioned is Trickery Across Three Generations', *The
      Chosun Ilbo*, 8 March 2018. <https://www.chosun.com/site/
      data/html_dir/2018/03/08/2018030800330.html>.
3   'Trump and North Korea talks: Strange optics of the North
      Korea announcement', BBC News, 9 March 2018. <https://
      www.bbc.com/news/world-asia-43340070>.
4   'Trump-Kim summit: Kim Jong Un's Air China ride is
      Chinese Premier Li Keqiang's private jet, says Apple Daily',
      The Straits Times, 11 June 2018. <https://www.straitstimes.
      com/asia/east-asia/trump-kim-summit-kim-jong-uns-air-china-
      ride-is-chinese-premier-li-keqiangs-private>.
5   Karamjit Kaur and Seow Bei Yi, 'North Korea leader Kim
      Jong Un arrives in Singapore, welcomed by Foreign Minister
      Vivian Balakrishnan', *The Straits Times*, 11 June 2018.
      <https://www.straitstimes.com/singapore/3-singapore-bound-
      aircraft-one-believed-to-be-carrying-kim-jong-un-departed-
      pyongyang-on>.
6   Huileng Tan, 'Singapore shelled out $15 million for the
      Trump-Kim summit. Some question that expense,' *CNBC*, 13

June 2018. <https://www.cnbc.com/2018/06/13/singapore-shelled-out-15-million-for-the-trump-kim-summit.html>.

7   Morgan Gstalter, 'Trump on North Korea's human rights violations: "It's rough in a lot of places, not just there"', *The Hill*, 12 June 2018. <https://thehill.com/homenews/news/391772-trump-on-north-koreas-human-rights-violations-its-rough-in-a-lot-of-places-not>.

8   Ed Pilkington, 'Donald Trump shakes off Kim's human rights record: "He's a tough guy"', *The Guardian*, 14 June 2018. <https://www.theguardian.com/world/2018/jun/13/donald-trump-kim-jong-un-fox-news-human-rights>.

9   Veronica Stracqualursi and Stephen Collinson, 'Trump declares North Korea "no longer a nuclear threat"', CNN, 13 June 2018. <https://www.cnn.com/2018/06/13/politics/trump-north-korea-nuclear-threat/index.html>.

10 'United States-North Korea Singapore Summit Video', Destiny Pictures Production, 12 June 2018. <https://www.youtube.com/watch?v=A838gS8nwas&t=233s>.

11 Peter Baker, 'Coming Attractions: Trump Showed Kim a Faux Movie Trailer About a Transformed North Korea', *The New York Times*, 12 June 2018. <https://www.nytimes.com/2018/06/12/us/politics/trump-kim-jong-un-north-korea-faux-movie-trailer.html>.

12 'Pyongyang Joint Declaration of September 19, 2018', *The Korea Times*, 19 September 2018. <https://www.koreatimes.co.kr/www/nation/2018/09/103_255848.html>.

CHAPTER 14: THE ASCENT: MOUNTED PAEKTU PRINCESS

1   Hyonhee Shin, 'Smoke Signal: Kim Jong Un's sister rushed off her feet on Vietnam trip', Reuters, 28 February 2019. <https://www.reuters.com/article/us-northkorea-usa-kim-sister/smoke-signals-kim-jong-uns-sister-rushed-off-her-feet-on-vietnam-trip-idUSKCN1QH11F>.

2   Amos Harel and Aluf Benn, 'No Longer a Secret: How Israel Destroyed Syria's Nuclear Reactor', *Haaretz*, 23 March 2018.

<https://www.haaretz.com/world-news/MAGAZINE-no-longer-a-secret-how-israel-destroyed-syria-s-nuclear-reactor-1.5914407>.

3   Robert Rampton, '"We fell in love": Trump swoons over letters from North Korea's Kim', Reuters, 20 September 2018. <https://www.reuters.com/article/us-northkorea-usa-trump/we-fell-in-love-trump-swoons-over-letters-from-north-koreas-kim-idUSKCN1MA03Q>.

4   Jung In-Hwan, 'Kim Jong-un complained of "unnecessary" interest from Moon in a 2018 letter to Trump', *The Hankyoreh*, 26 September 2022. <https://english.hani.co.kr/arti/english_edition/e_northkorea/1060192.html>.

5   'KCNA on appointment of new U.S. deputy secretary of state', Korean Central News Agency, 3 April 2001. <https://kcnawatch.org/newstream/1452002381-408519385/kcna-on-appointment-of-new-u-s-deputy-secretary-of-state/?t=1660914319592>.

6   John Bolton, *The Room Where It Happened: A White House Memoir* (New York: Simon & Schuster, 2020), 320–1.

7   John Bolton, *The Room Where It Happened*, 323.

8   David K. Li, 'Michael Cohen's testimony: The 10 best lines from his hearing before Congress', NBC News, 27 February 2019. <https://www.nbcnews.com/politics/politics-news/michael-cohen-testimony-10-best-lines-his-hearing-congress-n977116>.

9   John Bolton, *The Room Where It Happened*, 325.

10   John Bolton, *The Room Where It Happened*, 326.

11   Hyonhee Shin and Joyce Lee, 'North Korea execute envoy to failed U.S. summit – media; White House monitoring', Reuters, 30 March 2019. <https://www.reuters.com/article/us-northkorea-usa-purge/north-korea-executes-envoy-to-failed-u-s-summit-media-white-house-monitoring-idUSKCN1T02PD>.

12   'Kim Jong Un Leaves Russia After Summit with Putin', *Voice of America* (originally published in the Associated Press), 26 April 2019. <https://www.voanews.com/a/kim-jong-un-leaves-russia-after-summit-with-putin/4892424.html>.

13 David Nakamura, 'In a tweet, Trump appears to invite Kim Jong Un to meet him at the Korean demilitarized zone', *The Washington Post*, 29 June 2019. <https://www.washingtonpost. com/politics/in-a-tweet-trump-appears-to-invite-kim-jong-un-to-meet-him-at-the-korean-demilitarized-zone/2019/06/28/ 0e9fc900-99f9-11e9-830a-21b9b36b64ad_story.html>.

14 Translation into English by the author. See Audrey Yoo, 'North Korea Rewrites Rules to Legitimize Kim Family Succession', *South China Morning Post*, 16 October 2013.

15 'Let Us Steadfastly Continue the Bloodline of the Revolution' [in Korean], Uri Minzokkiri, 10 June 2020. <http://www. uriminzokkiri.com/index.php?ptype=cgisas&mtype=view&no= 1193416>.

16 Korean Central TV, 16 October 2019. Urimizokkiri.com; Photos Nos. 21 (4:32 min) and 23 (5:09 min). <http:// uriminzokkiri.com/index.php?ptype=ccentv&stype=0&mtype= view&no=46261>.

17 Korean Central TV, 16 October 2019. Urimizokkiri.com; Photo No. 5 (1:13 min). <http://uriminzokkiri.com/index. php?ptype=ccentv&stype=0&mtype=view&no=46261>.

18 Korean Central TV, 16 October 2019. Urimizokkiri.com; Photo No. 5 (0:34 min). <http://uriminzokkiri.com/index. php?ptype=ccentv&stype=0&mtype=view&no=46261>.

19 Author's translation from the Korean: '세계가 괄목하는 경이적인 사변들을 펼치며 폭풍쳐 용진하는 우리 조국의 도도한 기상을 안고 장엄히 솟아있는 백두성산에 절세의 위인이 펼치신 전설같은 화폭과 특기할 자욱이 뜻깊게 새겨져 천지를 진감시키였다.' Korean Central TV, 16 October 2019. Urimizokkiri.com; Photo No. 3 (0:42-1:00 min). <http://uriminzokkiri.com/index.php?ptype=ccentv& stype=0&mtype=view&no=46261>.

20 Author's translation from the Korean: '위대한 김정은동지께서 몸소 백마를 타시고 백두산정에 오르시여 새기신 심원한 뜻과 거룩한 자욱은 이 조선을 세계가 부러워하는 최강의 힘을 가진 사회주의강대국으로 더 높이

떨쳐가실 원대한 웅지로 빛날것이며 우리 혁명의
완전승리를 앞당기는 력사적인 장거로 불멸할것이다.'
Korean Central TV, 16 October 2019. Urimizokkiri.com;
Photo No. 25 (5:43–5:59 min). <http://uriminzokkiri.com/
index.php?ptype=ccentv&stype=0&mtype=view&no=46261>.

CHAPTER 15: WEAPONIZING FOOD: A FAMILY PRACTICE

1   William Elliot Griffis, *Korea, the Hermit Nation* (New York: Scribner's, 1888).

2   Sandra Fahy, *Marching through Suffering: Loss and Survival in North Korea* (New York: Columbia University Press, 2015).

3   United Nations, General Assembly, Human Rights Council, *Report of the commission of inquiry on human rights in the Democratic People's Republic of Korea* (A/HRC/25/63), 7 February 2014, para. 76, p. 14/36. <https://www.ohchr.org/en/hrbodies/hrc/coidprk/pages/commissioninquiryonhrindprk.aspx>.

4   'Kim Jong Il Berates Cadres for Food Anarchy' (in Korean), *Wolgan Chosun*, 20 March 1997, pp. 306–317; 'Kim Jong Il, Speech at Kim Il Sung University, December 1996', BBC, 21 March 1997, as cited in United Nations, General Assembly, Human Rights Council, *Report of the commission of inquiry on human rights in the Democratic People's Republic of Korea* (A/HRC/25/CRP.1), 7 February 2014, para. 598, p. 176/372. <https://www.ohchr.org/en/hrbodies/hrc/coidprk/pages/commissioninquiryonhrindprk.aspx>.

5   United Nations, UN News: Global perspective Human stories, 'North Korean families facing deep "hunger crisis" after worst harvest in 10 years, UN food assessment shows', 3 May 2019. <https://news.un.org/en/story/2019/05/1037831>.

6   Choe Sang-Hun, 'North Korea Is Facing a "Tense" Food Shortage', *The New York Times*, 16 June 2021. <https://www.nytimes.com/2021/06/16/world/asia/north-korea-food-shortage.html>.

7   United Nations FAO, IFAD, UNICEF, WFP and WHO. 2022.

The State of Food Security and Nutrition in the World 2022. Repurposing food and agricultural policies to make healthy diets more affordable'. Rome, FAO (162–173). <https://www.fao.org/documents/card/en/c/cc0639en>.

8   United Nations FAO, IFAD, UNICEF, WFP and WHO. 2019. *The State of Food Security and Nutrition in the World 2019*. Safeguarding against economic slowdowns and downturns. Rome, FAO (146–158). Licence: CC BY-NC-SA 3.0 IGO. <tinyurl.com/y63skjxd>.

9   Joshua Stanton and Sung-Yoon Lee, 'Pyongyang's Hunger Games', *The New York Times*, 7 March 2014. <https://www.nytimes.com/2014/03/08/opinion/pyongyangs-hunger-games.html>.

10   'Kim Jong Il Berates Cadres for Food Anarchy' (in Korean), *Wolgan Chosun*, 20 March 1997, pp. 306–317; 'Kim Jong Il, Speech at Kim Il Sung University, December 1996', BBC, 21 March 1997, as cited in United Nations, General Assembly, Human Rights Council, *Report of the commission of inquiry on human rights in the Democratic People's Republic of Korea* (A/HRC/25/CRP.1), 7 February 2014. See paragraphs 423, 681, 689, 716, 773, 787, 842, 1046, 1078, 1084, 1103, and 1220. <https://www.ohchr.org/en/hrbodies/hrc/coidprk/pages/commissioninquiryonhrindprk.aspx>.

11   United Nations, General Assembly, Human Rights Council, *Report of the commission of inquiry on human rights in the Democratic People's Republic of Korea* (A/HRC/25/63), 7 February 2014, para. 78, p. 14/36. <https://www.ohchr.org/en/hrbodies/hrc/coidprk/pages/commissioninquiryonhrindprk.aspx>.

12   'Consultative Meeting of Political Bureau of C.C., WPK Held', Korean Central News Agency, 14 May 2022. <https://kcnawatch.org/newstream/1652508387-842122486/consultative-meeting-of-political-bureau-of-c-c-wpk-held/?t=1676057141116>.

13   Victor Cha and Dana Kim, 'A Timeline of South Korea's Response to Covid-19', Center for Strategic International Studies, 27 March 2020. <https://www.csis.org/analysis/timeline-south-koreas-response-covid-19>.

14 R. Ghosh, 'Kim Jong-un Orders Officials to Kill Pigeons and Cats as He Believes They are Carrying COVID from China', *International Business Times*, 29 May 2021. <https://www.ibtimes.sg/kim-jong-un-orders-officials-kill-pigeons-cats-he-believes-they-are-carrying-covid-china-57805>.

15 Josh Smith, 'Kim Jong Un suggests North Korea may begin COVID vaccinations', Reuters, 8 September 2022. <https://www.reuters.com/world/asia-pacific/kim-jong-un-suggests-nkorea-may-begin-covid-vaccinations-2022-09-09/>.

16 Frank Smith, 'Reports of people "starving" as N Korea struggles to feed itself', Al Jazeera, 1 July 2021. <https://www.aljazeera.com/news/2021/7/1/humanitarian-disaster-looms-in-north-korea>. See also Kim Chae Hwan, 'Around 20 residents of South Hwanghae Province die due to starvation', *Daily NK*, 3 June 2022. <https://www.dailynk.com/english/around-20-residents-south-hwanghae-province-die-due-starvation/>; Jong So Yong, 'Hoeryong authorities cremated around 20 bodies in late May', *Daily NK*, 10 June 2022. <https://www.dailynk.com/english/hoeryong-authorities-cremated-around-20-bodies-in-late-may/>.

17 Scott Neuman, 'North Korea's Kim Alludes to 1990s Famine, Warns of "Difficulties Ahead of Us"', National Public Radio, 9 April 2021. <https://www.npr.org/2021/04/09/985743058/north-koreas-kim-alludes-to-1990s-famine-warns-of-difficulties-ahead-of-us>.

18 Carl Samson, 'North Korea urges citizens to eat less until 2025 – resorting to black swan for meat', Yahoo, 1 November 2021. <https://www.yahoo.com/now/north-korea-urges-citizens-eat-202541304.html>.

19 Ifang Bremer, '3 years into pandemic, fears mount North Korea is teetering toward famine', *NK News*, 15 February 2023. <https://www.nknews.org/2023/02/3-years-into-pandemic-fears-mount-that-north-korea-is-teetering-toward-famine/>.

20 Republic of Korea Ministry of Unification, 'Policy on North

Korea Defectors: Number of North Korean Defectors Entering South Korea'. <https://www.unikorea.go.kr/eng_unikorea/relations/statistics/defectors/>.

21 Hyonhee Shin, 'North Korea paper calls outside aid "poisoned candy", urges self-reliance', Reuters, 21 February 2023. <https://www.reuters.com/world/asia-pacific/north-korea-paper-calls-outside-aid-poisoned-candy-urges-self-reliance-2023-02-22/>.

CHAPTER 16: TWISTED SISTER

1 'First Vice-department Director of WPK Central Committee Kim Yo Jong Blasts Chongwadae's Foolish Way of Thinking', Korean Central News Agency, 3 March 2020.

2 'First Vice Department Director of Workers' Party of Korea Central Commission Issues Statement', Korean Central News Agency, 13 June 2020.

3 'Kim Yo Jong Rebukes S. Korean Authorities for Conniving at Anti-DPRK hostile Act of "Defectors from North"', Korean Central News Agency, 4 June 2020.

4 William Shakespeare, *Richard II*, 3.2. <https://stateofshakespeare.com/?page_id=5862>.

5 'North Korea: Kim Jong-un "suspends military action" against South', BBC News, 24 June 2020. <https://www.bbc.com/news/world-asia-53159577>.

6 Hwang In-Chan and Yoon Sang-Ho, 'To the North's "Block by Law" demand, [South Korea] officially pushes ahead with "North Korea Leaflets Prohibition Law"', *The Dong-A Ilbo*, 5 June 2020. <https://www.donga.com/news/article/all/20200605/101372136/1>.

7 Hyung-Jin Kim, 'S. Korea bans flying of leaflets toward N. Korea by balloon', Associated Press, 14 December 2020. <https://apnews.com/article/seoul-south-korea-north-korea-legislation-moon-jae-in-23e329d4e25a8711be1a06859613a317>.

8 Josh Rogin, 'South Korea's new anti-leaflet law sparks backlash in Washington', *The Washington Post*, 17 December 2020.

<https://www.washingtonpost.com/opinions/2020/12/17/south-koreas-new-anti-leaflet-law-sparks-backlash-washington/>.

9   Lord Alton of Liverpool et al., 'Representations Made To the UN Foreign Secretary about the Republic of Korea's "Gag Law"', 20 December 2020. <https://www.davidalton. net/2020/12/20/representations-made-to-the-uk-foreign-secretary-about-the-republic-of-koreas-gag-law/>.

10   Choe Sang-Hun, 'North Korean Accused of Plotting Against Fellow Defector', *The New York Times*, 16 September 2011. <https://www.nytimes.com/2011/09/17/world/asia/north-korean-arrested-in-alleged-plot-against-fellow-defector.html>.

11   Joshua Stanton, *Arsenal of Terror: North Korea, State Sponsor of Terror* (Washington, D.C.: Committee for Human Rights in North Korea, 2015), 65. <https://www.hrnk.org/uploads/pdfs/4_27_15_Stanton_ArsenalofTerror.pdf>.

12   Fabian Kretschmer, 'Fighting Kim Jong Un's regime with balloons', *Deutsche Welle*, 2 October 2017. <https://www.dw.com/en/fighting-kim-jong-uns-regime-with-balloons/a-40779878>.

13   'DPRK: CPUK', 31 July 2012.

14   'Statement of Kim Yo Jong, Vice Department Director of Workers' Party of Korea Central Committee', Korean Central News Agency, 2 May 2021.

15   Hyung-Jin Kim, 'S. Korea raids activist's office over anti-North leaflets', Associated Press, 6 May 2021. <https://apnews.com/article/asia-pacific-pyongyang-seoul-south-korea-north-korea-68dd5843d4ec408ba3f2cb76b59500c5>.

16   Choe Sang-Hun, 'Fiery North Korean Charged Under New Propaganda Law', *The New York Times*, 28 January 2022. <https://www.nytimes.com/2022/01/28/world/asia/korea-border-leaflets-speech-law.html>.

CHAPTER 17: THEY CALL HER 'DEVIL WOMAN'

1   Kim Yo Jong, 'Press Statement by the First Vice Department

Director of the Central Committee of the Workers' Party of Korea', Korean Central News Agency, 10 July 2022.

2   Euan McKirdy, 'North Korea state media celebrates "gift" to "American bastards"', CNN, 5 July 2017. <https://www.cnn.com/2017/07/05/asia/north-korea-missile-nuclear-gift/index.html>.

3   Choe Sun Hui, 'Statement of First Vice-Foreign Minister of DPRK', Korean Central News Agency, 4 July 2020.

4   Kim Yo Jong, 'Statement of Vice Department Director of the Workers' Party of Korea Central Commission (January 12)', Korean Central News Agency, 13 January 2021.

5   Republic of Korea, Cheong Wa Dae, '2020 New Year's Address by President Moon Jae In', 11 January 2021. <https://english1.president.go.kr/briefingspeeches/speeches/931>.

6   Mitch Shin, 'President Moon Is Still Hopeful for North Korea Talks', *The Diplomat*, 19 January 2021. <https://thediplomat.com/2021/01/president-moon-is-still-hopeful-for-north-korea-talks/>.

7   'Great Programme for Struggle Leading Korean-style Socialist Construction on Fresh Victory Report Made by Supreme Leader Kim Jong Un at Eight Congress of WPK', Korean Central News Agency, 10 January 2021. <https://tinyurl.com/v73s8ens>.

8   Mitch Shin, 'Seeking North Korea Breakthrough, Seoul Looks to Biden Administration', *The Diplomat*, 3 February 2021. <https://thediplomat.com/2021/02/seeking-north-korea-breakthrough-seoul-looks-to-biden-administration/>.

9   Kim Yo Jong, Vice Department Director of the Central Commission of the Workers' Party of Korea, 'It Will Be Hard to See Again Those Spring Days Three Years Ago', Korean Central News Agency, 16 March 2021.

10   'Vice-Director of Information and Publicity Department of WPK Central Committee Kim Yo Jong Releases Statement', Korean Central News Agency, 30 March 2021.

11   John Haltiwanger, 'North Korea's Kim Jong Un Promotes Ex-Girlfriend to Top Government Job', *Newsweek*, 10 October

2017. <https://www.newsweek.com/north-koreas-kim-jong-un-promotes-ex-girlfriend-top-government-job-681994>. That Ms Hyun was Kim Jong Un's girlfriend has been confirmed by former North Korean officials who have escaped their country of birth.

12   Hung-Jin Kim & Kim Tong-Hyung, 'Kim sister derides U.S. official, dismissed chances for talks', Associated Press, 22 June 2021. <https://apnews.com/article/kim-yo-jong-derides-us-offiicial-dismisses-chance-for-talks-cc6b22f5dd72151d8e6761ab244570f0>.

13   'Vice Department Director of the Workers' Party of Korea Central Committee Kim Yo Jong Releases Press Statement', Korean Central News Agency, 1 August 2021.

14   'Vice Department Director of the Workers' Party of Korea Central Committee Kim Yo Jong Releases Press Statement', Korean Central News Agency, 10 August 2021.

15   Choe Sang-Hun, 'North Korea Fires 2 Ballistic Missiles as Rivalry with South Mounts', *The New York Times*, 15 September 2021. <https://www.nytimes.com/2021/09/15/world/asia/north-korea-ballistic-missiles.html>.

16   'Kim Yo Jong, Vice Department Director of WPK Central Committee, Makes Press Statement', Korean Central News Agency, 15 September 2021.

17   'Kim Yo Jong, Vice Department Director of C.C., WPK, Issues Press Statement', Korean Central News Agency, 25 September 2021.

18   Hyung-Jin Kim, 'Kim's sister enraged by Seoul's preemptive strike comment', Associated Press, 3 April 2022. <https://apnews.com/article/business-moon-jae-in-kim-yo-jong-south-korea-north-korea-969792db0f11306ece138e5574058364>.

19   'Press Statement of Kim Yo Jong, Vice Department Director of C.C., WPK', *Rodong Sinmun*, 3 April 2022. North Korea's official English translation mistranslated Kim Yo Jong's original Korean phrase, '나도 위임에 따라 엄중히 경고하겠다' ('By the authority granted me I will give a serious warning') as 'I will

give a serious warning upon authorization.' <https://kcnawatch.
org/newstream/1648959613-495460960/press-statement-of-kim-
yo-jong-vice-department-director-of-c-c-wpk/>.

20 'Press Statement of Vice Director of C.C. WKP Kim Yo
Jong', *Rodong Sinmun*, 5 April 2022. <https://kcnawatch.org/
newstream/1649138673-332467186/press-statement-of-vice-
department-director-of-c-c-wpk-kim-yo-jong/>.

21 Yi Wonju and Chae Yun-hwan, 'In military parade, North
Korean leader vows to strengthen nuclear power', Yonhap
News Agency, 26 April 2022. <https://en.yna.co.kr/view/
AEN20220426005352325?section=nk/nk>.

22 Lili Pike, 'Why Kim Jong Un is "freaking out": North
Korea's covid nightmare', The Grid, 20 May 2022.

23 'Brilliant Victory Gained by Great People of DPRK:
National Meeting of Reviewing Emergency Anti-epidemic
Work Held, Respected Comrade Kim Jong Un Makes
Important Speech at Meeting', Korean Central News Agency,
11 August 2022. <https://kcnawatch.org/newstream/16603958
86-735757779/brilliant-victory-gained-by-great-people-of-
dprknational-meeting-of-reviewing-emergency-anti-epidemic-
work-heldrespected-comrade-kim-jong-un-makes-important-
speech-at-meeting/?t=1676054273682>.

24 Jeongmin Kim, 'Full Text: Kim Yo Jong's obscenity-laced
denunciation of South Korean "enemies"' (unofficial
translation), NK News, 12 August 2022. <https://www.
nknews.org/pro/full-text-kim-yo-jongs-obscenity-laced-
denunciation-of-south-korean-enemies/?t=1663326578647>.

25 'Full text of Yoon's Liberation Day speech', Yonhap News
Agency, 15 August 2022. <https://en.yna.co.kr/view/
AEN20220815001600315>.

26 Kim Yo Jong, 'Press Statement of Vice Department Director of
C.C., WPK Kim Yo Jong: Don't have an absurd dream', Korean
Central News Agency, 19 August 2022. <https://kcnawatch.org/
newstream/1660921729-881735367/press-statement-of-vice-
department-director-of-c-c-wpk-kim-yo-jong/>.

27   Jeongmin Kim, 'Full text: How North Korea transformed its nuclear doctrine law', NK News, 9 September 2022. <https://www.nknews.org/pro/full-text-how-north-korea-transformed-its-nuclear-doctrine-law/>.

28   Hyung-Jin Kim, 'N Korea's Kim orders "exponential" expansion of nuke arsenal', Associated Press, 1 January 2023. <https://apnews.com/article/politics-north-korea-south-895fb34033780fdafd5bf925b376a2c6>.

29   'Press Statement of Kim Yo Jong, Deputy Director of WPK C.C.', Korean Central News Agency, 22 November 2022. <https://kcnawatch.org/newstream/1669129874-63040339/press-statement-of-kim-yo-jong-deputy-department-director-of-wpk-cc/>.

30   'Press Statement of Kim Yo Jong, Deputy Director of WPK C.C.', Korean Central News Agency, 24 November 2022. <https://kcnawatch.org/newstream/1669259019-497600999/press-statement-of-kim-yo-jong-deputy-department-director-of-wpk-cc/>.

31   Hyung-Jin Kim, 'North Korea says latest launches tested 1st spy satellite', Associated Press, 19 December 2022. <https://apnews.com/article/seoul-south-korea-north-c971c80155b62ff11d0fb473cdd7f76f>.

32   'Press Statement of Kim Yo Jong, Vice Department Director of C.C., WPK Issued,' Korean Central News Agency, 20 February 2023.

33   'Statement of Kim Yo Jong, Vice-Department Director of C.C., WPK,' Korean Central News Agency, 19 February 2023.

34   'Press Statement by Kim Yo Jong, Vice Department Director of C.C., WPK', Korean Central News Agency, 7 March 2023.

35   Hyemin Son, 'Officials Scared After Sister of North Korean Leader Has Their Colleagues Executed', tr. Leejin Jun, Radio Free Asia, 18 May 2021. <https://www.rfa.org/english/news/korea/kyj-05182021171329.html>.

36   Hyemin Son, 'Officials Scared After Sister of North Korean Leader Has Their Colleagues Executed'.

Index

Page numbers in **bold** indicate photos.

Abe, Shinzo 5, 123
Afghanistan 62–3
Albright, Madeleine 68, 93
Alton, David, Baron 220
An Hak-Young 221
As I Saw It (Rusk) 30
assassinations 20, 85–7, 221

Bach, Thomas 5, 141
Baier, Bret 173
Baik Bong 31–2
Balakrishnan, Vivian 167
Band, Doug 100, 101–5
Band, Dr Roger 102, 103
Barrett, Edward 36
Biden, Joe 229, 232
Biegun, Stephen 102
Blue House, Seoul 4, 89, 131–4, **135**, 136–41, 142
Bolton, John 189–90, 225–6
Bonesteel, Charles 30
Brazil 78
Bush, George W. 99, 188

Carter, Jimmy 56, 100
Cheonan, ROKS 124, 141, 150
China
    Chairman's power 177
    Covid-19 pandemic 209
    Cultural Revolution 33
    human trafficking 98
    Kim family members visits to 54–6, 162–5
    Kim Jong Il's youth in 54, 55
    Korean War, role in 33–4, 35, 37
    Nixon's visit 67
    North Korea, relations with 6, 14–15, 32–5, 54–6, 67, 162–5, 167, 204
    Sino–Indian War (1962) 32
    Six-Party Talks 94
    South Korea, relations with 204
    UNSC resolutions 235, 244
    Westernization 201–2
Cho Myoung-gyon 3, 6, 8, 141
Choe Hwi 7, 9, 143
Choe Ryong Hae 76, 89
Choe Son Hui 165–6, 168, 226–7
Choe Thae Bok 111
Choe Yong Rim 112
Choi Eun-Hee 64–6
Chonlima horse 152
Christians, persecution of 61–2, 63
Chun Doo Hwan 64
Chung Eui-Yong 160–1, 162
Chung Sye-Kyun 229

Clark, Mark W. 37
Clinton, Bill 68, 97–105
Cohen, Michael 190, 191
Comedy of Errors, The (Shakespeare)
146
Covid-19 pandemic 19, 209–12, 238,
239, 240–1

Dae Jang Geum TV series 90
Dangun 15
Democratic People's Republic of
Korea (DPRK) *see* North Korea

Fahy, Sandra 204
Fighters for Free North Korea 221
'Footsteps' (Pochonbo Electronic
Ensemble) 96–7
France 47–8
Freedom House, South Korea 144,
147
Fujimoto, Kenji 44–7, 76–7

Gomes, Aijalon 56

Han Bok-Ryeo 90
Harrison, William K., Jr. 37
Heaven Lake, China–North Korea
border 14, 15
Ho Jong Man 46
Hong Il Chon 40
hostage diplomacy 56, 97–106, 121,
139
Hu Jintao 54, 56
human rights abuses 62–3, 98, 116,
120–1, 123, 124–5, 172–3, 204–8;
see also North Korea, executions
and disappearances
Hyon Song Wol 231
Hyon Yong Chol 110
Hyunseung Lee 20

Im Jong-Seok 142
inter-Korean summits
2000 68, 71–2, 88, 89, 91–2, 145
2007 88–96, 145, 178, 181–2
2018, April
crossing MDL 146–7
evening banquet and concert
156–9

handshake across MDL 144, 146
inter-Korean energy cooperation
153–4
Kim Jong Un's 'transformation'
145, 146–7, 148, 155
Kim Yo Jong's participation 144,
145–6, 147, 148, 149–50, 151–2,
154, 156–7, 158, 159
meetings in Peace House
149–52, 154
Panmunjom Declaration 154,
155–6
private conversation 153–4
public perception of 146–7, 148,
158–9
statements 154, 155
success for North 155–6, 156–7,
158–9
tree-planting 152
2018, May 166
2018, September 177–8, **179**,
180–3
Israel 188

Jang Song Thaek 22–3, 76, 110–11,
111–12, 114, 115
Japan
Kim family visits to 46
Kim Jong Nam's deportation from
79
Ko Yong Hui's birthplace 80
Korea as colony of 13–14, 15, 80,
180, 202
Korean emigrees to 80–2
Korean fight for independence
from 6–7, 13–14, 15, 31–2, 180
North Korea's abductions 66–7
Six-Party Talks 94
under US occupation 37
USSR, war with 29, 32
Westernization 201, 202
Ji Soeng-Ho 123
Jiang Qing 33
Jo Yong Won 231
Julius Caesar (Shakespeare) 108

Kang Ban Sok 83
Kang Kyung-wha 183
Khrushchev, Nikita 32–3

INDEX

kidnappings 52, 64–7, 97–105
Kim, Andrew 102
Kim Chang Son 8, 9, 10
Kim Chun Song 41, 48
Kim Dae Jung 68, 71–2, 88, 90, 91–2, 132–3
Kim Hye Kyong 40
Kim Hyok Chol 191–2
Kim Hyon 50, 86
Kim Hyong Jik 83–4
Kim Il Sung
  1953 armistice agreement 37–8
  Baik's biography of 31–2, 33–4, 34–5
  birthday 42, 230–2
  China, youth in 54, 55
  'Chonlima speed' 151–2
  death 13, 40
  'denuclearization' wish 160–1, 161–2
  divinity and infallibility 14
  executions 33, 191
  heroic narrative of 6–7, 13–14, 16, 31–2, 34–5, 195
  Hyon, birth of 50
  Korean War (1950–1953) 33–7, 53–4
  losing power to son 58–9
  mausoleum 76, 204
  parents, Christian 83–4
  'the press,' definition of 155
  religious persecutions 61–2, 81
  reunification goal 31, 36
  secrets kept from 41, 82
  Shin Young-Bok 139
  'side branches' of family 48–9
  South Korea, invasion of 1
  in Soviet army 16, 54
  Soviet support for 32–3, 52–3
  US view of 36–7
Kim Jong Chol 4, 20, 44, 45, 46–7, 50, 73–4, 76, 77, 86, 97, 167
Kim Jong Gak 110
Kim Jong Il
  accession 13, 16, 40
  assassinations, ordering 85–7
  birth 15–16
  birthday 42
  childhood 52–4, 55

children 20, 40–1, 42, 48, 50, 73–4; *see also* Kim Jong Un; **Kim Yo Jong**
children's education abroad 77, 78
China, 2010 visit to 54–6
death and funeral 13, 23, 107, 108–9, 112
death of Ko Yong Hui 47–8
executions and disappearances 50, 58–9, 59–61, 66–7, 86–7
exposés on 44–5, 51–2, 76–7, 85
father's 'denuclearization' wish 161–2
'food as weapon' scheme 204–6, 208
foreign relations
  hostage diplomacy 97–105
  South Korea 68, 71–2, 88–96, 145, 178, 181–2
  USA 68, 93, 97–105, 105–6, 187
  use of threats to achieve goals 69–70, 91–2, 99
hedonism 51–2, 57–8, 68–9, 73
human rights abuses 204–6, 208
international terrorism 63–4
Jong Il Peak 15
kidnapping foreigners 52, 64–7, 97–105
during Korean War 54, 55
minjok (ethnic Koreans) 156
named 'heir apparent' 41, 59
naming Jong Un as successor 77, 96–7
nuclear weapons 69, 90, 99
photographs 16, 74, 75–6, 97
power, consolidating 58–9
Propaganda and Agitation Department 23
public persona 57, 91–2, 145
'side branches' of family 49–50
Song Hye Rang 86
stroke 77
'Ten Principles' 195
women 40–2, 47, 79–80
Yo Jong, doting on 4, 45
Kim Jong Nam 20, 40, 41, 43–4, 50, 77, 78, 79, 82, 85–6, 125
Kim Jong Nyo 45–6
Kim Jong Suk 42, 53

Kim Jong Un
  2010 China visit 54–6
  2019 visits to Mount Paektu 196–8, **199**, 200
  absolute power 12, 26, 247–8
  accession 13, 23, 113
  birthday 42, 43
  children 20–2
  Covid-19 pandemic 209–12, 238, **239**, 240
  denuclearization promises 154, 160–1, 162, 166, 171, 172
  education abroad 77
  executions and disappearances 22–3, 60, 85–6, 109–11, 191–2
  father's funeral 107, 109
  'food as weapon' scheme 207
  foreign relations
    China 162–5
    hostage diplomacy 101–5, 121
    refusal to chat on phone 154–5
    Russia 192–3
    South Korea 11, 26, 141–2, 143, 166, 177–8, **179**, 180–3, 237–8; *see also* inter-Korean summits, 2018, April
    USA 38–9, 60, 102, 119, 120, 188–9, 193–4, 232; *see also* United States–North Korea relations, 2018 Summit
  use of threats to achieve goals 68, 141–2, 163–4, 187
  Fujimoto's exposé 44–5, 76–7
  General Secretary title 227
  grandfather's birthday 230–1
  health problems 19
  letter to President Moon 11, 134, 139
  mother's Japanese birth 79, 82
  Mount Paektu Bloodline, importance of 194–5
  name 74–5
  named 'heir apparent' 77, 96–7
  names, false 77–8
  nuclear weapons 20–1, 26, 68, 105, 120, 121, 163–4, 194, 226, 234–8, 242–3, 245–6
  photographs 16–17, 73–4, 75–6, 82–3, 97, **169**, **179**, 197–8, **199**

'side branches' of family 48–9, 50
sister as heir, designating 196–8, **199**, 200, 227–8
sister, promotion of 23, 25, 227–8
sister, trust in/closeness to 24, 176–7, 186, 196–8, 218, 238, **239**, 240
'Ten Principles' 195
Kim Ju Ae (Ju Un) 20–2
Kim Jung-Sook 156
Kim Ki Nam 74, 111, 132
Kim Kyong Hui 17, 54, 55, 75
Kim Ok 47, 48
Kim Shura 53
Kim Sol Song 41, 48
Kim Song Ae 48–9
Kim Song Gap 48–9
Kim Song Hye 9, 10
Kim Yang Gon 132
Kim Yo Jong
  at 2018 Winter Olympics *see* Olympics, 2018 Winter
  2021 celebration of grandfather's birthday 230, 231–2
  appointed 'First Secretary of the Party' 227–8
  brother's promotion of 23, 25, 227–8
  brother's trust in/closeness to 24, 176–7, 186, 196–8, 218, 238, **239**, 240
  character
    arrogance/rudeness 6, 127, 134, 226; *see also* **Kim Yo Jong**, vitriol targets
    carefree manner 114, 149, 168, 170
    minimising make-up and bling 8–9
    ruthlessness/cruelty 25–7, 61, 130, 215, 231–2, 234, 247–8
  China, diplomacy with 162–3, 164
  Covid-19 pandemic 238, **239**, 240–1
  Department of Organization and Guidance 23–4, 228
  'Deputy Dear Leader' 23, 24, 218
  education 77, 114–15
  father's funeral 73, 107, 112

INDEX

Fujimoto's exposé on 44–7, 76
'heir apparent' 17, 19–20, 22,
  196–8, **199**, 200, 227–8, 231
human rights abuses 106, 247–8
'Manlima Speed Battle' 151–2
marriage/family, secrecy about 115
mother's Japanese birth 79, 82
Mount Paektu, riding with brother
  on 17, 196, 197–8, **199**, 200
name 75
names, false 77–8
National Defence Commission 25
nuclear threats 25, 26, 236–8,
  245–6
parents doting on 4, 45
photographs 17, **18**, 20–1, 73–4,
  82–3, 97, **135**, **169**, 197–8, **199**
political power/infallibility 9–10,
  22, 23–7, 168, 176–7, 200,
  214–15, 216–18, 223–4, 232,
  247–8
Propaganda and Agitation
  Department 4, 23, 24–5, 27, 114,
  118, 151–2, 230
public's fascination with 1–2, 3, 7,
  8–9, 10–11, 124–5, 127, 131–2,
  141, 198, 200
public's misunderstanding of 6,
  185–6, 215–16
at Rungna People's Pleasure
  Ground 113–14
South Korea, demands/threats to
  26, 216–18, 222–3, 224, 233–4,
  235, 236–7, 245–6
South Korea, diplomacy with 166,
  177–8, 181, 183; *see also* inter-Korean summits, 2018, April;
  Olympics, 2018 Winter
South Korea's obedience to
  218–21, 223–4, 235, 236
State Affairs Commission 25
USA, demands/threats to the 27,
  161, 225, 226, 234
USA, diplomacy with the 177,
  185–7, 190, 193–4; *see also* United
  States–North Korea relations,
  2018 Summit
USA, hostage diplomacy with the
  101–2, 104

vitriol targets
  defectors 82, 85, 150, 216, 240–1
  Moon Jae-in 24, 26, 133, 184,
    213–14, 215–16, 228, 230, 234–5
  Park Geun Hye 27, 116–18
  South Korea's Defence Minister
    237
  South Korea's military experts
    244–5, 245–6
  USA/Americans 27, 118–19,
    225–6, 232–3, 243
  Yoon Suk Yeol 241–2, 244
Kim Yong Chol 141, 149, 166–7,
  168, 186, 190, 191
Kim Yong Chun 110
Kim Yong Ju 49
Kim Yong Nam
  Kim Jong Il's funeral 112
  Roh's visit to North Korea 90, 93
  South Korea, 2018 visit to 2, 3, 5,
    6–7, 9, 127, 133, 134, **135**, 137–8,
    141
  title 11
Kim Yong Suk 41
Kim, Yuri Irsenovich *see* Kim Jong Il
Kirby, Michael 116
Ko Kyong Thaek 80
Ko Yong Hui 20, 41–2, 45–6, 47–8,
  79–80, 82
Ko Yong Suk 43, 83
Koizumi, Junichiro 66
Korea; *see also* North Korea; South
  Korea
  1953 armistice agreement 37–8
  Demilitarized Zone (DMZ) 19
  'hermit nation' moniker 202
  inter-Korean energy cooperation
    153–4
  under Japanese rule 13–14, 15, 80,
    180, 202
  Joint Security Area 144
  March First Independence
    Movement Day 180
  Military Demarcation Line (MDL)
    19, 89, 144, 146, 147, 193
  Mount Paektu, importance of 16
  mythology 15, 16
  North–South conflicts
    abductions 63, 64–6, 67

Korea (*cont.*)
  attacks/incursions 19, 63–4,
    69–70, 93–4, 178, 209
  invective 117–18, 234–5, 237,
    240–1, 241–2, 244–6
  Korean War (1950–1953) 33–7, 53–4
  threats 26, 117–18, 214–15,
    215–16, 222–3, 229, 233, 234,
    236–8, 240–1, 243, 245
  North–South diplomacy *see*
    inter-Korean summits
  partitioning of 28–31
  reunification
    Moon's hope for 125, **135**,
      136–8, 139
    North's agenda 28, 31, 38–9, 94,
      133, 134, 151–2
  self-isolation policy, 19th-century
    201, 202
  thirty-eighth parallel 30
  Yi dynasty 203
Korean Central News Agency
  (KCNA) 55, 75, 116, 117–18, 119,
  196, 214, 218
KuenSaem 221

Lee, Euna 97–105
Lee Han-Young (Yi Il Nam) 43–4,
  51–2, 85–6
Lee Hsien Loong 168
Lee Myung Bak 132
Lee Nak-Yon 122
Lee, Sung-Yoon 78, 206–7, 211–12
Lee Young-Ae 90
Lincoln, George 30
Ling, Laura 97–105
Ling, Lisa 98
Llo Shin Yong 78

MacArthur, Douglas 53
McCaul, Michael 219–20
Man Gyong Bong ferry 46
Mao Zedong 33, 34, 35
Martyrs' Mausoleum, Rangoon,
  Burma 64
Military Demarcation Line (MDL)
  88–9, 144, 146, 193
minjok (ethnic Koreans) 156
Molotov, Vyacheslav 29

Moon Jae-in
  2021 missile tests 233–5
  Gag Law 219–21, 223
  Kim Yo Jong's diatribes against 24,
    133, 184, 213–14, 215–16, 228,
    230, 234–5, 241
  in Korean–USA relations 133,
    140, 165, 166, 188–9, 228–9
  Mount Paektu, visit to 182–3
  North Korea, diplomacy with
    131–4, **135**, 136–40, 166, 177–8,
    179, 180–3; *see also* inter-Korean
    summits, 2018, April
  North Korea, support for better
    relations with 71–2, 130, 139
  Olympics, 2018 Winter 5, 10, 11,
    122, 125, 127–8, 130, 141
Mount Kumgang 149, 180
Mount Paektu 14–15, 16, 17, 181–3,
  194, 196–8, **199**, 200
Mount Paektu Bloodline; *see also*
  North Korea; *specific family members*
  absolute power 13, 14, 43–4, 49,
    177, 194–6, 204, 208, 218, 247–8
  cruelty 60–1, 69, 247–8
  defectors 43, 85–6
  exposés on 43–4, 44–7, 76–7
  false names 77–9
  five-pointed star 16, 17, 198, **199**
  hedonism 51–2, 203, 208
  intra-family rivalry/threats 79,
    86–7, 115
  necessary to complete revolution
    194, 195–6, 200
  secrecy about family 69, 73, 74–5,
    77, 79–80, 82, 83–5, 87, 115, 200,
    203, 240
  self-isolation 202–3
  'side branches' 48–9, 49–50, 115

Nam Il 37
New York Times 145, 155
Nixon, Richard 67
No Kwang Chol 168
North Korea
  assassinations abroad 20, 85–7, 221
  Charter of the Workers' Party of
    Korea 28
  Christians, persecution of 61–2, 63

INDEX

counterfeiting US currency 158
Covid-19 pandemic 209–12, 238, **239**, 240–1
defections from
  family members 43, 77, 81–2, 83, 85–6
  others 39, 95, 98, 114, 150, 212, 216, 217, 221, 240
denuclearization of 71–2, 94, 154, 160–1, 162, 166–8, **169**, 170–6, 187–8, 188–90, 241–2
Department of Organization and Guidance (OGD) 23–4, 59, 77, 96, 228
Eighth Party Congress, 227–8
executions and disappearances 22, 50, 58–61, 62, 63, 66–7, 81, 82, 84, 109–11, 191–2, 247
food shortages 204–8, 211
foreign aid
  from China 164, 204
  food 205–6
  refusal of, during pandemic 210, 211, 212
  from Russia/USSR 32–3, 204
  from South Korea 91, 95, 132–3, 133–4, 187
  from USA 69, 99, 161–2, 187–8
foreign relations
  China 6, 14–15, 32–5, 54–6, 67, 162–5, 167
  Russia/USSR 27, 32–3, 35, 53, 192–3
  South Korea see inter-Korean summits; Korea, North–South conflicts
  USA see United States–North Korea relations
'guilt by association' 83
hostage diplomacy 97–106, 121
human rights abuses 62–3, 98, 116, 120–1, 123, 124–5, 172–3, 204–8, 220–1, 247–8
international terrorism 63–7, 187
KCNA see Korean Central News Agency (KCNA)
kidnapping foreigners 52, 64–7, 97–105
live-strike artillery drills 214

mass games 104–5, 181
Mount Paektu Bloodline see Mount Paektu Bloodline
Mount Paektu, importance of 16
National Defence Commission 25, 219
nuclear weapons see nuclear weapons, North Korea's
political classification system 79–81, 84, 212
'the press,' definition of 155
Propaganda and Agitation Department 4, 23, 24–5, 27, 82–3, 114–15, 132, 152, 230
reunification agenda 28, 31, 38–9, 94, 133, 134, 151–2
revolution, completing the
  Kim family as necessary for 194, 195–6, 198, 200
  USA as obstacle to 38–9, 229
royal birthdays 42–3
sanctions against 7, 140, 163, 166, 184, 187, 189, 207–8
secret police 58–9
self-isolation policy 202–3
sexual inequality 63, 112
Six-Party Talks 94
songbun ('birth status') 79–81, 84
South's obedience to 125, 127, 219–21, 223–4, 235, 236
spy satellite 244–5
state secrets
  assassination of defectors to keep 85–7
  Kim children 73–7
  Kim identities 77–9
  Kim Il Sung's Christian parentage 83–4
  Ko Yong Hui's origins 79–83
  Ko Yong Suk's defection 83
Supreme Leader's divinity and infallibility 14, 49, 62, 86, 177, 195, 247–8
surveillance 81, 82
'Ten Principles' 195
UNSC Resolutions 90, 133, 153–4, 235, 243–4
North–South Joint Liaison Building, Kaesong 215

nuclear weapons, North Korea's; *see also* North Korea, denuclearization of
Kim Jong Un's birthday speech 229
'law on the state policy on the nuclear forces' 242
missile tests
  under Kim Jong Il 69, 90, 99
  under Kim Jong Un 20–1, 68, 105, 120, 121, 163–4, 194, 226, 234–6, 242–3, 245–6
prioritized over food 207
threats 25, 26, 69, 95–6, 99, 120, 187–8, 236–8, 245–6
UNSC Resolutions, violations of 243–4

Obama, Barack 27, 98–9, 99–100, 100–1, 116–17, 118–19
Olympics, 2018 Winter
Kim Yo Jong
  arrival 1–6, 7–9
  cheering team 128, 140, 141
  Cho, dinner with 140–1
  Im, meeting with 142
  Moon, meeting with 131–4, **135**, 136–40
  North–South handshake 127
  not applauding USA team 129
  pregnancy speculations 131–2
  press and public fascination with 1–2, 3, 7, 8–9, 10–11, 124–5, 127, 141
  success of mission 142–3
  in VIP box **126**, 127
  Warmbier's appraisal 130
Kim Yong Chol at closing ceremony 141–2
the 'Peace Games' 122
Pence's attendance 122–4, 125, **126**, 127–9
'Unified Team Korea' 121–2, 128, 141
VIP box 125, **126**, 127–9
Warmbier's summary 129–30
Open Doors mission 61
Orient Express (Pulikovsky) 48

Paek Hwa Garden State Guest House, Pyongyang 103
Pak Hon Yong 191
Pak Jong Chon 231
Palace of the Sun, Mount Kumsu 76, 109, 112, 230–2
Panmunjom Declaration 154, 155–6, 217, 218–19
Park Chung Hee 117–18
Park Geun Hye 27, 116–17
Park Jung-Oh 221
Park Sang-Hak 221–3
Park Wang-ga 149
Peace House, South Korea 148, 149, 154
Pence, Karen 125, **126**, 128
Pence, Mike 5, 10, 122–5, **126**, 127–9, 165–6
Peng Dehuai 37
Peng Liyuan 164
Phanmun Pavilion, North Korea 144, 147
Pochonbo Electronic Ensemble 45, 96–7
Podesta, John 102
Pompeo, Mike 102, 171, 177, 190
Pulikovsky, Konstantin 48
Putin, Vladimir 192–3, 244
Pyongyang Declaration 178, **179**, 180–1, 217

Republic of Korea *see* South Korea
Ri Chun Hi 198, 200
Ri Jong Ho 114–15
Ri Myong Je 58–9, 59–60
Ri Sol Ju 20, 156, 197, 198, 231
Ri Son Gwon 7, 9, 143
Ri Su Yong 78, 168
Ri Ul Sol 54
Ri Yong Ho 60, 75–6, 110, 168
Rodman, Dennis 20
Rodong Sinmun 75–6, 117, 212, 216, 222, 226, 237, 241
Roh Moo Hyun 88–95, 178, 181–2
Rusk, Dean 30
Russia 27, 48, 94, 192–3, 243–4; *see also* USSR

INDEX

Samjiyeon Revolutionary Battlefield
   Monument 194
Sato, Ayako 134, 136
Shaw, George Bernard 188
Shin Sang-Ok 64–6
Shin Young-Bok 137–8, 139
Singapore 167–8
Six-Party Talks 94
Smith, Chris 220–1
Song Hye Rang 44, 77, 86
Song Hye Rim 41, 86
South Korea
   2018 Winter Olympics *see*
      Olympics, 2018 Winter
   anti-Pyongyang propaganda
      balloons 216–20, 222–3
   China, relations with 204
   Covid-19 pandemic 209
   defunding anti-North NGOs 221
   democracy 31
   Gag Law 219–21, 222–3
   KTX (Korea Train eXpress) 3
   Mount Paektu, importance of 16
   North Korea, aid to 91, 95,
      132–3, 133–4, 187
   North Korea, obeying 125, 127,
      219–21, 223–4, 235, 236
   North Korea, relations with *see*
      inter-Korean summits; Korea,
      North–South conflicts
   North Koreans escaping to 39, 43,
      85, 150, 212
   Six-Party Talks 94
   UN defence of 31, 33–4, 37, 38,
      53
   USA, combined military exercises
      with the 233–4
   USA defence of 34, 36–7, 38–9,
      161
   USA, relations with the 94,
      116–17, 138–9
   wealth 39
Stalin, Josef 27, 29, 30, 35, 36
*State of Food Security and Nutrition in
   the World, The* (UN) 206–7
Steinmeier, Frank-Walter 5
Suh Hoon 160–1
Sullivan, Jake 232
Switzerland 77, 78, 83, 132, 141, 208

Syngman Rhee 37–8
Syria 188

Taliban 62–3
'Ten Principles' 195
Trump, Donald 9, 68, 120–1, 172–3,
      185, 187–92, 193–4, 227; *see also*
      United States–North Korea rela-
      tions, 2018 Summit
Trump, Ivanka 193

U Dong Chuk 110
Ukraine 27, 244
United Nations
   deaths of Command personnel 19
   North Korea, sanctions against
      140, 187, 207–8
   North Korea's human rights abuses
      116, 205–7, 208
   Security Council Resolutions 90,
      133, 153–4, 235, 243–4
   South Korea, defence of 31, 33–4,
      37, 38, 53–4
   South Korea's Gag Law 220
United States
   China, relations with 67
   Korea, partitioning of 28–31
   North Korea, relations with *see* United
      States–North Korea relations
   South Korea, combined military
      exercises with 233–4
   South Korea, defence of 34, 36–7,
      38–9, 161
   South Korea, relations with 94,
      116–17, 138–9
   South Korea's Gag Law, response
      to 219–20, 220–1
United States–North Korea relations
   1953 armistice agreement 37–8
   2018 Summit
      'denuclearization,' North's defini-
         tion of 161
      Kim and Trump signing joint
         statement **169**, 171
      Kim–Trump meeting 170–1
      Kim Yo Jong's role 177
      Koreans' arrival 168
      Koreans visiting Marina Sands
         SkyPark Observation Deck 170

INDEX

United States–North Korea relations (*cont.*)
North Koreans' flight to Singapore 167
North Korea's success 172
pre-Summit manoeuvring 160–7
'reframing' human rights abuses 172–3
Singapore footing bill for 168
Trump's belief in Kim 173
US money-for-missiles scheme 174–6
US video 173–5
at 2018 Winter Olympics 122–4, 125, **126**, 127–30
2019 Summit, DMZ 193–4
2019 Summit, Hanoi 185–92
aid 69, 99, 161–2, 187–8
hostage diplomacy 97–106
insults 118–19, 120–1, 165–6, 184, 232–3, 243
Korean War (1950–1953) 33–7
North Korean disengagement 225–7, 232–3
nuclear threats 27, 99, 120, 226, 245–6

sanctions 7, 140, 163, 166, 184, 187, 189, 207–8
USA as 'principal enemy' 38–9
USSR 16, 28–33, 35, 36, 52–3, 54, 69, 204; *see also* Russia

Vietnam **18**, 19, 139, 184

Warmbier, Cindy 123
Warmbier, Fred 123, 128, 129–30
Warmbier, Otto 105–6, 121, 129, 187
Washington Post, The 8–9, 43, 145
Westernization of Asia 201–2

Xi Jinping 6, 54, 163–5, 177

Yanbian Korean Autonomous Prefecture, China 98
Yeonpyeong Island, South Korea 150
Yi dynasty 203
Yi Il Nam *see* Lee Han-Young
Yokota, Megumi 66–7
Yonhap News 97
Yoon Suk Yeol 236–7, 241–2

Credit: Alonso Nichols, Tufts University

Sung-Yoon Lee is a fellow at the Woodrow Wilson International Center for Scholars. Previously, he taught Korean history at Tufts University. He has written on the politics of the Korean peninsula for numerous publications including the *New York Times*, *Wall Street Journal*, and *Washington Post*. He has testified as an expert witness at the US House of Representatives Foreign Affairs Committee hearings on North Korea policy and has advised senior leaders, including the president of the United States.

PublicAffairs is a publishing house founded in 1997. It is a tribute to the standards, values, and flair of three persons who have served as mentors to countless reporters, writers, editors, and book people of all kinds, including me.

I. F. STONE, proprietor of *I. F. Stone's Weekly*, combined a commitment to the First Amendment with entrepreneurial zeal and reporting skill and became one of the great independent journalists in American history. At the age of eighty, Izzy published *The Trial of Socrates*, which was a national bestseller. He wrote the book after he taught himself ancient Greek.

BENJAMIN C. BRADLEE was for nearly thirty years the charismatic editorial leader of *The Washington Post*. It was Ben who gave the *Post* the range and courage to pursue such historic issues as Watergate. He supported his reporters with a tenacity that made them fearless and it is no accident that so many became authors of influential, best-selling books.

ROBERT L. BERNSTEIN, the chief executive of Random House for more than a quarter century, guided one of the nation's premier publishing houses. Bob was personally responsible for many books of political dissent and argument that challenged tyranny around the globe. He is also the founder and longtime chair of Human Rights Watch, one of the most respected human rights organizations in the world.

·   ·   ·

For fifty years, the banner of Public Affairs Press was carried by its owner Morris B. Schnapper, who published Gandhi, Nasser, Toynbee, Truman, and about 1,500 other authors. In 1983, Schnapper was described by *The Washington Post* as "a redoubtable gadfly." His legacy will endure in the books to come.

Peter Osnos, *Founder*